THE EGO
AND THE
DYNAMIC GROUND

THE EGO
AND THE
DYNAMIC GROUND

*A Transpersonal Theory
of Human Development*

Second Edition, Revised

Michael Washburn

STATE UNIVERSITY OF NEW YORK PRESS

Tables 1.4 and 1.5 adapted from *Eye to Eye: The Quest for the New Paradigm*, expanded edition, by Ken Wilber. © 1983, 1990 by Ken Wilber. Reprinted by arrangement with Shambhala Publications, Inc., 300 Massachusetts Avenue, Boston, MA 02115.

Published by
State University of New York Press, Albany

For information, address State University of New York Press,
State University Plaza, Albany, NY 12246

Production by Christina Tartaglia
Marketing by Nancy Farrell

Library Of Congress Cataloging-in-Publication Data

Washburn, Michael, 1943–
    The ego and the dynamic ground : a transpersonal theory of human development / Michael Washburn. — 2nd ed., rev.
        p.   cm.
    Includes bibliographical references and index.
    ISBN 0–7914–2255–0 (alk. paper).—ISBN 0–7914–2256–9 (pbk. : alk. paper)
    1. Transpersonal psychology.   2. Ego (Psychology).   I. Title.
BF204.7.W37 1995
150.19'8—dc20   94-1379
                                                                            CIP

10 9 8 7 6 5 4 3 2 1

FOR

Ione Rich Washburn
My mother, my friend

Contents

Preface to First Edition

IN TERMS OF THE disciplinary categories currently in use, this study falls within the field of transpersonal psychology. Transpersonal psychology is the study of human nature and development that proceeds on the assumption that human beings possess potentialities that surpass the limits of the maturely developed ego. It is an inquiry that presupposes that the ego, as ordinarily constituted, can be transcended and that a higher transegoic plane or stage of life is possible. The present study falls within this field of investigation because it postulates that the ego, despite pretensions of independence, is a grounded existent and, consequently, that the highest plane or stage of life is not one of egoic ascendancy but rather one in which the ego is properly rooted in its ground. Specifically, the present study postulates that the ego exists in essential relation to a superior *Dynamic Ground* and that the highest possible psychic organization is one in which the ego, itself fully developed and self-responsible, is a faithful instrument of this Ground.

Transpersonal psychology is less a subdiscipline of psychology than it is a multidisciplinary inquiry aimed at a holistic understanding of human nature. It is a synthesis of several disciplines, including most importantly not only the larger discipline of psychology but also the disciplines of religious studies and philosophy. Transpersonal psychology is concerned not only with psychological notions such as ego, the unconscious, and integration but also with spiritual notions such as fallenness, transcendence, and spiritual realization and with philosophical notions such as selfhood, existential project, and life-world. Transpersonal psychology is a comprehensive enterprise; it is a *Geisteswissenschaft* that draws upon several humanistic disciplines without itself being strictly subsumable under any of them. In light of this multidisciplinary character of transpersonal psychology, it would perhaps be better if transpersonal inquiry were to change its name from transpersonal *psychology* to, simply, transpersonal *theory*.

I have approached transpersonal theory from a psychodynamic and phenomenological orientation. For this reason my thinking, in drawing upon psychology, religion, and philosophy, has drawn most heavily upon dynamic depth psychology (especially Jung), psychospiritually oriented religion (such as ascetical and mystical theology, yoga, alchemy), and existential-phenomenological philosophy (especially Kierkegaard, Nietzsche, and Sartre). I trace the unfolding interaction between the ego and the Dynamic Ground from the ego's initial differentiation from the Ground (the period of the preoedipal body ego), through the ego's repressive dissociation from the Ground (the period of the Cartesian ego and the dynamic unconscious), to, finally, the ego's return to and reconstitution by the Ground (the period of spiritual regeneration and higher integration). And in tracing these stages of the ego-Ground interaction, I also speak to the different senses of selfhood, the different existential projects, and the different experiential lifeworlds that correspond to the stages.

I am aware of the ambitious nature of any attempt to formulate an encompassing transpersonal theory, so acutely aware, in fact, that I have been plagued with self-doubts throughout the writing of this book. There were countless times when, for lack of understanding or learning, I felt inadequate to the task and unable to proceed. Nevertheless, I persevered to the end. And on the whole I am pleased with the way the book has turned out. The book suffers from many weaknesses, I am sure. In particular, since my professional training is confined to philosophy, it is likely that my treatment of psychological and spiritual notions will in some cases seem unsophisticated to experts in these fields. However, notwithstanding these, and other, shortcomings, I am confident that the book at least presents a clear and fully developed point of view, and I am hopeful that it will make a significant contribution to transpersonal theory.

This book has been six years in preparation. During this time there have been many people who have given generously of their time and understanding in helping me. Richard Allen, Arthur Bohart, William Borden, David Eastman, James McGrath, Richard D. Mann, James Mosel, George Nazaroff, Pamela Washburn, and Ken Wilber all read and commented on portions of the book at various stages of its evolution. Their encouragements have sustained me, and their constructive criticisms have saved me from many errors and have challenged me to state my ideas as clearly and rigorously as I am able. The readers for the State University of New York Press offered many excellent suggestions, almost all of which have been followed. I would like to thank them for helping me make this a considerably better book than it otherwise would have been. Of the people I have mentioned so far, I am especially indebted to Richard Mann and Ken Wilber. Richard Mann warmly received the manuscript of this book and offered helpful advice about how it could be improved. And Ken Wilber has been an inspiring intellectual model. Wilber's books are powerful beacons that have led the way in the early years of transpersonal inquiry.

I am grateful to my school, Indiana University South Bend, for providing me with a Summer Faculty Fellowship (1981) and a sabbatical leave (1983–84) at crucial junctures in this project. Also, my colleagues in philosophy at IUSB—Andrew Naylor, Jon Ringen, and J. Wesley Robbins—have been a valued resource. They have all read parts of the book and have given me insightful feedback and suggestions. And appreciative acknowledgment is due, too, to Peter Blum, Craig Schroeder, and Michael van de Veire, friends in philosophy at IUSB with whom I have enjoyed many stimulating conversations on topics related to those dealt with herein.

I would like finally to thank the members of my family for their understanding and support, especially during the last year when I was so preoccupied with finishing the book. Kirsten, Tracy, and Alison, my daughters, were always willing to listen when I needed to express my hopes for the book or my frustrations in trying to write it. Pamela, my wife, helped me in all phases and aspects of the project. And Ione, my mother—to whom the book is dedicated—provided me with vital encouragements and insights.

Michael Washburn
1987

Preface To Second Edition

I AM GRATEFUL TO William Eastman, Director of the State University of New York Press, for his encouraging response to my inquiry about bringing out a second edition of *The Ego and the Dynamic Ground*. I am pleased, as most authors would be, to have had a second chance at a first book. I have tried to make the best use of the opportunity. This second edition of *The Ego and the Dynamic Ground*, I believe, presents a significantly improved and, for me, much more satisfying formulation of the ideas introduced in the first edition.

In going through the text for revisions, I have corrected errors of fact and interpretation, clarified key ideas, taken advantage of some recent developments in psychoanalytic theory, upgraded the scholarship, improved the prose throughout, and brought the text into agreement with my more recent book, *Transpersonal Psychology in Psychoanalytic Perspective* (SUNY Press, 1994). These revisions amount to a major reworking of the text. The entire book has been revised at least for style and clarity, and the introduction and chapters 2, 3, 4, and 6 have been substantially overhauled.

In addition to the people whose assistance was acknowledged in the preface to the first edition, I would like here to acknowledge the major contribution made to this edition by Ms. Cynthia Briggs, who copyedited the manuscript and suggested many ways in which I could improve not only the style of my exposition but also the substance of my thought. I profited immensely from her thorough and intelligent reading of the manuscript. I also would like to acknowledge the generous assistance provided by John Lewis, my friend and colleague at IUSB. John always took time to listen to my questions and offered valuable suggestions that helped me find more effective ways to express my ideas.

I would like to thank my school, Indiana University South Bend, for supporting me with a Summer Faculty Fellowship (1993). The fellowship made it possible for me to complete work on this new edition of *The Ego and the Dynamic Ground* much sooner than otherwise would have been possible.

A word of explanation is in order concerning the relation of *The Ego and the Dynamic Ground* to *Transpersonal Psychology in Psychoanalytic Perspective*. The two books cover a good deal of the same ground. They do so, however, in significantly different ways and with different emphases. *Transpersonal Psychology in Psychoanalytic Perspective* is geared more to academic and professional audiences. It focuses on theoretical debates within the psychoanalytic tradition, giving special attention to the debate, begun by Freud and Jung, over whether psychoanalysis (understood in the widest possible sense of the term) can be both scientific and transpersonal, both biologically grounded and open to spirituality. In addressing psychoanalytic perspectives, *Transpersonal Psychology in Psychoanalytic Perspective* gives extensive consideration to object relations theory and feminist theory and tries to explain why these orientations have important implications for a transpersonal understanding of human development. *The Ego and the Dynamic Ground*, in contrast, is directed to a more general audience and focuses more exclusively on issues within transpersonal psychology, especially the issue of competing paradigms within transpersonal theory. Also, *The Ego and the Dynamic Ground* devotes chapters to the unconscious and to the psychodynamics of meditation and is interested in how transpersonal theory can illuminate spiritual practice.

Introduction

A CHIEF OBJECTIVE OF transpersonal theory is to integrate spiritual experience within a larger understanding of human nature and human development. Transpersonal theory, that is, is committed to the possibility of unifying spiritual and psychological perspectives. In being committed to such a unification, however, transpersonal theory does not advocate a program of reduction, of the spiritual to the psychological, or, for that matter, of "promotion," of the psychological to the spiritual. Transpersonal theory is not a one-sided psychology of religion or an exclusively spiritual psychology. It is rather a project that attempts a true synthesis of spiritual and psychological perspectives, a synthesis that involves a thorough rethinking of each of these perspectives in terms of the other.

Although transpersonal theory aims at a genuine synthesis of spiritual and psychological perspectives, it nonetheless gives the spiritual perspective a theoretical priority. Transpersonal theory assumes that human development aims ultimately at a spiritual fulfillment and, therefore, that human nature can be properly understood only from a spiritual standpoint. Transpersonal theory, that is, holds that spirituality—understood experientially rather than doctrinally or historically— should play the role of guiding principle in a unified understanding of the human psyche.

Transpersonal theory was pioneered by Carl Jung, who parted company with Freud and psychoanalysis when he stressed that psychology is not only incomplete but fundamentally misconceived if it does not seek to understand human spiritual possibilities. Jung's analytical psychology, which focuses on the inherited depth potentials of the unconscious and on the numinous, archetypal, and mythological dimensions of spirituality, maintains that the drama of human development becomes fully intelligible only when seen in light of spiritual symbols. According to Jung, spiritual symbols speak so powerfully to us because they are embodiments of the archetypes that, rooted in the collective psyche, guide us on the path of self-realization or, as he calls it, individuation. Spiritual symbols point to the future and highest stages

1

of the developmental process; they are signposts that appear on the path leading from ego-centered existence to spiritually centered integration. They are waymarks that appear during the ego's redemptive return to and higher integration with the dynamic potentials of the collective psyche.

Jung's contribution to transpersonal theory is unsurpassed. Not only was he the chief pioneer of transpersonal thought but he also remains a towering figure in the field. The Jungian depth-psychological and archetypal approach to understanding our spiritual potentialities is presently one of the two major perspectives within transpersonal theory. Ken Wilber's structural-hierarchical approach is the other. (More on Wilber in a moment.)

A second major figure in the development of transpersonal theory is Roberto Assagioli, the Italian psychiatrist and founder of psychosynthesis. It was Assagioli's view that human beings have not only a lower (prepersonal) unconscious but also a higher (transpersonal) superconscious and, consequently, that psychotherapy needs to focus not only on alleviating disturbances connected with the former but also on facilitating spiritual possibilities connected with the latter. Also, in his main work, *Psychosynthesis* (1965), Assagioli defended the position that some psychological disturbances, even very serious ones, are better understood as crises of spiritual awakening than as symptoms of psychopathology. For Assagioli, then, it is the proper business of psychotherapy not only to treat psychopathology but also to foster spiritual awakening and to deal intelligently with the difficulties that such awakening can incur.

A third major contributor to the emergence of transpersonal theory is Abraham Maslow, a founding father of both humanistic and transpersonal psychology. In relation to transpersonal theory, Maslow's greatest contribution is his defense of the view that spiritual experience is a higher potentiality of human nature, a potentiality that belongs to us inherently as a biological species (1970, 1971). For Maslow, spirituality is innate, and spiritual experiences are "peak" or "plateau" experiences occurring at the "farther reaches of human nature." For Maslow, as for transpersonal theory generally, human developmental realization is ultimately a spiritual realization. For this reason Maslow believed that psychology, including humanistically oriented psychology, cannot be complete until it has been refocused and brought under a spiritual or transpersonal perspective. In one famous passage, for example, Maslow stated: "I should say also that I consider Humanistic, Third Force Psychology to be transitional, a preparation for a still 'higher' Fourth Psychology, transpersonal, transhuman, centered in the cosmos rather than in human needs and interests, going beyond humanness, identity, self-actualization, and the like" (1968, iii–iv). Transpersonal theory came into its own as a movement with the founding of the *Journal of Transpersonal Psychology* in 1969. In the early years transpersonal theory was predominantly humanistic in its psychology and Eastern in its religion, a synthesis of Maslow and Buddhism (primarily Zen). These identifications, however, have loosened over the years, and transpersonal theory is now more open to a diversity of psychological and spiritual perspectives. The principal figure in the field at this time is Ken Wilber (1980a, 1980b, 1983, 1990; Wilber et al. 1986), whose theory of the spectrum of consciousness is based on wide-ranging materials from contemporary psychology and comparative religion. Unlike Jung's work, which arose primarily out of depth-psychology and the Christian religious tradition, Wilber's work draws primarily on structurally oriented psychology (especially cognitive-developmental psychology) and the Indian (primarily Buddhist) religious tradition. Both Jung and Wilber are multicultural and inclusive in their work. Jung's work, though, is basically Western in its orientation, Wilber's basically Eastern.

In addition to Wilber, two other leading transpersonal theorists currently working in the field are Stanislav Grof and David M. Levin. Grof is a psychiatrist who has done extensive work in LSD psychotherapy, first in Prague in the 1950s and then as chief of psychiatric research at the Maryland Psychiatric Research Center in Baltimore in the late 1960s and early 1970s. Grof has published the dramatic findings of this research in a series of important books (1975, 1985, 1988) that greatly expand our understanding of the human unconscious, and its transpersonal potentials in particular. Grof has gone farther than anyone else in exploring the numinous and archetypal experiences that lie in store in the deeper strata of the unconscious. In recent years, Grof, in collaboration with Christina Grof (Grof and Grof 1989, 1990), has written extensively on difficulties that can accompany spiritual awakening, bringing much-needed clarity to a vitally important class of developmental phenomena first recognized by Assagioli.

David M. Levin (1985, 1988, 1989) is a transpersonal philosopher who draws on the hermeneutical and phenomenological work of Martin Heidegger and Maurice Merleau-Ponty. Levin agrees with Heidegger that our metaphysical tradition has alienated us from the deepest sources of our being. It has transformed us into ego-centered subjects estranged from our bodies, from each other, and from the world. In the modern era in particular, he believes, we have become nihilistic selves driven by the will to power, the need to fix, secure, and master. Levin, drawing on Merleau-Ponty, suggests that the key to overcoming our estrangement lies in our bodies. In *The Body's Recollection of Being*, Levin presents a phenomenology of embodiment that reveals that our bodies, unbeknownst to our egos, are already attuned to the world and to others. As embodied beings, we are already grounded in the earth, open to the dynamic sources of life, and intimately interlinked with other human beings. If we are to overcome our alienation, then, we need to retrieve the life of the body. This retrieval is a hermeneutical process, Levin stresses. It is no mere return to bodily life as it was experienced during early childhood but is rather a regathering of this life at a higher transpersonal level, a level that integrates bodily life with our cultural and personal histories. Levin's work is full of deep insights, and his phenomenology is sensitive to the many turns and nuances of transpersonal experience.

The view formulated in this book is much closer to the views of Jung, Grof, and Levin than it is to Wilber's view. The ways in which my view differs from Wilber's are discussed in chapter 1. Basically, I think Wilber loses sight of the transpersonal potentials of the deep unconscious and consequently mistakenly conceives the course of (ontogenetic) development as a straight ascent to higher levels rather than as a spiral loop that, after departing from origins, bends back through origins on the way to transpersonal integration. Similar to the views of Jung, Grof, and Levin, the view presented here is one that postulates the existence of an original dynamic, creative, spontaneous source out of which the ego emerges, from which the ego then becomes estranged, to which, during the stages of ego transcendence, the ego returns, and with which, ultimately, the ego is integrated. Jung, Grof, Levin, and I differ in the specific ways in which we describe the basic source of the ego's existence and the ego's spiral journey of departure from and higher return to this source; nevertheless, the underlying paradigm is substantially the same.

In this book, then, I shall be presenting a formulation of the view that human development follows a spiral path of departure from and higher return to origins. Specifically, I shall be formulating this view from a perspective that, broadly stated, is *dynamic, triphasic,* and *dialectical.*

The perspective of this book is *dynamic* in that the primary focus is on the ego's interaction with dynamic life (energy, power, spirit), the source of which is referred to as the *Dynamic Ground* (or, more simply, the *Ground*). Accordingly, I shall be focusing, in matters more narrowly psychological, on the ego's interaction with libido or psychic energy and, in matters more properly spiritual, on the ego's interaction with numinous power or spirit. One of the basic assumptions of this book is that these two general types of dynamic expression, psychic and spiritual, derive from a single source. These two types of dynamic expression, I propose, are not manifestations of two different powers but are rather two different manifestations of a single fundamental power. Libido or psychic energy on the one hand and numinous spirit on the other, I propose, are different manifestations of the power of the Dynamic Ground.[1]

The perspective of this book is *triphasic* in that it divides human development into three principal stages: the preegoic, egoic, and transegoic stages. This triphasic perspective is common to all transpersonal theories that postulate not only a stage after the transcendence of the ego (a transegoic stage) but also a stage prior to the consolidation of the ego (a preegoic stage). What distinguishes the triphasic view set forth here is that the three basic stages of development are seen as reflecting three different positions in the ego's unfolding interaction with dynamic life. The preegoic stage, which corresponds roughly to prelatency childhood, is conceived as a period during which the Dynamic Ground has a strong and frequently overpowering influence on a weak and undeveloped ego. The egoic stage, which corresponds roughly to the long period running from the beginning of latency to midlife, is conceived as a period during which a maturing ego is protectively separated (i.e., repressively disconnected) from the Dynamic Ground. And the transegoic stage, which corresponds to later adulthood—in most of the cases in which this stage emerges—is conceived as a period during which a strong and mature ego is returned to and finally integrated with the Dynamic Ground.[2] In sum, the three basic stages of life are understood as reflecting three basically different forms of relationship between the ego and the Dynamic Ground. As a brief preview, the three stages of life can be described as follows.

THE PREEGOIC STAGE

The preegoic stage, which will also be called the stage of the *body ego*, is the stage of prelatency childhood. This stage is preegoic not because it is lacking altogether in an ego but rather because the ego is only in the process of emerging and has not yet fully differentiated itself from the inner and outer sources of its being. The ego's existence during this stage is intimately interlinked with and strongly influenced by both the Dynamic Ground and the primary caregiver—the inner and outer dimensions, respectively, of the preoedipal Great Mother. Although the ego, as body ego, does not have clear-cut self-boundaries, it nonetheless vaguely apprehends its existence as an embodied being. The body ego is an incarnate subject. The body ego does not *have* a body; it *is* the body.

Among the primary features of the preegoic or body-egoic stage are (1) inner openness to the power of the Dynamic Ground and corresponding intimacy with the primary caregiver; (2) a predominantly somatic, instinctually governed, and polymorphously sensual character; (3) numinously charged experience (awe, wonder, enchantment); and (4) a creative but crude cognitive life, conducted primarily in the medium of images.

THE EGOIC STAGE

The egoic stage, which will also be called the stage of the *mental ego*, is the stage that is by far of the longest duration. Indeed, this stage is so inclusive that its status *as a stage* has been overlooked by most developmental theorists. The egoic stage has three principal substages: latency, adolescence, and early adulthood. The consolidation of the ego as the executive agency of consciousness is established with the resolution of the Oedipus complex, which ushers in the period of latency. The ego's primacy within consciousness is challenged during adolescence by the awakening of sexuality and corresponding intimacy needs. The upheavals of adolescence bring about a destabilization and restructuring of the egoic system leading to a reconsolidation of the ego in early adulthood. The organization of the egoic system introduced in early adulthood typically lasts at least until midlife.

The primary characteristics of the egoic stage are (1) a deeply underlying repressive infrastructure that supports the mental ego and insulates it from the deep unconscious and therefore from the Dynamic Ground; (2) self-contained, privatized consciousness associated primarily with mental life and dissociated from physical and instinctual life; (3) apparent ego independence, self-control, and command of will; (4) secondary-process or operational cognition (whether the concrete operations of the latency years or the formal operations of adolescence and later years); and, as the egoic stage moves into midlife, (5) a sense of emptiness and alienation together with a corresponding impetus toward transcendence.

THE TRANSEGOIC STAGE

The transegoic stage, which will also be called the stage of *integration*, is a stage that usually begins—in those cases in which it does begin—at midlife or later, after the ego-developmental tasks of early adulthood have been completed. The beginning of movement toward the trans-egoic or integrated stage is frequently marked by an existential trans-valuation of values: one's worldly goals and priorities lose their meaning and one begins to hunger for spiritual possibilities. This transvaluation of values can lead to spiritual awakening, which in turn can lead to spir-itual transformation, which in its turn can lead to transegoic integration. As I shall be explaining it, the process of spiritual transformation leading to transegoic integration consists of two substages: regression in the ser-vice of transcendence and regeneration in spirit. Regression in the ser-vice of transcendence is the process by which the ego, spiraling back to origins, is returned to the Dynamic Ground; and regeneration in spirit is the process by which the ego, spiraling up to transegoic integration, is spiritually transformed and uplifted by the power of the Ground.

The transegoic or integrated psyche that emerges from these two transformative processes possesses the following principal features: (1) transcendence of the major dualisms that plague the mental ego—namely, the dualisms of mind and body, thought and feeling, logic and creativity, will and spontaneity, self and other, and, most basically, ego and Ground; (2) empowerment of the ego by the Ground; (3) spiritual presence; (4) awakened imaginal, intuitive, and contemplative capabil-ities; (5) rediscovered openness and spontaneity; and (6) an outreaching closeness to and love of others. To these facts about the transegoic or integrated stage should be added one more, namely, that it is the stage that is least frequently attained. Many people experience a midlife transvaluation of values and even some degree of spiritual awakening. For reasons unknown, however, few people experience spiritual awak-enings of great power, and even fewer undergo spiritual transforma-tion all the way to the goal of transegoic integration.

As this brief sketch indicates, the stages of the triphasic division of human development are markedly disproportionate. The first stage is short; most people have little recollection of it. And the third stage is rare; few people embark upon it. In contrast, the second, egoic, stage lasts for most people very nearly the whole of their lifetimes. Given this disproportion, it is understandable that prior to transpersonal theory the triphasic model would not have recommended itself as a likely basis for developmental stage theory.

Finally, the perspective of this book is *dialectical* in that movement through the three stages of life is seen as following a course of departure (thesis), return (antithesis), and higher integration (synthesis). Devel-opment involves a departure in that the ego, in the first half of life (egoic stage), departs from the Dynamic Ground and, in doing so, repressively separates itself from the Ground. Development involves a return in that the ego, usually at or after midlife, is sometimes reopened to the Dynamic Ground and regressively reclaimed by the Ground. And development involves a higher integration in that the ego's return to the Dynamic Ground is a redemptive return—a regression *in the service of transcendence*—that leads to regenerative transformation and, ultimately, to ego-Ground integration. According to the view that I shall be presenting, then, triphasic development is not a unidirectional ascending process but is rather a dialectical spiral played out between the ego and the Dynamic Ground.

1

Transpersonal Theory: Two Basic Paradigms

WE SHALL BEGIN BY formulating and contrasting two basic transpersonal paradigms, the *dynamic-dialectical* paradigm and the *structural-hierarchical* paradigm. The dynamic-dialectical paradigm, introduced in a preliminary way in the introduction, is the paradigm on which the ideas of this book are based. The discussion of the dynamic-dialectical paradigm that follows can therefore serve as a condensed preview of the perspective to be developed in later chapters. Although the dynamic-dialectical paradigm derives originally from Jung, the ensuing formulation of this paradigm is my own and is not intended to be an exposition of Jung's or anyone else's views.

The version of the structural-hierarchical paradigm to be presented here, on the other hand, is closely geared to an already existing formulation, namely, that of Ken Wilber.[1] Wilber is presently a leading figure in the transpersonal field. His work is distinctive in its coherent integration of extremely diverse psychological and spiritual sources within a single theoretical structure: the structural-hierarchical paradigm. This paradigm is one that, in its basic conception, combines structurally oriented psychology (in particular of the Piagetian, cognitive-developmental, type) with hierarchically oriented metaphysics (especially in Indian—for example, Buddhist and Vedantic—variations). This combination is in itself a powerful one, and Wilber presents it in a lucid and forceful way.

As transpersonal paradigms, both the dynamic-dialectical and the structural-hierarchical paradigms divide human development along

9

triphasic (preegoic, egoic, transegoic) lines. In doing so, however, they have very different conceptions of the psychic constitution that under-lies the stages of triphasic development. Consequently, they also have very different conceptions of how these stages are related to each other.

The dynamic-dialectical paradigm is based on a bipolar conception of the psyche, and it sees triphasic development as proceeding by way of a dialectical interplay between the two psychic poles. One of these poles is the seat of the ego, the other the seat of the Dynamic Ground. The dialectical interplay between the two psychic poles is therefore a dialectical interplay between the ego and the Dynamic Ground. Specif-ically, it is an interplay according to which (1) the ego initially emerges from the Ground (the preegoic or body-egoic stage); (2) the ego asserts its independence and develops itself in repressive disconnection from the Ground (the egoic or mental-egoic stage); (3) the ego undergoes a regressive return to the Ground (regression in the service of transcen-dence); (4) the ego, in touch with the Ground, is spiritually transformed by the power of the Ground (regeneration in spirit); and, finally, (5) the ego is "wedded" to the Ground in a higher ego-Ground synthesis (the transegoic stage). The dialectic of dynamic-dialectical development is thus a departure-and-higher-return, negation-and-higher-integration interplay between the ego and the Dynamic Ground.

The structural-hierarchical paradigm, in contrast, is based on a multitiered structural conception of the psyche, and it sees triphasic development as proceeding by way of a level-by-level movement through ascending structural tiers. At first the structures of the lowest level are developed; then the structures of the next higher level are developed, incorporating and reorganizing within themselves the structures of the preceding level; then the structures of the next higher level are developed, incorporating and reorganizing within themselves the structures of the preceding two levels. And so the process unfolds, level by level, each level at once developing its own structures and incorporating and reorganizing within itself the structures of the pre-ceding levels. Development proceeds in this fashion in principle until the structures of the highest level have been developed and, thereby, complete psychic differentiation and integration have been accom-plished. According to Wilber, the psyche is complexly layered, consist-ing of ten or eleven structural levels depending on how they are counted (see tables 1.4 and 1.5). For the structural-hierarchical para-digm, then, the triphasic framework divides human development only into its most basic stages, as each of the triphasic stages spans several psychic levels.

Although both of the transpersonal paradigms here under consideration divide development along broad triphasic lines, they diverge considerably in their interpretations of what triphasic development is really about. The dynamic-dialectical paradigm interprets triphasic development as a dialectically spiraling movement of departure, return, and higher synthesis played out between the ego and Dynamic Ground. The structural-hierarchical paradigm, in contrast, interprets triphasic development as a step-by-step climb up a psychic ladder.

THE DYNAMIC-DIALECTICAL PARADIGM

In presenting the dynamic-dialectical paradigm, the main ideas to be covered are (1) the bipolar constitution of the psyche, (2) the dialectical interplay between the two psychic poles, and (3) unfolding selfhood according to the dynamic-dialectical paradigm.

THE BIPOLAR CONSTITUTION OF THE PSYCHE

As set forth in table 1.1, the bipolar conception divides the psyche into egoic and nonegoic poles. The egoic pole is the seat of the ego, of ego functions (reality testing, self-control, reflective self-awareness, operational cognition), and of personal, that is, biographical, experience. In contrast, the nonegoic pole is the seat of the Dynamic Ground (libido, psychic energy, numinous power or spirit), of somatic, instinctual, affective, and creative-imaginal potentials, and of collective (inherited) memories, complexes, and archetypes. The egoic pole, which will also be called the *mental-egoic* pole, is the seat of rational cognition and volition, discursive thought and deliberative will. In contrast, the nonegoic pole, which will also be called the *physicodynamic* pole, is the source of upwelling dynamism, spontaneous impulse, feeling, and creatively forged images. The bipolar structure, then, encompasses many of the most basic dualities of life: form and dynamism, mind and body, thought and feeling, logic and creativity, self-control and spontaneity.

The bipolar structure is implicit in classical psychoanalysis in the structural (id-ego-superego) model of the psyche. Although the structural model divides the psyche into three tiers, it is more fundamentally a division of the psyche into two poles. For the superego is a subsystem of the ego, and therefore the id-ego-superego tripartite division is more basically an id-ego bipolar division. Conceived in this simplified structural way, the Freudian ego clearly corresponds to the egoic pole of the bipolar structure of table 1.1; the description of the egoic pole in table

TABLE 1.1

The Bipolar Structure of the Psyche

Nonegoic or Physicodynamic Pole	Egoic or Mental-Egoic Pole
Dynamic Ground: dynamism, libido, energy, spirit	Ego as organizing and controlling center of consciousness
Somatic, sensual experience	Reflective self-awareness
Instinctuality	Impulse control
Affect, emotion	Self-control, deliberative will
Imaginal, autosymbolic cognition	Operational cognition
Collective memories, complexes, archetypes	Personal, biographical experience

1.1 is a straightforward description of the ego as conceived by psychoanalysis. Less clearly, but still quite evidently, the Freudian id corresponds to the nonegoic pole of the bipolar structure. For the id as conceived by classical psychoanalysis is the seat of psychic energy (libido, aggressive energy), bodily experience (infantile polymorphous sensuality), instinctual drives (sexual and aggressive drives), affect or emotion (sublimated instinctual drives), imaginal, autosymbolic cognition (the primary process), and collective memories and complexes (the killing of the primal father, the Oedipus complex).

The correspondence of the Freudian id with the nonegoic pole of the bipolar structure is less clear than the correspondence of the Freudian ego with the egoic pole because the id is a one-sidedly preegoic, or subegoic, interpretation of the nonegoic pole. Table 1.1 describes the nonegoic pole in neutral terms, leaving it unspecified whether that pole is to be interpreted in a lower or higher, preegoic or transegoic, manner. The Freudian conception of the id, however, clearly interprets the nonegoic pole as a psychic realm or system of a lower, preegoic status. The id is inherently unconscious; its dynamism consists solely of sexual and aggressive energies; its bodily experience is conceived as infantile polymorphous "perversity"; its affective expressions are transformations of the sexual and aggressive drives; its imaginal, autosymbolic cognition is the creative but prelogical primary process; and its collective memories and complexes are exclusively archaic or infantile in character. Freud, then, in effect reduces the nonegoic pole of the bipolar structure to the preegoic level, which means that the psychoanalytic id-ego duality can more accurately be said to be a preegoic-egoic than a nonegoic-egoic bipolar structure.

Turning to Jung's theory, the bipolar structure is reflected in the fundamental division between the ego and the collective unconscious (or objective psyche). The Jungian ego corresponds unproblematically to the egoic pole of the bipolar structure. The Jungian ego is the center of consciousness and the agency responsible for reality testing, logical thinking, and rational exercise of will. And the Jungian collective unconscious corresponds to the nonegoic pole of the bipolar structure. For the collective unconscious is the seat or source of psychic energy, instinctual life, feelings, and archetypes and creative images. The collective unconscious as conceived by Jung matches almost all of the features of the nonegoic pole as set forth in table 1.1.

The Jungian collective unconscious more accurately represents the nonegoic pole of the bipolar structure than does the Freudian id, for the collective unconscious as conceived by Jung is by no means exclusively preegoic in nature. Jung describes the collective unconscious as having both "pre-" and "trans-" expressions. For instance, he holds that psychic energy is not just sexual or aggressive drive energy, as Freud held, but is rather an energy that empowers all modes of experience—even spiritual experience—without being inherently of the nature of any particular mode of experience. He interprets instinctuality in an inclusive sense that covers not only primitive "pre-" instincts governing basic life needs such as food, safety, and reproduction but also higher "trans-" instincts guiding the process of individuation. He interprets feelings nonreductionistically to include both lower (infantile or malevolent) feelings associated with the shadow and higher numinous feelings associated with spiritual development. He interprets the imaginal or autosymbolic process as the source not only of fantasies and dreams of a prelogical (archaic or infantile) sort but also of mythic symbols of a genuinely transcendental stature. And he interprets collective memories and complexes in terms of the archetypes of the collective unconscious, which include both "pre-" archetypes reflecting our phylogenetic past and "trans-" archetypes reflecting our spiritual future.

Although Jung's conception of the nonegoic pole is not one-sidedly negative like Freud's, it is still problematic. For although Jung acknowledges both "pre-" and "trans-" expressions of the collective unconscious, he frequently leaves it unclear—as Wilber (1980b) has observed—whether these expressions are to be understood in a constitutional sense (as expressions of basic, permanent psychic sources or structures) or in a developmental sense (as stage-specific phenomena). "Pre-" and "trans-" expressions of the collective unconscious, I suggest, are properly understood in a developmental sense as stage-specific expressions of the nonegoic pole of the psyche, which itself is properly understood in a constitutional rather than a developmental sense. Jung makes no clear distinctions of this sort, and therefore his notion of the collective unconscious, although not reductionistically one-sided like Freud's notion of the id, is still far from an adequate conception of the nonegoic pole. Jung's conception of the collective unconscious, I suggest, confuses a number of developmental and constitutional matters.

A psychic duality that should be distinguished from the bipolar structure is a duality that Deikman (1971) has designated the *bimodal* structure of consciousness. The two modes of the bimodal structure are engaged activity (active mode) and open receptivity (receptive mode). The primary features of these modes are outlined in table 1.2.

The bimodal structure belongs to the egoic side of the bipolar structure: it is the ego or egoic pole of the psyche that has two basic modes, active and receptive. It is the ego that either asserts itself by exercising ego functions (active mode) or "lets go" and opens itself to nonegoic influences (receptive mode). These two modes of the ego reflect the ego's status as one end of a bipole, as something that is at once individuated and part of a larger whole. For as one end of a bipole, the ego has two stances it can adopt: it can either assert itself in its status as an individuated existent or it can surrender itself in its status as a part of a larger whole. In adopting the former stance, the ego takes initiative and exercises its own functions; in adopting the latter stance, the ego relinquishes hold of itself and allows itself to be influenced by nonegoic or physicodynamic potentials: dynamism, instinctual impulses, affect, the creative process, collective cognitions and complexes. Or in bimodal terms, in adopting the former stance, the ego functions in the active mode; in adopting the latter stance, it "switches off" the active mode and enters the receptive mode.

A qualification is in order: in saying that the ego can switch back and forth between the active and receptive modes, I do not mean to suggest that these two modes are necessarily mutually exclusive. It must be left open as a possibility that the ego, in a completely integrated psyche,

TABLE 1.2

The Bimodal Structure of Consciousness

Receptive Mode	Active Mode
Receptive openness Ego yields to experience. Infusion, absorption, merger, fusion	Active engagement Ego centered in itself. Ego autonomy, self-possession, independence

can exercise ego functions effectively while at the same time being open to the full range of nonegoic potentials. Such bimodal integration, I shall propose, is indeed possible, but only on the basis of a more fundamental bipolar integration. The ego, as we shall see, can indeed be open to the nonegoic pole without loss of its own functions, but only if it is first both fully developed and harmoniously rooted in the nonegoic pole.

In sum, the dynamic-dialectical paradigm sees the psyche as being bipolar in its basic constitution. The distinction between the ego and the Dynamic Ground is at the same time a distinction between egoic and nonegoic poles of the psyche, the egoic pole being the seat of the ego and ego functions and the nonegoic pole being the seat of the Dynamic Ground and associated nonegoic or physicodynamic potentials. In dividing the psyche in this bipolar manner, the dynamic-dialectical paradigm at the same time divides the ego, or the egoic pole of the psyche, in a bimodal manner. The ego can either assert itself within the limits of its semi-independence (active mode) or it can open itself to nonegoic potentials (receptive mode). If the ego opens itself to nonegoic potentials, it allows itself to be affected in a variety of ways. For example, the ego might be (1) entranced, absorbed, infused, inflated, or inspired by the power of the Dynamic Ground, (2) played upon by erotogenic or sensual sensations, (3) moved by instinctual urgings, (4) uplifted or overswept by feelings, (5) made witness to vivid images, or (6) brought under the influence of collective memories, archetypes, or complexes. In the dynamic-dialectical view, the ego, in entering the receptive mode, opens itself to the diverse potentials of the nonegoic pole and is affected accordingly.

THE DIALECTICAL INTERPLAY BETWEEN THE TWO PSYCHIC POLES

The dynamic-dialectical paradigm holds that triphasic development is governed by a dialectical interplay between the two poles of the bipolar structure, as schematized in figure 1.1.

In this bipolar dialectic, life begins with the egoic pole only minimally active: the ego is only minimally differentiated from the Dynamic Ground. Psychoanalysts have debated for many years whether an ego and object relations exist at birth. The current consensus is that the neonate does have an active ego (or self) and is involved in object relations to a significant degree.[2] Acknowledging this very likely fact, it remains true that the ego is at first only *minimally* active. The ego during the first months of life, although almost surely not absent, nonetheless exists for the most part only as a potentiality for further development. The ego at this point is for the most part an ego germ not yet differentiated from the Dynamic Ground. This initial condition of ego-Ground merger I shall call *original embedment*.

The egoic pole of the psyche, as can be seen from figure 1.1, is soon significantly differentiated from the nonegoic pole and begins to participate in a lifelong developmental interaction with the nonegoic pole. Human development very soon becomes an interplay between the ego and the Dynamic Ground. If human development is an interplay between the two poles of the bipolar structure, however, it is by no means always a balanced or harmonious interplay. On the contrary, according to the dynamic-dialectical paradigm, the two psychic poles are never in a state of parity, and they are harmoniously related only at the very beginning and end of human development, in the first year and a half of the preegoic (or body-egoic) stage and in the transegoic stage of development. Throughout most of human development, the two psychic poles are neither equal nor balanced in their relation to each other.

The preegoic stage—which succeeds original embedment after the first weeks of life—is a stage during which the nonegoic pole prevails over the egoic pole. During this stage physicodynamic potentials have a strong and frequently overpowering influence on a weak and undeveloped ego. The egoic (or mental-egoic) stage, in turn, is a period during which the nonegoic ascendancy of the preegoic stage is brought to an end and the ego assumes a one-sided control of consciousness. The egoic pole frees itself from the direct influence of the nonegoic pole, but only by repressing the nonegoic pole and banishing physicodynamic potentials from consciousness. The egoic stage is for this reason one that is unbalanced in the direction of the ego. The egoic pole is developed and functions to a significant extent independently of the nonegoic pole, which is submerged and becomes the deep unconscious. Finally, in the transition to the transegoic stage this egoic one-sidedness of the egoic stage is brought to an end and the nonegoic pole of the psyche once again gains ascendancy. During the transitional stages of regression in the service of transcendence and regeneration in spirit, the egoic pole loses its independence and comes once again under the direct influence of the nonegoic pole. The ego, no longer repressively insulated from the nonegoic pole, is regressively reclaimed and then regeneratively transformed by nonegoic potentials and by the power of the Dynamic Ground in particular. This regressive-regenerative transformation reroots the ego in the Dynamic Ground and culminates in bipo-

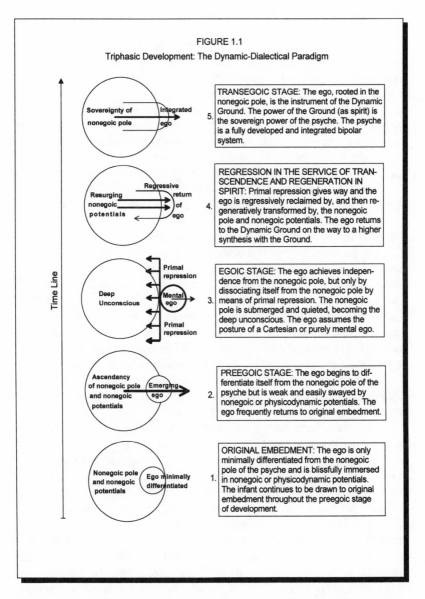

FIGURE 1.1

Triphasic Development: The Dynamic-Dialectical Paradigm

lar integration. The ego is in this way finally brought into a harmonious relationship with the Dynamic Ground, and the transegoic stage commences.

This harmony of transegoic integration, however, is not a harmony of equals. It is a state of interpolar balance but not of interpolar parity.

For according to the dynamic-dialectical paradigm, the two psychic poles are inherently unequal: the nonegoic pole is superior in both power and authority. This superiority is evident whenever the egoic pole is open to the nonegoic pole, as is the case in both the preegoic and transegoic stages. In the preegoic stage, as just noted, the nonegoic pole has a strong and frequently overpowering influence on a fledgling ego; and in the integrated stage the nonegoic pole, without any longer over-powering the ego, still possesses primacy in that it empowers, grounds, and guides the ego. Accordingly, transegoic bipolar integration is an integration in which the ego is once again the lesser of two psychic poles. It is an integration in which the ego accedes not only to the actual felt power but also to the legitimate supremacy of the Dynamic Ground. Transegoic integration is an integration in which the nonegoic pole, without being dominant, is nonetheless sovereign and in which the egoic pole, without being subjugated, is nonetheless subject.

Given that, in the dynamic-dialectical view, the three stages of triphasic development reflect reversals in which psychic pole has ascendancy, it follows that the transitions between these stages are developmental intervals during which these reversals occur. During the transition from the preegoic to the egoic stage the original ascen-dancy of the nonegoic pole is brought to an end and the ego achieves a one-sided control of consciousness. And during the transition from the egoic stage to the transegoic stage this egoic one-sidedness is in its turn brought to an end and the nonegoic pole becomes ascendant once again, this time in a harmoniously integrated way, in a way that empowers rather than overpowers the ego.

The shift from nonegoic ascendancy to egoic one-sidedness that occurs during the transition to the egoic stage is predicated on a repressive separation of the ego from the nonegoic potentials of life. Following Freud, I shall call the repression that occurs at this point *primal repression*. Freud maintained as early as *The Interpretation of Dreams* (1900) that the secondary process cannot accommodate primary-pro-cess materials and, therefore, that a repressive elimination of these materials from awareness occurs as soon as the system of conscious-ness is formed. Freud (1911b) later termed this initial, infantile form of repression primal repression. After he introduced the (id-ego-super-ego) structural model (1923), Freud explained primal repression in terms of the ego's emergence from the id. Instinctual impulses of the id, Freud explained (1926, 1933), overwhelm the fledgling ego, trigger-ing severe anxiety. The immature ego is unable to deal with these impulses in any way other than by repressing them and thereby keep-ing them contained within the id. Freud (1926) stated that this original and basic repression likely occurs before the end of the oedipal period. The resolution of oedipal conflicts and the emergence of the superego, however, reinforce the id-ego separation initiated by primal repression.[3]

In adopting Freud's notion of primal repression, I depart slightly from Freud by adding an object-relational account of primal repression to his primarily psychodynamic account. In chapter 2 I propose that the ego, in emerging from the Dynamic Ground, experiences nonegoic potentials as elements or aspects of the primary libidinal object: the primary caregiver—or rather, in Jungian terminology, the Great Mother, the primary caregiver as empowered and magnified by nonegoic potentials. Accordingly, the crisis that, according to Freud, the ego experiences in relation to id impulses—that is, in relation to nonegoic or physicodynamic potentials—is not just an intrapsychic affair; it is part of a larger crisis that the ego experiences in relation to the Great Mother. And, in corresponding fashion, the repressive act by which the ego finally separates itself from nonegoic potentials is not just an intrapsychic act; it is at the same time an interpersonal act by which the ego separates itself from the Great Mother.

The young child, I shall propose, has no choice but finally to separate itself from the inner-outer, intrapsychic-interpersonal, Ground-caregiver Great Mother. It accomplishes this separation by severing any remaining ties of symbiotic merger or union with the primary caregiver and, as the inner side of this very act, by repressing the nonegoic pole of the psyche. This response, primal repression, initially emerges at about the beginning of the third year, near the end of what Margaret Mahler (Mahler, Pine, and Bergman 1975) calls the *rapprochement subphase* of the separation-individuation process. This initial response, however, is not final. The child continues to crave intimate union with the Great Mother—both interpersonal merger with the primary caregiver and intrapsychic merger with the Dynamic Ground (reembedment). Primal repression, then, is at first only a tentative and halting separation of the ego from the Great Mother. It does not become final—as Freud suggests—until the end of the oedipal period. In chapter 2 I shall argue that primal repression does not become decisive and irreversible until the oedipal father enters the scene and forces the child's hand by making the child's choice for or against the Great Mother at the same time a choice against or for the father. The resolution of the Oedipus complex, predicated on a capitulation to the father and on emulation of him as model of egoic independence, finalizes the child's separation from the Great Mother in both her inner and outer dimensions. The resolution of the Oedipus complex, that is, finalizes primal repression and consolidates it as a psychic structure.

Primal repression has both positive and negative consequences. Its primary positive consequence is that it frees the developing ego from the strong and frequently overpowering influence of the Great Mother and thereby confers upon the ego the self-possession needed for its continued development. Primal repression is at the basis of both latency and libidinal object constancy, both of which, according to psychoanalysis, are necessary conditions for continued ego development. Primal repression is at the basis of latency because the inner side of this act submerges and therefore quiets nonegoic potentials. And primal repression is at the basis of libidinal object constancy because the final severing of symbiotic ties with the primary caregiver gives the child the emotional distance needed to relate to the caregiver, and therefore to others generally, in a stable and consistent manner. Primal repression both calms the ego's intrapsychic experience and stabilizes the ego's primary relationships. Such calm and stability are necessary for continued ego development, and therefore primal repression serves a positive developmental end.

The primary negative consequence of primal repression is that in protecting the ego from nonegoic and interpersonal influences it also *closes* the ego to these influences and thereby disconnects the ego from the original bases of its being. It requires the ego to forfeit both radical nonegoic spontaneity and unconditional interpersonal intimacy. These sacrifices are developmentally necessary, but they are sacrifices— immense sacrifices—nonetheless. The ego is free to develop, but only because it has disconnected itself from the nonegoic pole of the psyche, which is submerged and becomes the deep unconscious, and because it has withdrawn from its primary other and therefore from others generally, who become "merely other." The egoic stage is for these reasons a stage not only of freedom from overawing nonegoic and interpersonal influences but also of egoic-nonegoic and self-other dualism.

The egoic stage as here described lasts from the beginning of latency throughout much of the rest of life. In classical psychoanalysis, of course, the egoic stage is the final and highest stage of development. The egoic-nonegoic dualism of the stage is, for psychoanalysis, a permanent psychic structure. Jungian psychology, on the other hand, acknowledges transegoic possibilities beyond the egoic stage. According to Jung, there is a tendency at midlife or later for egoic-nonegoic dualism to give way and for the ego to undergo a reversal (an *enantiodromia*) in its relation to the nonegoic sphere. Jung believed that this reversal is a natural part of the movement of life, the first half of which is devoted to ego development and the second half of which is devoted to a return of the ego to its underlying source in the collective unconscious or objective psyche.

The dynamic-dialectical view presented here is close to Jung on this issue, holding that the ego, once mature, may be drawn back toward the nonegoic pole of the psyche. Around midlife, according to the dynamic-dialectical view, primal repression may begin to dissolve, reopening the ego to nonegoic life. When such a reopening occurs, the ego is exposed to the power of the Dynamic Ground and to other nonegoic potentials and is drawn into the nonegoic sphere. The ego, drawn toward the Ground, undergoes a *regressus ad originem*. It returns to the deepest inner source of its being.

The dynamic-dialectical paradigm conceives of this return of the ego to the Ground not only as a regression to origins but also as a potentially redemptive process.[4] The return is conceived as the first phase of a transformation that, in reopening the egoic pole to the nonegoic pole, leads ultimately to a dialectical synthesis of these poles. That is, the return is seen as the first phase of a two-phase, return-then-higher-synthesis spiral. Jung recognized this phase of development, which, following Leo Frobenius (1904), he referred to as the "night sea journey," the period during which the sun (ego) descends into the sea and is devoured by a water monster, a whale or dragon, only later to be reborn for the dawn of a new day. In Jung's interpretation of the night sea journey, the sun's descent beneath the sea is the ego's descent into the collective unconscious, wherein the ego is engulfed only to be reborn in a new empowered and transfigured form. In other mythic or symbolic expressions, this regressive return is depicted as the odyssey of a hero into the underworld, as the journey of a saint into the lower regions of hell, as the awakening of the "serpent power" *kundalini*, and as the alchemical reduction of base metal into prime matter. In the terms of St. John of the Cross, this descent into the deep is the dark night of spirit, which is the most difficult phase of the dark night of the soul. Drawing on psychoanalytic terminology, I shall call the ego's regressive return to the nonegoic sphere, and to the Dynamic Ground in particular, *regression in the service of transcendence*.

Once the ego has returned to the Ground, the second, redemptive phase of the return-then-higher-synthesis process begins. At this point descent gives way to ascent, darkness to light, regression to regeneration. Having weathered the resurgence of nonegoic potentials, the ego here ceases being overpowered by these potentials and begins being empowered by them instead. The difficulties experienced during the regression to the Ground abate, and the ego, now rooted in the Ground, begins to be infused and redemptively transformed by the power of the

Ground. This redemptive transformation of the ego has been described in many ways; for example, as the liberation of the sun from the belly of the sea monster, as the triumphant return of the hero or saint from infernal regions, as the awakening of the *chakras* by ascending *kundalini*, as a purgative transformation of the soul, as a spiritual betrothal presaging full spiritual union, and as the alchemical transubstantiation of base metal into gold. Using traditional terminology, I shall call this higher rebirth and redemptive transformation of the ego *regeneration in spirit*.

According to the dynamic-dialectical paradigm, the goal aimed at by regeneration in spirit is a condition of fully actualized and integrated bipolarity. This condition is one in which the two poles of the psyche finally become a true two-in-one; it is a condition in which ego functions and nonegoic potentials at last function harmoniously and on a higher plane. Bipolar integration is a *coincidentia oppositorum* that transcends all of the elements that enter into it. The stipulation needs to be added, however, that integration, as a higher unity of opposites, is not a unity of equals. For, again, in the integrated psyche the nonegoic pole has primacy; the egoic pole accedes to the nonegoic pole as a superior power and authority. The egoic pole is an instrument of the nonegoic pole; the ego is a servant of the power of the Ground as spirit.

UNFOLDING SELFHOOD ACCORDING TO THE DYNAMIC-DIALECTICAL PARADIGM

The bipolar dialectic is at the same time a dialectic of unfolding selfhood. The dialectical interplay between the two poles of the psyche is a dialectic of selfhood because each of the two psychic poles is in a sense a self, the nonegoic pole being the original, deeper, and (potentially) higher self and the egoic pole being a secondary but still essential self. Each of these two selves, like its corresponding pole, is incomplete without the other and is fully itself only in harmonious integration with the other. Accordingly, the dialectical process that leads ultimately to bipolar integration also leads to an integrated duality of selfhood, as represented in figure 1.2.

Dynamic-dialectical development begins with original embedment: the egoic pole is at first only minimally differentiated from the nonegoic pole. The ego is at first essentially an ego germ gestating within the Dynamic Ground, which at this point is the original source of life prior to the articulation of selfhood. This initial condition of merger, however, lasts for only a short time, because the egoic pole develops rapidly and is soon significantly differentiated from the non-

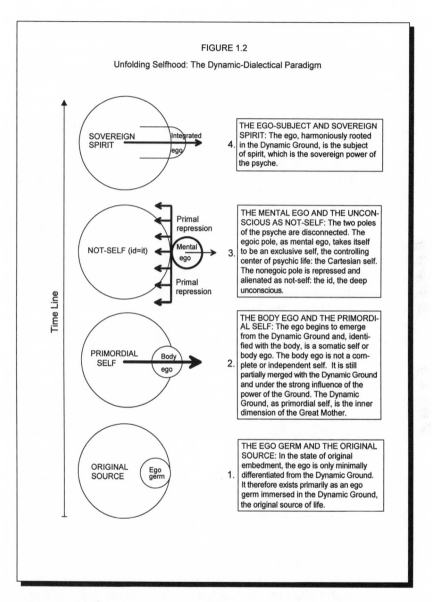

FIGURE 1.2

Unfolding Selfhood: The Dynamic-Dialectical Paradigm

THE EGO-SUBJECT AND SOVEREIGN SPIRIT: The ego, harmoniously rooted in the Dynamic Ground, is the subject of spirit, which is the sovereign power of the psyche.

THE MENTAL EGO AND THE UNCONSCIOUS AS NOT-SELF: The two poles of the psyche are disconnected. The egoic pole, as mental ego, takes itself to be an exclusive self, the controlling center of psychic life: the Cartesian self. The nonegoic pole is repressed and alienated as not-self: the id, the deep unconscious.

THE BODY EGO AND THE PRIMORDIAL SELF: The ego begins to emerge from the Dynamic Ground and, identified with the body, is a somatic self or body ego. The body ego is not a complete or independent self. It is still partially merged with the Dynamic Ground and under the strong influence of the power of the Ground. The Dynamic Ground, as primordial self, is the inner dimension of the Great Mother.

THE EGO GERM AND THE ORIGINAL SOURCE: In the state of original embedment, the ego is only minimally differentiated from the Dynamic Ground. It therefore exists primarily as an ego germ immersed in the Dynamic Ground, the original source of life.

egoic pole. As the ego emerges and begins to grow, the virtually undivided state of original embedment is split into a lopsided duality; it is split into a primitive Ground-dominant bipole. This primitive Ground-dominant bipole is at the same time a primitive Ground-dominant dyadic self.

The ego at this point is only in the process of being individuated and is still to a large extent enfolded in the Dynamic Ground. The Ground, as inner core of the Great Mother, remains the principal reality in the ego's life, not only as the original source from which the ego has sprung but also, now, as the primordial self with which the ego is partially merged and to which it returns again and again to reexperience the bliss of original embedment. Partially merged with the Ground as primordial self, the ego during the preegoic stage has only incomplete self-boundaries. The ego at this point does have a differentiated sense of itself as a *bodily self* or *body ego*, but this sense is vague and shifting, because no clear line has yet been drawn separating the ego from the Dynamic Ground—or from the outer correlate of the Ground, the primary caregiver.

The strong and frequently overpowering influence that the Ground has on the ego comes to an end only when the ego finally perpetrates the act of primal repression and thereby divorces itself from its nonegoic origins. Primal repression marks the transition to the egoic stage. In embarking upon this transition, the ego asserts it independence, but only by dissociating itself from the nonegoic pole, which is submerged beneath consciousness and negatively interpreted as the id or not-self. According to the dynamic-dialectical paradigm, then, the ego becomes an independent self only by assuming the posture of an exclusive self, a self that is no longer identified with or tied to physicodynamic life. The ego severs its connection with the primordial self and takes on airs of being the only self. It fancies itself to be a self-subsistent mental self that is the exclusive owner and controller of psychic life. The egoic stage of development is therefore a period during which the ego ceases being a body ego still partially merged with the Ground and becomes a purely mental ego that, disjoined from the Ground, acts as if it were a completely independent and autonomous self.

At first, during the latency period, the mental ego does not yet clearly conceive of itself as a mental ego. Limited to concrete operational thought, the latency child is still prone to think of itself in concrete material terms. Accordingly, although the ego of the latency period no longer identifies with the body, it nonetheless does not yet conceive of itself as a purely psychomental or Cartesian subject. Rather, it conceives of itself, vaguely and confusedly, as a *something* inside the head—some object or substance, perhaps the brain itself. Not until adolescence does the mental ego begin to be reflectively aware of itself as a purely psychomental subject or Cartesian ego. This Cartesian self-reflection of adolescence is a source of both certainty and anxiety, certainty because it confirms the fact that the mental ego exists (*cogito ergo sum*) and anxiety because the mental ego confirmed by Cartesian self-reflection is never directly intuited by means of Cartesian self-reflection. The mental ego of adolescence is therefore a self-certain *absence*, an ego certain *that* it exists but completely unsure of *what*, if anything, it is.

The anxiety of Cartesian self-reflection is a primary motivating cause of the adolescent and young-adult pursuit of identity. The mental ego that is absent to itself in introspection needs to give its existence some kind of recognizable form. It responds to this need by fashioning an identity, which, recognized by others, confers upon the mental ego a sense of worldly being. The mental ego in adolescence experiments with identity possibilities without committing itself to any of them; then, in the transition to early adulthood, it commits itself to a long-term identity project. The forging and defense of ego identity, of being-in-the-world, is one of the main developmental tasks of early adulthood.

The mental ego's assumption that it is a Cartesian subject completely independent of physicodynamic life is false. It is false because the mental ego, as a specific developmental expression of the egoic pole of the psyche, remains one end of a bipole. Even in its stance of independence, the mental ego remains internally connected to and dependent for its very being upon the nonegoic pole of the psyche. Consequently, despite its seeming self-sufficiency, the mental ego is vulnerable to feeling unwhole, to sensing that it is somehow out of touch with a deep and vital part of itself. This feeling of unwholeness typically does not begin to plague the mental ego in a serious way until after it has completed the developmental tasks of the first half of adult life. Once these tasks have been completed, however, the mental ego frequently becomes prone to feelings of emptiness and incompleteness. At midlife or later, the mental ego frequently becomes susceptible to feeling that its stance of independence may be only a false pose and that its worldly identity may be only an inauthentic mask hiding a buried, "true" self.

Although the mental ego's stance of independence can lead to these disturbing feelings, it is not for that reason a posture that is easily let go. On the contrary, it is a posture that, according to the dynamic-dialectical paradigm, is deeply entrenched and extremely difficult to surmount. The undoing of the ego's stance of independence requires an undoing of primal repression. Primal repression, however, rarely gives way, and therefore movement beyond the egoic stage into transegoic realms is an infrequent occurrence.

In those instances when primal repression is undone, however, the mental ego's stance of independence is undermined and the mental ego is set on the course of regression in the service of transcendence. No longer supported by the false ground of primal repression, the mental ego comes into direct contact with the Dynamic Ground, which reclaims the mental ego and disabuses it of its pretension of being an independent, incorporeal substance. The mental ego facing this situation has no choice but to confess the falseness of its posture of self-sufficiency and to yield to the superior power and authority of the Dynamic Ground. No longer undergirded by primal repression, the mental ego loses its self-possession; it is drawn out of its own sphere and begins the odyssey of return to the Dynamic Ground, the power of which is the ego's higher self.

The ego's return to the Ground involves a regression: regression in the service of transcendence. The undoing of primal repression reopens the ego to nonegoic potentials, which spring to life in dramatic fashion. The ego experiences the return of the repressed. In particular, the power of the Ground reawakens and challenges the ego's hold on consciousness. From the dynamic-dialectical perspective, then, the ego's return to the Ground involves a regression that brings the ego into contact with powerful derepressing forces.

This regression-derepression process continues until the power of the Ground and other nonegoic potentials have fully reasserted themselves and the ego has finally overcome its resistance to these potentials. At this point the transition from regression to regeneration occurs: the power of the Ground ceases posing a threat to the ego and begins to support and heal the ego. The ego here realizes that the power of the Ground is not an alien invading force but is rather a spiritual power that is both superior and essential to the ego. The ego, having been regressed to the Ground, here begins to undergo a regenerative transformation that brings it into harmony with the Ground and that in general brings the egoic pole of the psyche into harmony with the nonegoic pole. This regeneration process leads ultimately to a complete union of the two psychic poles, a union that is at the same time a wedding of the ego (as lesser self) to spirit (as greater self). Full self-realization conceived in dynamic-dialectical terms is, accordingly, a condition of perfected ego-Ground, self-Self bipolarity: the two psychic poles function as one and the two selves that correspond to these poles are joined as one. The ego, as subject, becomes the instrument of sovereign spirit.

Table 1.3 reviews and summarizes the dynamic-dialectical conception of human development.

TABLE 1.3

The Dynamic-Dialectical Paradigm

Time Line		
INTEGRATION	The two poles of the psyche are harmoniously united and their potentials and functions are effectively integrated. The two poles begin functioning as a true bipolar system, a coincidence of opposites. The power of the Ground, as spirit, is the sovereign power of the psyche.	
REGENERATION IN SPIRIT	The ego, having yielded to the Dynamic Ground, now begins to be empowered rather than overpowered by nonegoic potentials. The ego begins to be regenerated by the power of the Ground as spirit.	
REGRESSION IN THE SERVICE OF TRANSCENDENCE	Primal repression gives way and the ego is regressively reclaimed by the Dynamic Ground. The ego is unseated as the central power of consciousness and challenged by awakening nonegoic potentials. The ego undergoes a regression to origins.	
EGOIC OR MENTAL-EGOIC STAGE	The ego develops its own functions in relative independence from the nonegoic pole, which underlies the ego as the deep unconscious. The nonegoic pole is not-self or id; the egoic pole is a mental ego or Cartesian self.	
PRIMAL REPRESSION	The ego finally wins its independence from nonegoic potentials, but only by repressively disconnecting itself from the nonegoic pole, which is submerged and becomes the deep unconscious.	
PREEGOIC OR BODY-EGOIC STAGE	The preegoic stage is a period during which the ego is progressively differentiated from the Great Mother but is still under the sway of nonegoic potentials. The nonegoic pole is the primordial self; the egoic pole is a bodily self or body ego.	
ORIGINAL EMBEDMENT	The ego at birth is only minimally differentiated from the Dynamic Ground and exists as an ego germ immersed in the Ground, which here is the original source of life prior to selfhood. Original embedment is a blissful condition to which the ego frequently returns throughout the preoedipal period.	

THE STRUCTURAL-HIERARCHICAL PARADIGM

The structural-hierarchical paradigm differs from the dynamic-dialectical paradigm both in its conception of the psychic constitution and in its conception of how the stages of development are related to each other. Moreover, as a consequence of these differences, the structural-hierarchical paradigm has a very different conception of unfolding self-hood as well. The structural-hierarchical paradigm shares with the dynamic-dialectical paradigm the triphasic or transpersonal perspective. Beyond this point of agreement, however, it has little in common with the dynamic-dialectical view.

The account of the structural-hierarchical paradigm presented here is based on the work of Ken Wilber, who first formulated this paradigm in *The Spectrum of Consciousness* (1977). Wilber has since reformulated the paradigm in a number of different places (1980a, 1980b, 1981a, 1981b, 1990; Wilber et al. 1986). The ensuing exposition draws on all of these sources but especially on the statement of the paradigm in the collection of papers published under the title *Eye to Eye* (1990).

THE HIERARCHIAL CONSTITUTION OF THE PSYCHE

The structural-hierarchical paradigm conceives of the psyche as a hierarchy of structural levels, each higher level of which surpasses the ones below it in representing both greater psychic differentiation and greater psychic integration. Each higher level represents greater differentiation in that once a higher level emerges, the structures of that level are articulated and added to the structures of the levels beneath it. And each higher level represents greater integration in that each such level has a significant degree of access to and command over the structures of lower levels and therefore effectively integrates those structures within itself.

Wilber holds that each level of the psychic hierarchy is distinguished by a set of basic or defining structures (functions, potentials, capabilities, predispositions). These basic structures, in being inherent to a level of the psychic hierarchy, are thereby inherent to the psyche itself. They are deep structures that are part of the psyche's original endowment and that, as such, are transcultural, universal to human experience. As deep structures, these basic structures are to be distinguished from surface structures, which are the merely contingent ways in which the psyche's basic structures happen to be expressed and implemented in life. Whereas basic structures are the innate underlying patterns of life, surface structures are the particular social and thematic manifestations of those patterns. Unlike basic structures, which are original and universal, surface structures are derivative and variable, differing widely in cultural form and focus.

According to the structural-hierarchical paradigm, the levels of the psychic hierarchy are related in the following fundamental ways: (1) lower levels support and subserve higher levels, and (2) higher levels subsume and control lower levels. Lower levels support and subserve higher levels because the structures of lower levels are necessary foundations upon which the structures of higher levels are built. Lower levels are more than foundations, however; they are also integral parts of higher levels. Higher levels subsume the structures of lower levels, utilizing them as elements or modules of higher-level functions. In subsuming lower levels in this way, higher levels reorganize lower levels and exercise control over them. Lower levels retain a significant degree of autonomy, but to a significant degree their functioning is subject to the control of the higher level under which they are subsumed. This model is clearly organic and holistic. The levels of the structural-hierarchical paradigm are related in ways that are similar to the ways in which the levels of an organic hierarchy—such as the hierarchy of cell, organ, and organ system—are related.

Given that higher psychic levels incorporate lower levels, it follows that the highest active psychic level is in effect the whole of the psyche. That is, each level (except the lowest) is not only a single psychic tier but also a multitiered totality including within itself all lower levels. The structural-hierarchical paradigm therefore conceives of the psyche not just as a hierarchy but more specifically as a hierarchy that is organized in a top-down fashion. Each level of the hierarchy retains a significant degree of autonomy, and the top-down organization of the hierarchy in no way precludes bottom-up causality; nevertheless, the point remains that the psyche is a hierarchy the highest active level of which superintends the whole. The highest active level is the seat of psychic agency.

Wilber's account of the principal psychic levels and their corresponding basic structures is summarized in table 1.4. As can be seen from table 1.4, Wilber divides the psyche into many levels and groups these levels within the three stages of the triphasic framework. In making the triphasic division, Wilber extends Piaget's distinction between sensorimotor and preoperational levels of cognition on the one hand and operational levels on the other by adding several transoperational levels. Wilber also extends Piaget's thought by conceiving of psychic levels not only as levels of cognitive attainment but also as levels of instinctual, affective, or spiritual expression.

Extending the Piagetian perspective in these ways, Wilber describes the three levels of triphasic development as follows: The pre-egoic levels, up to and including the phantasmic level (representational mind being a transitional level), correspond to the infantile rudiments of life: sensorimotor and preoperational cognition, instinctually governed dynamism and affect. The egoic levels, up to and including

TABLE 1.4

Wilber's Hierarchical Psyche*

	Psychic Level	Basic Structures
Transegoic Levels	ULTIMATE UNITY	Complete psychic integration and coincidence of individual with reality. Unity beyond all division and duality.
	CAUSAL (35 years and up)**	Unitive consciousness; contemplation of unity of human and divine; radiant absorption in the godhead.
	SUBTLE (28 years and up)**	Paranormal psychic abilities; archetypal, visionary intuition; spontaneous devotional and altruistic feelings.
Egoic Levels	VISION LOGIC (21 years and up)**	Holistic-synthetic thinking; mind-body, thought-feeling integration; existential wholeness and authenticity.
	REFLEXIVE-FORMAL MIND (11 to 15 years)**	Formal operational (Piaget) or secondary-process (Freud) cognition: abstract, analytical, inferential, hypothetical thinking. Self-consciousness combined with ability to assume perspective of others.
	RULE-ROLE MIND (6 to 8 years)**	Concrete operational thinking (Piaget); initial command of basic laws of the logic of classes and propositions. Ability to assume role but not perspective of others.
Preegoic Levels	REPRESENTATIONAL MIND (15 months to 2 years)**	Preoperational thinking (Piaget); rudimentary conceptual thought. Narcissistic; inability to assume role of others.
	PHANTASMIC (6 months to 12 months)**	Primitive imaginal or "picture" thinking.
	EMOTIONAL-SEXUAL (1 month to 6 months)**	Basic organismic dynamism (bioenergy, libido, *prana*) and its basic instinctual modes of expression.
	SENSORIPERCEPTUAL (Prenatal to 3 months)**	Simple sensorimotor skills (Piaget).
	PHYSICAL (Prenatal)**	Basic physical substratum of organism.

* Reconstructed from table by Wilber (1990, p. 285).
** Wilber's estimate of ages at which levels are developmentally achieved.

reflexive-formal mind (vision logic being a transitional level), correspond to the spectrum of operational competencies: concrete and formal operational cognition, rational control of feelings, and rule-governed action. Finally, the transegoic levels, up to and including ultimate unity,[5] correspond to possibilities of life beyond the spectrum of operational competencies: visionary and mystical cognition, devotional and altruistic feeling. In sum, Wilber conceives of the psychic hierarchy as being at once complexly multitiered and yet fundamentally triphasic in its constitutional organization.

DEVELOPMENT FROM LOWER TO HIGHER LEVELS

According to the structural-hierarchical paradigm, all of the levels of the psychic hierarchy are implicitly or potentially present at the outset of development. The explicit or actual emergence of the levels of the hierarchy, however, occurs only over time, starting with the lowest level and proceeding one level at a time to each higher level. The psychic hierarchy is therefore not only a constitutional hierarchy but also a developmental hierarchy. Wilber holds that typical human development proceeds through the initial levels of the psychic hierarchy up to the level of reflexive-formal mind, or in some cases to the level of vision logic. In exceptional cases, however, Wilber says, human development, starting at the lowest or physical level, proceeds all the way to the highest transpersonal level, ultimate unity.

In holding that lower levels are prerequisites of higher levels, the structural-hierarchical paradigm also holds that no stages can be skipped as development proceeds up the psychic hierarchy: a higher level cannot be attained until the basic structures of the level below it have emerged and been established. Or as Wilber states this point, *transformation* to a new level cannot occur until the *translations* (the basic structural procedures and manipulations) of the immediately preceding level have been mastered. A developmental transformation occurring before such mastery would be dangerously premature: lacking the requisite foundations, it would likely fail.

In addition to not skipping levels, normal structural-hierarchical development does not abandon levels. Because lower levels serve as functional components of higher levels, movement to higher levels normally assimilates rather than alienates lower levels. For this reason developmental transformation or transcendence is normally of an incorporative rather than dissociative sort. It would be an exception to the rule if some part of a lower level were alienated or repressed. Moreover, if such an exception were to occur, the higher level attained would be deficiently and precariously attained, because it would be missing an ingredient necessary to its proper functioning.

Normal structural-hierarchical development, then, neither skips nor abandons psychic levels. It does not skip levels because each level of the psychic hierarchy is a prerequisite of the level above it. And it does not abandon levels because each level of the psychic hierarchy subsumes the level below it. Normal structural-hierarchical development moves according to a definite sequence of stages and in a direction of increasingly inclusive wholeness. Preceding stages lay the foundation for succeeding stages by articulating basic structures that are indispensable to succeeding stages. And succeeding stages preserve the fruits of preceding stages by reorganizing the basic structures of preceding stages within higher levels of psychic functioning.

Human development, according to the structural-hierarchical paradigm, is simply a sequential unfolding of the structural-hierarchical constitution of the psyche. The sequence of stages corresponds to the hierarchy of psychic levels, and the principal developmental relations that obtain between succeeding stages are temporal manifestations of the constitutional connections that obtain between adjacent levels.

UNFOLDING SELFHOOD ACCORDING TO THE
STRUCTURAL-HIERARCHICAL PARADIGM

As each ascending hierarchical level is developmentally achieved, it becomes, according to the structural-hierarchical paradigm, not only a new center of psychic agency but also a new center of selfhood. The locus of selfhood changes with each change of psychic level; each change of psychic level reconstitutes the sense of self. Conceived in this fashion, the self is what Wilber (1981a, 1990) calls a *transition* or *replacement* structure.

Transition structures are structures that are not only level specific but also stage specific; they are structures that come into existence only when the basic structures of the psychic level to which they correspond are developmentally activated. Transition structures are not inherent to the psychic constitution; rather, they result from an organism's seeing or acting upon the world through the basic structures of a particular psychic level. Transition structures therefore exist only when the psychic level to which they correspond is the highest active level. Once this level is developmentally superseded, the transition structures that obtained during its ascendancy are dissolved and new transition structures, appropriate to living at the next higher level, come into being.

Unlike basic structures, transition structures are not preserved in developmental transformation from one psychic level to the next.

Transition structures, then, are developmental expressions of basic structures. Accordingly, whereas basic structures are innate and present (whether in active or potential, enfolded form) at the outset of life, transition structures do not exist in any sense until the psychic level to which they correspond is developmentally achieved. And even then transition structures come into existence only in a virtual sense; they exist only as "the way things seem" when the world is engaged through the basic structures of that level. Transition structures are epiphenomena that arise from the employment of their corresponding basic structures. Unlike basic structures, then, transition structures exist only derivatively, temporarily, and virtually.

Although transition structures are derivative and merely temporary, they are nonetheless, according to Wilber, developmentally required. They are unavoidable in the sense that they are "the way things *necessarily* seem" when the world is engaged through the basic structures of the level to which transition structures correspond. Transition structures are stage specific but nonetheless universal modes of experience. They are necessary, even if temporary, appearances.

Among the transition structures discussed by Wilber are (1) *worldview*: the fundamental character of the world as it happens to appear when viewed through the basic cognitive structures of a particular level; (2) *needs*: the primary types of felt needs that are characteristic of life at a particular level; (3) *morality*: the kinds of behaviors and values that are implied by the basic structures of a particular level; and (4) *selfhood*: the organization of self that is characteristic of a particular level.

All of these structures have been the subjects of developmental studies, on which Wilber draws in formulating his views. Regarding worldview, for example, he draws on the cognitive-developmental studies of Piaget. Regarding needs, he accepts the hierarchical framework formulated by Abraham Maslow (1968). Regarding morality, he adopts the developmental scheme of Lawrence Kohlberg (1969, 1976, 1984). And regarding selfhood, he utilizes the timetable of ego growth formulated by Jane Loevinger (1976). Wilber provides many different tables that correlate these developmental accounts with his own model of structural and developmental levels; table 1.5 is one of these, slightly reformatted.

For Wilber, then, worldviews, needs, moralities, and self-structures change with each transition to a higher psychic level. For example, in the transition from the level of representational mind to that of rule-role mind, the worldview changes from being mythical (prelogical, preoper-

TABLE 1.5

Wilber's Psychic Hierarchy and Related Transition Structures

	LEVELS	MASLOW (NEEDS)	LOEVINGER (SELF-SENSE)	KOHLBERG (MORAL SENSE)
TRANSEGOIC STAGE	ULTIIMATE	Self-transcendence		
TRANSEGOIC STAGE	CAUSAL	Self-transcendence		
TRANSEGOIC STAGE	SUBTLE	Self-transcendence	Integrated	
	VISION LOGIC	Self-actualization	Autonomous	
			Individualistic	
EGOIC STAGE	REFLEXIVE-FORMAL MIND	Self-esteem	Conscientious	Individual principles of conscience Individual rights POSTCONVENTIONAL
EGOIC STAGE			Conscientious-conformist	
EGOIC STAGE	RULE-ROLE MIND	Belongingness	Conformist	Law and order Approval of others CONVENTIONAL
			Self-protective	
	REPRESENTA-TIONAL MIND	Safety	Impulsive	Naive hedonism Punishment/obedience PRECONVENTIONAL
PREEGOIC STAGE	PHANTASMIC	(Physiological)	Beginning impulsive	
PREEGOIC STAGE	EMOTIONAL-SEXUAL	(Physiological)	Beginning impulsive	
PREEGOIC STAGE	SENSORI-PERCEPTUAL	(Physiological)	Symbiotic	
	PHYSICAL		Autistic	

Time Line

Adapted from Wilber 1990, p. 298.

ational, protoconceptual) to being rational (logical, operational, conceptually organized) in character. Correspondingly, the primary felt need changes from a need for safety to a need for belonging. Morality changes from a preconventional standpoint, stressing desires and self-interested consequences of behavior, to a conventional standpoint, stressing moral rules and social norms. Finally, the self-structure changes from what Loevinger calls the impulsive self (identified chiefly with the impulses and feelings of immediate bodily life) to what she calls the conformist self (identified chiefly with stereotypical social labels, which confer a definition and sense of belonging). In each of these examples, the transition involves a dissolution of structures that had existed when development was at the level of representational mind and a replacement of those structures with completely new ones that are expressive of living at the level of rule-role mind. The basic structures of the level of representational mind are preserved in the movement to the level of rule-role mind, but the transition structures corresponding to the level of representational mind are not.

Turning now to the matter of selfhood, the most important implication of Wilber's conception of the self as a transition structure is that the self is not part of the inherited psychic apparatus. The self is not part of the furniture of existence; it is not an entity of any kind. Rather, the self exists only in a virtual sense, as a subjective experience accompanying the basic structures of a particular psychic level. The self is not a pre-given structure present at birth or waiting to become active at the appropriate developmental moment. It is rather something merely derivative and stage specific, the distinctive way consciousness experiences itself through the basic structures of the highest active psychic level. The self is therefore a mere, albeit developmentally unavoidable, appearance. On this point Wilber and the structural-hierarchical paradigm concur with the principal Eastern view espoused by Buddhism and nondualistic Vedanta: the individual self, although seemingly real, is ultimately illusory.

Wilber explains the self's virtual existence as a transition structure in terms of the phenomenon of *identification*. The self is not an actually existing basic structure but is rather the identification of consciousness with such structures. Specifically, it is the identification of consciousness with the basic structures of the highest active psychic level. Because the highest active level of the psychic hierarchy is the locus of psychic agency, it is therefore also the vantage point from which life is lived, which means that the highest active level is the seat of the sense of self. In functioning at a certain level, consciousness inevitably identifies with that level; consciousness effectively *is* the basic structures of that level. For the structural-hierarchical paradigm, then, the self exists only as a species of identification rather than as a substantive component of the psychic apparatus. The self exists only as self-identity, the content and boundaries of which are determined at each psychic level by the basic structures of that level.

It is clear from this account that the self exits only as a series of stage-specific epiphenomena. If the self exists only as identification with the basic structures of the highest active psychic level, it follows that the self must be dissolved when, in developmental transformation, that identification is dissolved. Developmental movement from one psychic level to another breaks the identification that had obtained with the basic structures of the transcended level and brings into existence a new identification with the basic structures of the transcending level.

Developmental transformation to a new psychic level thus eliminates an old self and creates a new one. The old self is not preserved, as basic structures are; instead, the old self is replaced by a new one.

Wilber holds that self-unfolding can in principle proceed in this fashion all the way to the highest psychic level: ultimate unity. In arriving at ultimate unity, however, the process necessarily comes to an end. It does so not only because ultimate unity is the highest and therefore final psychic level to be attained but also because ultimate unity is universal in scope and therefore transcends all possible boundaries of individual selfhood. Ultimate unity is a structural level that not only subsumes the whole of the psyche within itself but also brings the psyche into coincidence with reality itself. Ultimate unity is all-inclusive and therefore transcends all divisions, including the self-other division. In arriving at ultimate unity, therefore, not only is the previous level-specific sense of selfhood dissolved and dispelled, but so, too, is the very sense that there is a self. At ultimate unity, one is no longer a self vis-à-vis reality; rather, Wilber says (1982, p. 66), "one becomes reality."

CHOOSING BETWEEN THE PARADIGMS

Having set forth the basic features of the dynamic-dialectical and structural-hierarchical paradigms, I now want to sharpen the contrast between them by considering five main points of disagreement. Discussion of these points of disagreement will help clarify what is at stake in choosing between the two paradigms.

THE PREEGOIC STAGE: HOW CENTRAL A ROLE DOES CONFLICT PLAY?

The two paradigms disagree on whether the preegoic stage is normally plagued with conflict. The dynamic-dialectical paradigm sees conflict as a primary theme of the preegoic stage. It sees the preegoic stage as a period fraught with intense and unavoidable conflicts, both intrapsychic and interpersonal. The structural-hierarchical paradigm, in contrast, sees the preegoic stage not as a period of conflict but rather as a period of structural articulation, a period during which lower-level basic structures are developed.

In the dynamic-dialectical view, early childhood is a time of instability and turbulence. Intrapsychically, it is a period during which the Dynamic Ground both sustains and eclipses an emerging ego, which, accordingly, is torn between desires for reembedment in the Ground and for independence from the Ground. Moreover, because the Ground is experienced by the child as an integral dimension of the child's primary "object" or "other," the primary caregiver as Great Mother, this intrapsychic conflict is at the same time an outer-directed or object-related conflict. It is not only a tension between desires for reembedment and for independence in relation to the Dynamic Ground but also a tension between desires for intimacy and for distance in relation to the primary caregiver. And it is both of these tensions at once without any distinction. The fact that the preegoic child's primary object is the inner-outer, Ground-caregiver Great Mother means that the basic conflict of the preegoic period is a conflict that is at once bivalent in its options (reembedment versus independence, intimacy versus distance) and bidirectional in its sources (intrapsychic and object related, interpolar and interpersonal).

According to a widely accepted psychoanalytic view, this basic conflict of the preegoic stage comes to a head during the rapprochement subphase of the separation-individuation process.[6] At this point—beginning around the middle of the second year—the conflict is expressed in an intense ambivalence on the part of the child toward the primary caregiver. The child in the rapprochement subphase of the separation-individuation process awakens to the magnitude of its need for the caregiver and therefore begins to experience an especially strong desire for intimacy with the caregiver, without, however, relinquishing its continuing desire for distance and independence. In consequence, the child's desires for intimacy and distance here begin to clash in a serious way, each one undermining the other: the desire for intimacy making distance seem like alienation and the desire for distance making intimacy seem like engulfment. The rapprochment child is caught in a powerful crosscurrent of feeling; it experiences the basic conflict of the preegoic period in its most severe form.

The conflict of the preegoic stage, which, interpersonally, is played out in dyadic form during the preoedipal period, is reorganized in triadic form during the oedipal period. For in the oedipal period the child begins to perceive the father in rapprochement terms: the child begins to see the father at once as a rival for intimacy with the caregiver and as a model of egoic independence. Accordingly, the child's choice between intimacy with and distance from the caregiver here becomes at the same time a choice between confrontation with and acceptance by the father: to pursue intimacy with the caregiver is to risk confrontation with the father as rival, and to pursue distance from the caregiver is to win acceptance from the father as role model. The basic conflict of the pre-egoic stage is in this way intensified and the child's development now moves irreversibly in a direction away from the caregiver and toward the father. Accordingly, the ego, which had already begun to withdraw from completely open intimacy with the caregiver, is eventually forced to finalize this withdrawal and to commit itself decisively to the father. In this process the ego is forced as well to finalize its repression of nonegoic potentials (which had been associated with the caregiver as Great Mother) and to commit itself decisively to ego functions (which are represented by the father as model of independence).

The structural-hierarchical paradigm gives considerably less emphasis to the theme of conflict than does the dynamic-dialectical paradigm. The structural-hierarchical paradigm does not deny that difficulties occur during the preegoic stage, but it does not place conflict at the center of the developmental stage. Instead, the focus is on structural development, especially cognitive development. The focus is on the development of sensorimotor skills and rudimentary representational cognition. In contrast to the dynamic-dialectical paradigm, which interprets such structural developments as steps in the ego's struggle for independence from its intrapsychic and interpersonal sources, the structural-hierarchical paradigm interprets such developments as unfolding without serious countervailing challenges. Clearly, for the structural-hierarchical paradigm there is no interpolar tension to complicate structural articulation. Wilber (1980a) acknowledges the phenomenon of interpersonal ambivalence and splitting during the preoedipal period. He does not, however, assign as much theoretical importance to this aspect of preegoic development as he does to the more basic aspect of structural development. The main theme of the preegoic period, for Wilber, is the development of lower-level basic structures.

TRANSITION TO THE EGOIC STAGE:
ARE PREEGOIC POTENTIALS LOST OR RETAINED?

The two paradigms disagree on whether psychic resources belonging to the preegoic stage are lost or retained in the transition to the egoic stage. The dynamic-dialectical paradigm holds that the transition to the egoic stage normally involves a repressive forfeiture of the physicodynamic potentials of the nonegoic pole of the psyche. The structural-hierarchical paradigm, in contrast, holds that the transition to the egoic stage normally involves an incorporation and higher reorganization of preegoic psychic resources rather than any significant forfeiture of them.

According to the dynamic-dialectical paradigm, the ego resolves the basic interpolar-interpersonal conflict of early childhood by perpetrating primal repression, which, intrapsychically, submerges nonegoic potentials into unconsciousness. At first the child's commitment to primal repression is incomplete; the child remains drawn to the (inner-outer) Great Mother and to the bliss of original embedment. The child's tentativeness, however, comes to an end when the child is confronted with the challenge of the oedipal father, whose presence as perceived by the child forces the child to finalize its withdrawal from the Great Mother and therefore also, as the inner dimension of this withdrawal, to consolidate primal repression. This consolidation of primal repression performs a positive developmental function. The child's choice between yielding to the Great Mother and asserting its independence, it turns out, is a choice between regression and repression: in order to continue on the course of development, the child must disconnect itself from the original sources of its being. Intrapsychically, it must repress physicodynamic potentials, which are in this way lost to consciousness.

Not deeming conflict to play a central role in the preegoic stage, the structural-hierarchical paradigm does not see repression as a necessary aspect of the transition from the preegoic to the egoic stage. Indeed, according to Wilber, repression is not normally a part of any developmental movement from one psychic level to the next. Rather than entailing repression and consequent loss of psychic resources, all such developmental movements are based on a preservation of the basic structures of the superseded psychic level. The basic structures of the superseded level constitute the necessary foundation on which the basic structures of the superseding level are built. Under normal circumstances, then, the basic structures developed during the preegoic stage are not repressed and lost but are rather carried over into the egoic stage.

The structural-hierarchical paradigm acknowledges that the transition to the egoic stage does require a forsaking of some structures belonging to the preegoic stage. The structures forsaken, however, are *transition* structures, not basic structures. The worldview, distinctive needs, morality, and sense of self that prevail during the preegoic stage are ordinarily dissolved and hence "lost." This "loss," however, is really a gain, because basic structures are preserved and because new and higher transition structures replace the transition structures that are "lost." Wilber (1980a) acknowledges that the mental ego screens and therefore loses awareness of some preegoic basic structures (which cannot be expressed in formal operational or secondary-process terms). He acknowledges as well that the mental ego is prone to certain types of repression (repression of the shadow, for instance). However, he clearly rejects the idea that repression and consequent forfeiture of psychic resources is in any way a normal or necessary part of any developmental transformation to a higher psychic level.

The two paradigms disagree on whether the mental ego is alienated from or rooted in the original sources of its being. The dynamic-dialectical paradigm holds that the transition to the egoic stage entails a repression of the Ground and of the nonegoic pole of the psyche and therefore that the mental ego is out of touch with its deepest sources. The structural-hierarchical paradigm, in contrast, holds that the mental ego, in rising above the preegoic level, continues to stand on the structural foundations laid down during the preegoic stage.

According to the dynamic-dialectical paradigm, primal repression is a developmentally necessary and therefore warranted act. Faced with a choice between regression and repression, the ego legitimately chooses repression. Moreover, the ego initially experiences the choice of repression not as the lesser of two evils but as something entirely positive, namely, as independence from overawing nonegoic (and interpersonal) influences. This fact notwithstanding, primal repression *is* an act that sacrifices vital psychic resources, and this sacrifice eventually makes itself felt. It does so typically later in life after ego development is complete. For once the ego has completed its development, it no longer needs to be repressively protected from physicodynamic potentials and is ready to reopen itself to the nonegoic pole of the psyche. Once ego development is complete, then, primal repression ceases being necessary and loses its developmental warrant. It ceases being a way in which an immature ego protects itself from physicodynamic potentials and becomes a way in which a mature ego avoids a redemptive reunion with those potentials. Primal repression, no longer needed as a support for ego development, at this point becomes an obstruction to ego transcendence. Accordingly, as this transvaluation of primal repression occurs, the mental ego undergoes a reversal of feeling: it ceases feeling independent and begins feeling out of touch with the sources of its being. The mental ego at midlife frequently feels detached, unwhole, and empty, as if it were cut off from a deeper and truer self. In the dynamic-dialectical view, then, the mental ego is alienated from its sources, and it is prone to begin experiencing this alienation at or around midlife.

The structural-hierarchical paradigm sees things very differently. It sees the mental ego as remaining in touch with its foundations. Preegoic basic structures are preserved within the more inclusive bound-aries of egoic life. For this reason the structural-hierarchical paradigm does not see the mature mental ego as being predisposed to feelings of being out of touch with earlier sources of experience. The mental ego does not rest on a repressive foundation, and therefore it is not predis-posed to suffer from a sense of having forfeited psychic resources.

If, however, the structural-hierarchical paradigm does not see the mental ego as experiencing disconnection from preegoic foundations, it does have a way of explaining midlife existential difficulties. According to Wilber (1981b), these difficulties can be understood as growth pains of a mature mental ego that, still limited to egoic basic structures, is on the verge of moving toward new and higher, transegoic basic struc-tures. As Wilber puts it, the mental ego's existential difficulties at midlife do not express alienation from a preegoic Eden but rather reflect the fact that the mental ego has not yet reached transegoic heaven. The mental ego's sense of alienation arises in relation to future possibilities not yet realized rather than past actualities that have been repressed and submerged. They arise not because the mental ego has "sinfully" alienated itself from its sources but rather because the mental ego has not yet ascended all the way to the top of the developmental ladder: ultimate unity.

TRANSITION TO THE TRANSEGOIC STAGE:
STRAIGHT ASCENT OR SPIRAL MOVEMENT THROUGH ORIGINS?

The dynamic-dialectical paradigm holds that the transition to the trans-egoic stage involves a double reversal or spiral loop, a going back on the way to a going beyond, a regressive return to the preegoic in prepara-tion for a regenerating ascent to the transegoic. The structural-hierarchi-cal paradigm, in contrast, holds that the transition to the transegoic stage—as is true of all developmental advances—is a straightforward ascending movement to higher psychic levels.

According to the dynamic-dialectical paradigm, the lifting of pri-mal repression leads to a regressive reopening of the egoic pole of the psyche to the nonegoic pole, of the ego to the Dynamic Ground. The ego is returned to the sources from which it originally emerged and from which it had been alienated. This return is a regressive process in that the ego is disempowered, stripped of its defensive insulation, and brought into direct contact with resurging nonegoic life: the return of the repressed. This return to origins, however, is not a *merely* regressive process. Although the return can abort into regression pure and simple, such a result is not the normal outcome for the ego that is "seaworthy."

For the ego that is ready for the "night sea journey," the return to origins is a regression *in the service of transcendence*. It is the first, descending phase of a spiraling movement that leads to a second, ascending phase: regeneration in spirit. Accordingly, the ego's regression to the Ground is followed by a regenerative transformation of the ego by the power of the Ground. For the dynamic-dialectical paradigm, then, the transition from the egoic to the transegoic stage is not a straightforward ascending movement but is rather a spiraling movement that follows a regressive-regenerative course.

The structural-hierarchical paradigm, in contrast, sees the transition from the egoic to the transegoic stage as a direct ascent to higher psychic levels. Because, according to the structural-hierarchical paradigm, preegoic basic structures are not repressed in the transition to the egoic stage, they do not need to be regressively derepressed in the transition to the transegoic stage. Preegoic basic structures are not lost and therefore do not need to be regained as a precondition of reaching the transegoic stage. Instead, the transition to the transegoic stage is a direct climb, rung by rung, to higher levels of the psychic hierarchy, from reflexive-formal mind to vision logic and from there to subtle and causal realms.

None of these developmental steps requires a redeeming of resources that had been lost or forsaken; rather, they all involve a realizing or gaining access to higher resources that previously were only implicit or potential. Wilber acknowledges that developmental movement to a higher level can be fraught with difficulties in that one has to "die" to one's identification with the basic structures of the level being transcended before one can move to the next higher psychic level. This struggle for disidentification and then higher reidentification is a death-rebirth process of a sort. It is not, however, a process that follows a regressive-regenerative course like that postulated by the dynamic-dialectical paradigm.

Indeed, Wilber states that the transition to the transegoic stage normally involves no regression. He says:

> Now I believe there is most definitely such a regression, in both its useful forms—called regression in the service of the ego, wherein the ego can occasionally relax its upward growth by slipping back to lower levels, gathering strength and moving forward again—and in its pathological forms—mild regression/fixations in neurotic symptoms and full-scale regression/fixation in psychotic reactions. But the transpersonal Self—and

true mystic union—lies in *precisely* the opposite direction. As *Atman Project* tried to suggest, mysticism is not regression in the service of the ego, but evolution in transcendence of the ego. (1990, p. 240)

For Wilber, and for the structural-hierarchical paradigm, the transition to the transegoic stage requires no backward movement as a condition of forward movement. This transition is not a spiraling movement. It is rather a direct forward movement. New basic structures, which are both superior to and more inclusive than preceding basic structures, emerge, and consciousness identifies with these new basic structures as its new self.

THE TRANSEGOIC STAGE: ARE THERE TWO SELVES OR NONE?

The two paradigms agree that the ego of the egoic stage of development is a small-*s* self that needs ultimately to be transcended. However, whereas the dynamic-dialectical paradigm conceives of this small-*s* self as a real thing (one pole of a bipole) that needs to be transformed and reunited with a large-*S* self (the power of the Ground as spirit), the structural-hierarchical paradigm conceives of this small-*s* self as an illusion that needs to be dispelled (a transition structure that needs to be dissolved).

For the dynamic-dialectical paradigm, the small-*s* self of the egoic stage, the mental ego, is an actually existing self but not a complete self. It is one pole of a bipole, which, as such, is something that possesses real but not self-subsistent existence. To be sure, the mental ego acts as if it were an independent and complete self. This posture of independence, however, is only a false pose supported by primal repression. The mental ego's stance of independence does not change the fact that the mental ego is inherently linked to the nonegoic pole of the psyche, which is at once the mental ego's ultimate Ground and deeper self: the big-*S* self. The ego of the egoic stage is therefore something real; it is not an illusion. Although real, however, it is not exactly what it takes itself to be. For it takes itself to be an independently existing entity when in fact it is only the lesser pole of a bipolar duality.

Wilber's structural-hierarchical paradigm advances the contrasting view that the small-*s* self of the egoic stage is not anything real. It is not among the basic structures that make up the psychic constitution. Rather, this self is merely a transition structure, something that exists only virtually, as the "way things seem" at the egoic level of development. Specifically, the mental ego exists only as a level-specific identification of consciousness with egoic basic structures. And this identification, it should be added, is a false identification, because the only ultimately true identification is the all-inclusive identification of ultimate unity, which transcends all selfhood.

For the structural-hierarchical paradigm, then, there is no separate self because one's true existence coincides with reality itself. One's true existence is none other than the Brahman of Upanishadic Hinduism, the Void of Mahayana Buddhism. The mental ego, *qua* separate self, is an illusion. It is not any existing thing—not even, as the dynamic-dialectical paradigm maintains, a partial and incomplete thing. It is rather only a case of mistaken identity. It is a case of developmentally necessary and warranted mistaken identity, to be sure, but a case of mistaken identity nonetheless.

Following from these differences concerning the mental ego as a small-*s* self, the two paradigms have correspondingly different prescriptions for ego transcendence. The dynamic-dialectical paradigm, viewing the egoic self as a real but pseudo-independent self, prescribes a transcendence that would reunite and "alchemically" bond the egoic self with its missing, superior half. Such a reconnection and fusing would bring into existence a higher synthesis of the egoic and nonegoic poles of the psyche. This synthesis would be a union of opposites, a union of small-*s* and large-*S* selves, of the ego and the power of the Ground as spirit.

The structural-hierarchical paradigm, in contrast, viewing the egoic self as a transition rather than "real" or basic structure, does not prescribe any such realignments of the psychic constitution. The small-*s* self is not considered a part of the psychic apparatus that needs somehow to be reconnected and redeemed. It is rather seen only as a level-specific identification of consciousness that needs to be outgrown. Ego transcendence, then, for the structural-hierarchical paradigm, is not a matter of grounding and transforming a small-*s* self but rather of awakening to the fact that there is no such self to ground or transform. Self-realization is not a matter of yoking a lesser self to a greater self but rather of seeing that the very notion of selfhood has no basis in reality. Granted, such an insight is by no means easily attained; a whole sequence of transition selves must be formed and dissolved before the selflessness of ultimate unity can be appreciated. This fact notwithstanding, it remains true for Wilber that the highest attainment of selfhood coincides with the understanding that, truly, there is no self at all.

The choice between the dynamic-dialectical and structural-hierarchical paradigms, therefore, is a choice between two selves or none. The dynamic-dialectical paradigm sees development as leading ultimately to a goal in which two selves are united as one, the higher self of spirit and the lower self of the ego-subject. The structural-hierarchical paradigm, on the other hand, sees development as leading ultimately to a goal that lies beyond all selfhood, a goal at which the root illusion of selfhood has finally been dispelled.

CONCLUSION

In presenting the foregoing account of the dynamic-dialectical and structural-hierarchical paradigms, my purpose has been to sketch their essential lineaments, to point out their most important differences, and thereby to indicate what is at stake in choosing between them. Both of the paradigms are coherent; both are well grounded in psychological theory; both provide a framework for understanding the emergence and unfolding of transpersonal experience; and both (in one or another version) have many illustrious adherents. I myself have chosen the dynamic-dialectical paradigm—not because I know of any compelling criticisms of the structural-hierarchical paradigm, but because I believe the dynamic-dialectical paradigm is more sensitive to the dynamic potentials of spiritual life, to the transvaluations and reversals that frequently punctuate spiritual development, and to many of the most important features of the phenomenology of spiritual development. I hope these strengths of the dynamic-dialectical paradigm become evident in the chapters that follow, in which I shall be presenting this paradigm as rigorously as I am able.

2

The Body Ego

THE CLASSICAL PSYCHOANALYTIC VIEW that human life begins in a state of egoless absorption altogether without relation to the outside world has been the target of criticism in recent years. The view was in fact already criticized long ago by Melanie Klein, who argued that an ego involved in object relations is present even in the neonate. More recently, in the psychoanalytic community, Joseph Lichtenberg (1979, 1981, 1983, 1987) and Daniel Stern (1985) have challenged the classical view. Lichtenberg, drawing on the latest results of neonatal research, has argued that the newborn is vastly more differentiated, object related, and interactive than traditional psychoanalytic theory had realized. And Stern has argued that the newborn enters the world already situated in the context of self-other differentiation and relationship.[1]

The ensuing discussion pursues a position between the opposing sides of this discussion, a position, however, that is closer to the classical side. Acknowledging with the critics of the classical view that the newborn is not *completely* egoless and absorbed, that the newborn, that is, is *significantly* differentiated and object related, the position I shall pursue is that the newborn is nonetheless *nearly* egoless and *mostly* absorbed and consequently only *minimally* differentiated and object related. Criticism of the classical view, I suggest, requires a qualification, not a rejection, of the classical view.

We need to remember that the classical view was formulated from the adult perspective. When we, as adults, look at newborns, we see raw potentiality not yet individually shaped and not yet able to interact with the world and with others in the ways we do. This perspective of course carries with it a tendency toward exaggeration, a tendency to see in the newborn more potentiality and less actuality, more absorption and less object relatedness than is actually the case. The newborn is not a *tabula rasa* completely disconnected from the world. The critics of the classical view have demonstrated some of the many ways in which the newborn is cognitively competent and interactive with the world of objects and primary others. They have added many valuable insights to our understanding of infants and, in doing so, have corrected much of the exaggeration of the classical view. In correcting this exaggeration, however, the critics of the classical view have tended to overplay their hand and, in doing so, to speak as if the classical view were entirely wrong. This counterexaggeration itself needs to be corrected. The classical view needs to be restated in qualified form, as a relative rather than absolute truth.

In what follows, I shall be using the language of the classical view, speaking of the newborn's lack of differentiation and involvement in object relations, its absorption, immersion, embedment (in the Dynamic Ground), and so forth. In speaking in this way, I do not mean to endorse the exaggeration associated with the traditional view, much less to ignore the valuable findings of more recent infant researchers. I mean only to preserve the essential core of the traditional view, the insight that the infant is *minimally* differentiated and object related and *mostly* absorbed, immersed, and embedded.

ORIGINAL EMBEDMENT

Intrapsychically, the newborn is absorbed in the Dynamic Ground and in the numinous power resident in the Ground. This state of absorption, which I shall call *original embedment*, is a condition of dynamic plenitude. It is a state that is overflowing with upwelling energy. The newborn is bathed in the "water of life," which rises from the Ground and flows freely through the newborn's body.

The unrestricted circulation of the power of the Ground within the newborn's body affects the newborn in two primary ways. First, the power of the Ground potentiates the newborn's experience across all dimensions, amplifying all contents of consciousness and quickening all psychic processes. The power of the Ground is an energy that intensifies experience in all its aspects. And second, the power of the Ground, as an energy that has fluidic and magnetic properties, has the effect of buoying, lulling, and entrancing the newborn, drawing the newborn into states of self-contained absorption. To be sure, the newborn is keenly aware of the world and finely attuned to the actions and gestures of the primary caregiver. The newborn is by no means autistic, as Freud (1911a) suggested and as Margaret Mahler (Mahler, Pine, and Bergman 1975) believes; nevertheless, the newborn is prone to yield to states of absorptive envelopment. Original embedment is psychologically analogous to the intrauterine state. It is a womb outside the womb, a state sustained and suspended in a psychic "amniotic" fluid.

It follows from the fact that original embedment is a condition of dynamic plenitude that it is a state that is contented and fulfilled, without felt lack or need, and therefore that it is a condition that is psychically (although not physically) self-sufficing. Original embedment is then a state that, subjectively speaking, is whole as well as absorbed. The metaphor that best captures this self-sufficiency of original embedment is that of the fertilized egg.

Freud acknowledged the aptness of this metaphor. In a frequently quoted passage, he observed that "a neat example of a psychical system shut off from the stimuli of the external world, and able to satisfy even its nutritional requirements autistically...is afforded by the bird's egg with its food supply enclosed in its shell; for it, the care provided by its mother is limited to the provision of warmth" (1911a, p. 220). Erich Neumann (1954), Margaret Mahler (Mahler, Pine, and Bergman 1975), and others have followed Freud in using the image of the egg to describe the state of original embedment. The egg metaphor is useful, but it is not completely satisfactory. For, as we have noted, studies indicate that the newborn is not autistic or totally self-encapsulated, as the egg metaphor (expressing the classical view) suggests; the newborn is actively differentiated, object related, and cognitively discriminating in many ways. Nevertheless, the egg metaphor remains apt in giving expression to the energic saturation of original embedment and the consequent tendency of the newborn to yield to states of dynamic plenitude. Although alert, engaged in complex interactions with caregivers, and otherwise responsive to its environment, the newborn is prone to give way to states of undivided, boundless fullness. It is prone to "dissolve" into states of blissful absorption in the Dynamic Ground.

Although the state of original embedment is soon abandoned by the developing ego, traces of it remain as an archetype of the collective unconscious. The images issuing from this archetype are many and varied. Among them, the egg image, owing to its particular fittingness, is perhaps the most common; the picture of a cosmic egg out of which is hatched the world of multiplicity and change appears in mythologies around the world. Other images in which the archetype frequently is expressed are those of (1) a primordial chaos preceding the separation of heaven (consciousness) and earth (the unconscious); (2) an oceanic depth out of which are born the myriad forms of life; and (3) the *uroboros* (the world-encircling serpent eating its own tail) and other symbols portraying wholeness and self-sustenance.

The dynamic plenitude and blissful well-being characteristic of original embedment are never entirely forgotten; a faint memory of the "perfection" of the original, embedded state remains alive in later life. Our nostalgia for paradise reflects a longing for this original state, the wholeness, fullness, and bliss of which are implicit in our ideal of happiness. This nostalgia, however, is misleading if it is taken to imply that original embedment is the proper standard of maximal human well-being. For original embedment is only a primitive preegoic precursor of what is possible on the transegoic plane. Although original embedment is a state of wholeness, fullness, and bliss, it is also a state of egolessness prior to ego development rather than of ego transcendence subsequent to ego development. The real point of the nostalgia for paradise, then, is not to return to a state of egoless absorption in the Dynamic Ground but rather to achieve a state in which the ego, fully developed, is rooted in the Ground.

THE EMERGENCE OF THE EGO FROM THE DYNAMIC GROUND AND THE INITIAL APPEARANCE OF THE GREAT MOTHER

To the extent that the ego is differentiated from the Dynamic Ground, it possesses a primitive sense of its own existence. This initial sense of self is understandably grounded in the body, the boundaries of which are the most evident demarcations of the infant's existence. In the beginning, the ego is a *body* ego. This body ego is at first only vaguely delineated; it consists of little more than undefined physical sensations and somatic feeling states. Time and experience, however, articulate the ego's sense of somatic existence. The boundaries of the body are brought into sharper focus; its motor and perceptual capabilities are mastered; its limbs and parts are explored; and its basic desires and feelings are recognized. These aspects of embodied existence constitute what the fledgling ego *is*. The newly emerged ego relates to the body *as* self and not at all as an object *for* self. The body's life is the ego's own life.

Initially, the body ego is only minimally differentiated from the Dynamic Ground and is periodically reembedded in the Ground. Moreover, this relationship of partial fusion with the Dynamic Ground is at the same time a relationship of partial fusion with the primary caregiver, who is the outer or object-relational correlate of the body ego's inner experience. The body ego is at first only minimally differentiated from both the Dynamic Ground within and the primary caregiver without. Moreover, because the body ego knows no difference between these two sources of its experience, it in effect conflates the two into a single reality. In this way the Dynamic Ground and the primary caregiver interpenetrate and coalesce into a unity that is the principal "object" of the infant's experience.

This Ground-caregiver object possesses both numinous-archetypal and personal qualities, the numinous-archetypal qualities deriving from the Dynamic Ground and related nonegoic (somatic, energic, instinctual, affective, imaginal) potentials and the personal qualities deriving from the primary caregiver. The power of the Ground imbues the primary caregiver with magical and archetypal dimensions, and the primary caregiver in turn gives the Dynamic Ground a human face and form. The first object of the infant's experience is therefore one that, unbeknownst to the infant, has both inner and outer, both depth-psychological and object-relational dimensions. This object is not just an impersonal power (the Dynamic Ground); nor is it "merely" a human person (the primary caregiver). It is rather at once both and neither.

The body ego's emergence from the Dynamic Ground is at the same time a progressive articulation of this object—the Great Mother.[2] This object is the Great *Mother* because, historically, the primary caregiver has been female; and it is the *Great* Mother because it is not just the primary caregiver but rather the primary caregiver as numinously charged and magnified by the Dynamic Ground. In the ensuing discussion, then, I shall be leaning in a Jungian direction in speaking of the body ego's primary object as the numinous-archetypal Great Mother rather than simply as the primary caregiver.

We have already seen that the body ego is drawn to the power of the Ground and frequently yields to this power, which dissolves the body ego and returns it to the blissful state of original embedment. We can now add that the body ego experiences the same dynamic in relation to the primary caregiver. For the primary caregiver, like the Dynamic Ground, is not only a source from which the body ego emerges but also a source to which the body ego is drawn for sustenance and blissful absorption. The primary caregiver is a person to whom the body ego is attracted and in whose embrace the body ego is liable to dissolve. The inner and outer dimensions of the Great Mother thus have the same effects upon the body ego; they both attract the body ego and lead it toward reembedment. By the combined influence of the inner and outer dimensions of the Great Mother, then, the body ego is kept within the orbit of the Great Mother's influence and is repeatedly reabsorbed within the primordial unity of her being.

In addition to having identical effects upon the body ego, the inner and outer dimensions of the Great Mother are themselves causally interactive; the power of the Ground and the love of the primary caregiver are interfluent, mutually eliciting forces. They are forces that, in affecting the body ego, also affect each other, in somewhat the following way: The Dynamic Ground releases effluences that well up in the body ego as eddies or waves of bliss. The body ego responds to these effluences with cooing sounds and gestures of delight. These behaviors prompt the primary caregiver to bestow playful affection upon the body ego. The affection of the primary caregiver in turn captivates and dissolves the body ego, melting it to its core—the Dynamic Ground. The Dynamic Ground, stirred in this way by the love of the primary caregiver, again releases blissful effluences; again the body ego coos and gestures with delight, and again the primary caregiver plies loving attention, and so on. In this way a circuit is established between the inner and outer dimensions of the Great Mother. The power of the Ground and the love of the primary caregiver work in turn to stir and elicit each other.

The life of the body ego is played out against the background of the Great Mother. The Great Mother has a bearing upon all of the body ego's experiences. So much, in fact, does the body ego partake of the Great Mother that it is more accurate to conceive of the body ego as one side of a body ego–Great Mother duality than as an entity in its own right. The body ego and the Great Mother are *internally* connected: their subjectivities are to a significant extent merged. They constitute an indivisible dyad. To be sure, the Great Mother exists as an "object" for the body ego. This object, however, is not an entity altogether separate from the body ego. It is rather an object in which the body ego is grounded and in whose being the body ego intimately participates, especially when the body ego yields to reembedment. To use Heinz Kohut's term, this object is a *selfobject*

Margaret Mahler (Mahler, Pine, and Bergman 1975), in her now-classic account, holds that the infant in the first months of life exists in a symbiotic relationship of shared experience with the primary caregiver.[3] According to Mahler, the infant gradually differentiates itself from this state of symbiotic merger during the first two or three years of life, during which the child undergoes a process of separation and individuation from the primary caregiver. Although Mahler dates the completion of the separation-individuation process at about 24 to 36+ months, I suggest that some degree of child-caregiver symbiosis remains even into the oedipal period, because, as we shall see later, the child's withdrawal from symbiotic intimacy with the primary caregiver is not final until it is reinforced by a decisive commitment to the oedipal father.

In sum, the Great Mother is at once the source, foundation, and center of gravity of the body ego's life. She is the womb, physical and psychic, from which the body ego emerges. As provider and enlivener, she is the body ego's continuing support, indeed the very basis of its being. And as a power that has both gravitational and solvent effects, she is an attractive force that captivates the body ego and returns it again and again to the state of original embedment.

The Great Mother is an object of ambivalence for the body ego. The body ego has divided feelings for the Great Mother because she not only satisfies but also, at times, frustrates the body ego's needs and desires. To be sure, the Great Mother sustains the body ego and invites it into the blissful absorption of original embedment. She also, however, limits the body ego's behaviors, and the irresistibility of her power sometimes reduces the body ego to original embedment against its will. The body ego for these reasons is prone to perceive the Great Mother in both positive and negative guises, as both a Good Mother and a Terrible Mother.

Notwithstanding this ambivalence, the body ego's feelings for the Great Mother are at first weighted heavily in the positive direction. During the first year of life, despite occasional experiences of frustration and self-loss, the body ego experiences the Great Mother primarily as a Good Mother. The body ego experiences the inner dimension of the Great Mother, the power of the Dynamic Ground, primarily as a force that enlivens the body ego and graces it with feelings of fullness and bliss. And the body ego experiences the outer dimension of the Great Mother, the primary caregiver, primarily as a being who feeds and protects the body ego and showers it with "unmerited" love. In the first year of life, the body ego experiences the Great Mother primarily in a positive light, as a source of life, nurture, and well-being.

The benefits bestowed upon the body ego by the primary caregiver are fairly obvious. Those bestowed by the Dynamic Ground are more subtle but every bit as important. We have already seen how the Ground emits pulsations that bathe the body ego in waves of delight. Other positive expressions of the Ground in the body ego's life are (1) polymorphous sensuality, (2) superabundance in all dimensions of experience, and (3) numinosity (in the form of enchantment).

In saying that the body ego is polymorphously sensual, I am in substance following Freud's view that the prelatency child is capable of general bodily arousal—disagreeing only with Freud's narrowly sexual interpretation of polymorphous "perversity." The body ego, owing to its direct openness to the Dynamic Ground, is energized throughout its entire being by the power of the Ground. All of the body is supercharged with the power of the Ground, which means that any bodily limb, part, or "zone," upon being caressed or stimulated, can become a seat of somatic ecstasy. This fact is of course especially evident in the case of the erotogenic zones, which are sequentially dominant in the order explained by Freud in his theory of psychosexual development. The body ego's capacity for somatic ecstasy, however, is not limited to the erotogenic zones. The body ego is supercharged from head to toe and in all of its senses, and therefore any part of the body ego can be a vehicle of transport and delight.

The power of the Dynamic Ground is also manifested in the all-around abundance and aliveness of the body ego's experience. All dimensions of the body ego's life are potentiated by the power of the Ground, which is not only a gravitational-solvent power but also an amplifying power. All the body ego's perceptions are rich in qualities—full of deep colors, reverberating sounds, and pungent smells. The body ego's feelings are powerful currents that ripple or surge through the body. And the body ego's cognitions, although primitive, are insights that arrive with great impact and sense of significance, sometimes assuming the magnitude of astounding realizations. Every aspect of the body ego's experience, I suggest, is accentuated by the power of the Ground, which energizes and therefore enhances consciousness across all dimensions.

The power of the Ground also expresses itself in a positive way by imbuing the body ego's world with a numinous aura. The body ego's world, saturated with the power of the Ground, is enchanted: it is alluring, entrancing, awesome, mysterious, full of hidden depths and meanings. The body ego's world is magical, and the body ego itself, correspondingly, is enthralled. The body ego is prone to being captivated, as everything in its world is cathected—charged, amplified, and magnetized—with psychic energy. The world in general shimmers with aliveness, and specific objects in the world emanate a power that beckons, and sometimes commands, the body ego's attention. The body ego's world is permeated with an invisible power that, issuing from the Dynamic Ground, extends to the farthest reaches of perception.

A qualification is in order: the effects of the Dynamic Ground just described are not completely positive. For instance, polymorphous sensuality is a matter not only of somatically generated ecstasies but also of vulnerability, as the body ego is easily absorbed and dissolved, even against its will, in bodily sensations. The amplification of perception, feeling, and cognition is a matter not only of experience being enhanced but also, sometimes, of it being rendered painfully acute, even over-whelming, in its power and impact. And the numinous quality of the body ego's world is a matter not only of enchantment and rapture but also, sometimes, of eerie strangeness and bone-chilling dread. The Dynamic Ground can affect the body ego's experience in a dramatically bivalent manner.

This qualification acknowledged, the fact remains that the *young* body ego experiences the power of the Dynamic Ground primarily in positive ways. The young body ego's life is full of ecstasy, intensity, and wonder. Accordingly, the Great Mother appears to the young body ego for the most part in her Good Mother rather than in her Terrible Mother guise. For the young body ego, the negative side of the Great Mother (in both her inner and outer dimensions) remains in the background for the most part. The body ego–Great Mother relation is initially a relation that altogether favors the body ego.

As the body ego matures, however, the negative side of the Great Mother gradually emerges. The body ego's ambivalence toward the Great Mother begins to have a more pronounced negative accent. Even-tually, sometime in the second half of the second year, the negative side of the body ego's ambivalence becomes sufficiently strong to precipi-tate what Margaret Mahler (Mahler, Pine, and Bergman 1975) calls the *rapprochement crisis*. At this point, as we shall see shortly, the body ego's intensely opposed feelings for the Great Mother cause the body ego to split the Great Mother (the child's primary object representation) into two seemingly independent and antagonistic halves: the Good Mother and the Terrible Mother are completely disjoined and become appar-ently independent realities. This splitting of the Great Mother creates an impasse that threatens to bring ego development to a halt.

THE SPLITTING OF THE GREAT MOTHER

The Great Mother system has two axes, a positive-negative axis and an inner-outer axis. The Great Mother is both positive and negative because the body ego, in its ambivalence toward the Great Mother, is disposed to perceive her in both positive and negative guises, as both a Good Mother and a Terrible Mother. And the Great Mother is both inner and outer because she is at once the inner power of the Dynamic Ground and the outer person who is the primary caregiver. The Great Mother, then, is a double duality—which makes her very complex indeed. To avoid confusion, I shall distinguish the two axes of the Great Mother system by referring to the positive-negative axis as the *bivalent* axis and the inner-outer axis as the *bidirectional* axis.

Among psychoanalysts, Melanie Klein more than anyone else stressed the acute ambivalence-bivalence of the infant's experience. She held that the child, driven by life and death instincts, experiences both intense love and intense hate for the primary caregiver from birth on. Klein believed that the splitting of the primary object representation into a "good" (ideally nurturing) breast and a "bad" (persecutory) breast occurs in the earliest months of life. She also believed that the child has already moved beyond this splitting (characteristic of the "paranoid-schizoid" position) and has attained some degree of whole-object integration (characteristic of the "depressive" position) before the end of the first year of life.

These Kleinian views have been immensely influential. The consensus, however, is that Klein's dates are much too early. The more accepted view is that although ambivalence toward the primary caregiver is evident to some degree very early, acute ambivalence sufficient to split the child's world into powerful antagonistic opposites typically does not occur until sometime in the second half of the second year of life.[4] The second half of the second year, as noted earlier, is the time at which, in Mahler's terms, the child enters the rapprochement crisis.

The rapprochement subphase of the separation-individuation process is preceded by a "practicing" subphase (from eight to fifteen months). This practicing subphase is a period during which the young body ego explores its environment with reckless abandon. The practicing toddler knows no fear, for it assumes that the primary caregiver is so much a part of its world that, regardless of what might happen, the primary caregiver will always be available to provide help, support, and comfort. This confidence, however, collapses sometime around the middle of the second year of life. The body ego loses its confidence at this point because it begins to understand that the presence of the primary caregiver cannot be taken for granted.[5] Around age fifteen months, then, the body ego begins to feel insecure and begins to cling to the primary caregiver and to engage in behaviors that demand the caregiver's attention. The body ego at this point no longer assumes that the caregiver will always be available and begins to feel a strong need to reestablish closeness with the caregiver. The emergence of this felt need marks the transition to the rapprochement subphase of the separation-individuation process.

The movement toward rapprochement leads to a crisis because the body ego's reawakened need for the caregiver runs into contradiction with its continuing drive toward independence. This contradiction is exhibited in a variety of ways. The body ego begins both to cling to and assert itself against the caregiver, both to demand the caregiver's loving attentions and, responding to these attentions, to strike out against the caregiver in a show of independence. The body ego wants both closeness to and distance from the caregiver. Feeling insecure, the body ego seeks the loving embraces of the caregiver. In being embraced, however, the body ego feels as though it is being engulfed, and consequently the body ego pushes the caregiver away in a show of independence, only again to suffer from a sense of insecurity, and so on. The body ego wants both intimacy with and independence from the primary caregiver, who, reflecting these contradictory desires, begins to appear to the body ego in contradictory, split guises. The caregiver is split into a "good object" and a "bad object": the Great Mother is split into a Good Mother and a Terrible Mother, into powerfully opposed and apparently independent beings.

The splitting of the Great Mother is captured in a great many archetypal and mythological images. To the extent that the two sides of the bidirectional axis of the Great Mother system can be conceptually separated from each other, the splitting of the outer or personal dimension of the Great Mother is typically depicted in the form of female figures of either wholly good or wholly evil nature, and the splitting of the inner or intrapsychic dimension of the Great Mother is typically depicted in the form of elemental forces of either wholly pleasant or wholly inclement character.

In its outer dimension, the splitting of the Great Mother is expressed in images of good and evil guardians: fairies, witches, enchantresses. The good guardians are characteristically portrayed as wise, kind, and graceful maidens who protect and provide for young children. The evil guardians, in contrast, are characteristically portrayed as ugly crones who gain pleasure in deceiving and harming young children. As expressions of the Great Mother, both of these types of figures are magnetically or gravitationally attractive. The good guardians are so by virtue of the reassuring grace of their countenance and by magic charms. The evil guardians, being repellent in appearance, must rely on magic and deceptions (e.g., the house made of candy in the story of Hansel and Gretel).

The splitting of the inner dimension of the Great Mother, on the other hand, is depicted in terms of elemental forces of friendly or hostile character, especially forces such as water, fire, and wind, which provide the best metaphors for the movement of the power of the Ground. As archetypal symbols, these forces are always either completely gentle, soothing, and life-supporting or utterly violent and destructive. They are never neutral. So, for example, the power of the Ground is pictured as both good and evil waters, as both the water of life (virgin springs, clear streams, and serene lakes) and water with great destructive power (floods, raging seas full of tempests and whirlpools). Or the power of the Ground is pictured as both good and evil fires, as both a vital warmth (the fire of the hearth) and a scorching heat (infernos, volcanoes). Or the power of the Ground is pictured as both good and evil winds, as both a caressing zephyr and a raging whirlwind or gale. These elemental forces are in all cases extreme; they are forces that either assuage or assail, sustain or slay. As expressions of the inner dimension of the Great Mother, they indicate that the body ego's subjective atmosphere is volatile and subject to dramatic shifts from positive to negative.

Because the bidirectionality of the Great Mother is unrecognized by the body ego, many of the images of the Great Mother, and many of her bivalent manifestations in particular, stress neither her outer nor her inner dimension but rather reflect a fusion of features deriving from both of these dimensions. A typical image that results from such a fusion, combining as it does an external life form with an internal force or power, is that of a subhuman animal, characteristically either a furry mammalian comforter or a devouring monster (perhaps a wolf or reptile). The furry mammalian comforter is, of course, the Good Mother. It plays the role of a constant companion and guardian of the body ego—in the form, for instance, of the "transitional objects," the stuffed animals, to which the body ego clings. And the devouring monster is the Terrible Mother. It is imagined typically as a beast or serpent that lurks in darkness waiting for a chance to snatch the body ego unawares—in the form, for instance, of the monsters that, in the body ego's imagination, exist under the bed. Animals such as these constitute perhaps the very best symbols of the Great Mother, who, to the body ego, is not clearly a person in the full sense or simply a bare force or power, but is rather a being that approximates both of these. The mammalian comforter–devouring monster antithesis may therefore be the most representative expression of the bivalence of the Great Mother.

Because she is both bidirectional and bivalent, the Great Mother assumes virtually an infinite number of forms. She is a person, power, creature, friend, and foe. She is a multifaceted living presence embodying a complex array of archetypal images. She is, in short, a profusion of diverse and conflicting manifestations. These manifestations, however, are by no means random or unconnected. Understood in terms of the Great Mother's biaxial character, they observe an inner logic; they fit together as an ordered series or coherent constellation of forms.

CONFLICT WITH THE GREAT MOTHER AND PRIMAL REPRESSION

The bivalent axis of the Great Mother, expressing the body ego's ambivalence toward her, is the key to understanding the body ego's fundamental existential project. The body ego wants to be an "independent intimate" of the Great Mother, to be independent of the Great Mother *qua* Terrible Mother and intimate with the Great Mother *qua* Good Mother. This pursuit of "independent intimacy" commences as soon as the body begins to experience the Great Mother's bivalence, which is very early in life indeed. However, because the positive side of the Great Mother is primary in the early preoedipal period, the body ego's project to be an independent intimate of the Great Mother is at first only partially articulated. In the early preoedipal period, the body ego for the most part just strives to be intimate with the Great Mother, to surrender to her power of attraction and solvent embrace and thereby to return to the bliss of original embedment. But when, in the rapprochement subphase of the separation-individuation process, the body ego begins increasingly to experience the negative side of the Great Mother, both the bivalence of the Great Mother and the two-sidedness of the body ego's fundamental project become more pronounced. To the observer, it becomes increasingly clear that the body ego wants not only intimacy with the Great Mother but also independence from her. At this juncture, the body ego's increasing sense of need for the primary caregiver, running into contradiction with its ongoing drive for independence, intensifies the body ego's ambivalence to such a degree that the body ego splits its primary object representation into "good" and "bad" contrary opposites. The negative side of the Great Mother is in this way both magnified and hypostatized; to the body ego, the negative side of the Great Mother becomes a terrifying independent reality. This emergence of the negative side of the Great Mother as a magnified, split-off "bad object" heightens the body ego's drive for independence. Independence at this point becomes not only a continuing goal of development but also a means of escape from a negative reality that has now grown to ominous proportions: the Terrible Mother.

The body ego's fundamental project aims at something impossible. The goal of being both intimate with the Good Mother and independent of the Terrible Mother is not possible, because the Good Mother and the Terrible Mother are in fact one being. The body ego's fundamental project is therefore based on a contradiction. This contradiction is for the most part merely implicit prior to the rapprochement period, because the body ego's project is itself more implicit than explicit prior to this period. With the beginning of the rapprochement period, however, the impossibility of the body ego's project becomes fully explicit. During the rapprochement period, and during the rapprochement crisis in particular, the impossibility of being an "independent intimate" of the Great Mother is dramatically played out.

The impossibility of the body ego's fundamental project is expressed perhaps most dramatically in sudden reversals along the Great Mother's bivalent axis: the Good Mother is suddenly transformed into the Terrible Mother and the Terrible Mother into the Good Mother. In need of intimacy, the body ego seeks closeness with the Good Mother— only, in yielding to the Good Mother's gravitational-solvent embrace, to experience that embrace as a threat to independent existence. As this sense of danger arises, the Good Mother is suddenly transmogrified into the Terrible Mother, a being whose gravitational power is experienced as engulfing rather than inviting and whose solvent power is experienced as lethally disintegrative of self rather than as blissfully releasing of self. Frightened by this unanticipated encounter with the Terrible Mother, the body ego desperately struggles for independence. It strikes out against the very embrace it had sought out; it struggles to establish maximum distance between itself and the Terrible Mother. In asserting itself in these ways, however, the body ego succeeds only in exacerbating its need for intimacy, for safe and nourishing closeness with its primary other. Accordingly, the Terrible Mother is transfigured back into the Good Mother, whose embrace the body ego once again pursues. And so it goes, in sudden reversals back and forth between pursuit of the Good Mother and flight from the Terrible Mother. The body ego is in this way caught in a repetition of self-defeating behaviors that exhibit the impossibility of its fundamental project in dramatic fashion.

Because the body ego's project is an impossible one, it must in time be given up. A choice must ultimately be made between the two incompatible desires that motivate the project. And the choice is really predetermined: independence is the goal of development, and therefore unitive intimacy must be relinquished. The body ego must eventually sever its last remaining ties of symbiotic union with the Great Mother; it must relinquish its desire to yield to the Great Mother's gravitational-solvent influence. The choice between independence and intimacy is, for the body ego of the rapprochement period, a choice between growth and regression. The body ego must choose independence.

The choice of independence emerges from a two-sided struggle, a struggle that reflects the bidirectional nature of the Great Mother. This struggle is at once an interpersonal conflict by which the child seeks to extricate itself from the overawing influence of the primary caregiver and an intrapsychic conflict by which the child resists, and finally insulates itself from, the power of the Dynamic Ground. The first or interpersonal side of the struggle has as its chief consequences a withdrawal by the child from symbiotic intimacy with the caregiver and a corresponding burying by the child of its needs (felt as vulnerabilities) for openly flowing and intermingling love. And the second or intrapsychic side of the struggle has as its chief consequences a repressive sealing of the Dynamic Ground and, as instrument of this sealing, a repression of the body and physicodynamic life. Let us see how these consequences take shape.

Interpersonally, the body ego's struggle with the Great Mother is waged in response to two principal perceived dangers. One of these has already been noted, namely, the danger perceived to lie in the gravitational-solvent power of the Great Mother. The body ego undergoing the rapprochement crisis desires intimate union with the Great Mother, but it also fears such union as self-loss. Accordingly, the body ego at this stage perceives the Great Mother's gravitational power not only as an inviting but also as an engulfing power, and it perceives the Great Mother's solvent power not only as a power leading to blissful absorption (reembedment) but also as a power leading to dreadful dissolution (death). When the body ego perceives the Great Mother's gravitational-solvent power in these negative ways, it perceives the Great Mother as the Terrible Mother, as an ugly, massive, inescapable, engulfing, consuming being from whom the body ego desperately needs safe distance. In its interpersonal struggle with the Great Mother, therefore, the body ego feels itself at risk of being engulfed and destroyed.

This fear of engulfment and destruction, however, is just one aspect of the interpersonal conflict. For the emergence of the Terrible Mother is not just a consequence of the body ego's perceiving the Great Mother's gravitational-solvent power in a negative way. It is also a consequence of an objective change in the primary caregiver herself, whose *discipline* at this juncture becomes increasingly severe. The primary caregiver, who in the beginning attends to all of the body ego's needs and blesses the body ego with unconditional and uninterrupted love, has by this time begun to adopt definite expectations of the body ego. By about eighteen months of age the body ego is expected to control some of its negative outbursts and to take care of some of its own needs. And depending upon whether or not the body ego fulfills these expectations, the primary caregiver responds in markedly different ways. The primary caregiver ceases being simply an all-loving refuge and becomes in growing measure a power that praises and rewards the body ego when it is "good" and that scolds and perhaps even physically punishes the body ego when it is "bad." Beginning sometime in the middle of the second year, then, the Great Mother, in her interpersonal aspect, assumes a pronounced double negativity for the body ego. She becomes both a subversive and a coercive power; she becomes both a gravitational-solvent force that undermines the body ego's independence and a harsh judge who disapproves of, and seeks to change, much of what the body ego says and does.

The body ego continues to be attracted to the Great Mother and to crave intimacy with her even as she undergoes these negative changes in appearance and behavior. If the body ego now feels seriously endangered by the Great Mother in her Terrible Mother manifestation, it still strongly desires intimacy with the Great Mother in her Good Mother manifestation. This desire for intimacy with the Good Mother, however, is the body ego's Achilles' heel. For it is just this desire that brings the body ego under the subversive-coercive influence of the Terrible Mother. Moreover, the severity of the danger perceived to lie in the Terrible Mother's subversive-coercive power is directly proportional to the intensity of the desire for blissful intimacy with the Good Mother. The Great Mother could not have anywhere nearly as great a negative impact on the body ego if the body ego did not continue deeply to desire unity with her. Even the punishments of the primary caregiver would lose much of their sting if they were not perceived as the opposite of something—interflowing, boundary-melting love—that the body ego both wants and needs. It is therefore attachment to the Great Mother (as Good Mother) that leads repeatedly to the body ego's undoing, its dissolution and self-loss. For this reason the body ego, if it is truly to have a life and will of its own, must somehow put a stop to its yearning for loving, symbiotic intimacy with the Great Mother (as Good Mother).

And the body ego does precisely this. It distances itself; it braces itself; it holds itself back in defensive reserve; it no longer allows itself unconditionally to yield or surrender. In short, the body ego escapes from the Great Mother by withdrawing from her and by stifling its desire for her. The body ego closes itself to the primary caregiver's gravitational-solvent pull, and in this way it "wins" the outer or interpersonal battle with the Great Mother. To be sure, the body ego continues to need the primary caregiver and to interact with the primary caregiver in an affectionate manner. It never again, however, surrenders itself totally to the caregiver; the period of completely intimate mutuality is over. This interpersonal closing of the body ego to the Great Mother I shall call *primal alienation*. It is the act—which hardens into a psychic structure—that initiates self-other dualism. I shall have more to say about primal alienation later. First, however, we need to consider the inner or intrapsychic side of the body ego's struggle with the Great Mother.

What the body ego accomplishes interpersonally by severing its remaining ties of symbiotic union with the primary caregiver, it accomplishes intrapsychically by repressively insulating itself from the Dynamic Ground. These two acts go hand in hand. For the body ego, the primary caregiver and the power of the Dynamic Ground are outer and inner dimensions, respectively, of the single reality of the Great Mother. From the very beginning, it is one and the same thing for the body ego to yield to the primary caregiver and to surrender itself to the power of the Dynamic Ground. The body ego knows nothing of the difference between these two dimensions of the Great Mother, and even if it did, their intimate interaction as gravitational-solvent powers would preclude the possibility of the body ego's undertaking an action in relation to one dimension of the Great Mother without simultaneously undertaking fundamentally the same action in relation the other. Moreover, as we shall see in a moment, the body ego's action against the primary caregiver is of necessity also an action against the Dynamic Ground because the very bodily posture that distances the body ego from the primary caregiver also has the consequence of disconnecting the body ego from the Ground. For these reasons, then, the body ego's interpersonal alienation of the Great Mother *qua* primary caregiver is at the same time an intrapsychic repression of the Great Mother *qua* Dynamic Ground. Having termed the interpersonal alienation of the primary caregiver primal alienation, I shall, following Freud, call the corresponding intrapsychic repression of the Dynamic Ground *primal repression*.[6]

Primal repression insulates the body ego from the Dynamic Ground by creating a countercathectic barrier that contains, and thereby quiets, the power of the Ground. This power is from the outset of life an integral part of the body ego's experience. Earlier, we saw how the power of the Ground affects the body ego by rendering its experience polymorphously sensual, superalive in all dimensions, and numinously charged. We also saw how these effects are double-edged and can make themselves felt not only in a positive manner, as ecstasy, intensity, and enchantment, but also in a negative manner, as vulnerability, overstimulation, and estrangement. The point to be made here is that the negative side of this bivalent manifestation of the power of the Ground, in the background at first, begins to play a more prominent role once the rapprochement crisis splits the Great Mother. From the ego's point of view, for example, the power of the Ground begins at this point to manifest itself much more emphatically as hostile and destructive elemental forces, forces that fill the body ego's subjective atmosphere with violent storms. Also, in its gravitational effect, the power of the Ground now begins much more emphatically to manifest itself as an abyssal force, that is, as a force that threatens to captivate and engulf the body ego in a terrifying underlying darkness. In the face of these accentuated negative manifestations of the power of the Ground, the body ego feels more and more imperiled, so much so, in fact, that the body ego eventually begins to feel that it has no choice but to remove itself from further contact with the Ground—or, more accurately, from the Ground-caregiver Great Mother. The body ego therefore undertakes a repressive action against the Ground, which results in the sealing of the Ground and the submerging of the power of the Ground (together with physicodynamic potentials generally) into unconsciousness. This repressive action is primal repression.

The struggle with the Great Mother therefore culminates in primal alienation and primal repression. Primal alienation and primal repression are two sides of a single act, corresponding to the bidirectional two-sidedness of the Great Mother. Primal alienation–primal repression is the act by which the body ego simultaneously closes itself to the primary caregiver and covers over the Dynamic Ground. It is at once an interpersonal and intrapsychic act, involving both a withdrawal from outer affections and a containment of inner power and potentials. For the sake of simplicity, I shall henceforth dispense with the clumsy expression *primal alienation–primal repression* and, unless otherwise indicated, use the term *primal repression* to refer to both the outer and inner dimensions of the body ego's bidirectional disconnection from the Great Mother.

Primal repression is a physical as well as a psychic act—which brings into being a chronic physical as well as psychic posture. In committing itself to the act of primal repression, the young child physically separates itself from the gravitational-solvent influence of the Great Mother. The child accomplishes this separation by tensing the body, especially the anus, abdomen, chest, and shoulders, thereby holding itself in taut, girded and armored, reserve. This rigid stance shields the child from both the outer and inner dimensions of the Great Mother. Interpersonally, the armoredness of the body steels the body ego and renders it untouchable by, and therefore invulnerable to, the felt subversive-coercive influences of the Great Mother *qua* primary caregiver. And intrapsychically, the anal, abdominal, and other tensions inherent to the posture create a countercathectic barrier that blocks the release of energy from the Dynamic Ground. Primal repression is an act that establishes a posture of defensive self-containment. In bracing the body, it armors the child against gravitational-solvent emotional solicitations. And in "girding the loins," it seals the Ground and thereby protects the child from gravitational-solvent upwellings.

Intrapsychically, the posture of primal repression is a structure that closes the ego to the Dynamic Ground. The inner tensions, constrictions, and occlusions that make up the posture constitute a hierarchy of barriers that block the circulation of the power of the Ground in the body and restrict the power of the Ground to its point of origin—which, I suggest, lies in the sexual system.[7] Primal repression, then, closes the ego to the Ground by transforming the body from a vehicle receptive to the free upflow of the power of the Ground into an instrument that opposes the power of the Ground. This repressive transformation of the body will be discussed in greater detail in chapter 5, where I shall explain how primal repression, as a countercathexis, works not only in "hydraulic" fashion to restrict the power of the Ground to its point of origin in the sexual system but also, and perhaps more importantly, in "thermostatic" fashion to reduce the power of the Ground from an active to a latent ("sleeping," "coiled") state. For the present suffice it to say that the net effect of primal repression is that it disconnects the ego from the Ground by restructuring the body against the Ground. The body becomes impervious to the power of the Ground, and the ego is confined to the mental space associated with the head.

Because it contains the power of the Ground within its point of origin in the sexual system, primal repression marks the point at which polymorphous sensuality ends and genitally based latency begins. Polymorphous sensuality is an expression of the free circulation of energy in the body. Hence, because primal repression renders the body unreceptive to the movement of energy, it at the same time divests the body of its generalized arousability and capacity for ecstasy.[8] Primal repression both hardens and deadens the body; it transforms the body from a supple and sensitive vehicle of the power of the Ground into a "thing" that disallows the active expression of the power of the Ground. Primal repression, then, involves not only a negation of the Ground but also, as instrument of this negation, a negation of the body and of polymorphously sensual life. In using the body against the Ground, primal repression effects a thoroughgoing psychosomatic split. It effects a split not only between the ego and the Ground but also between mind and body and in general between ego-centered consciousness and the physicodynamic potentials of life.

Clearly, there is no longer a *body* ego once the repression of the body has occurred. The final divorce from the Great Mother, and the psychosomatic split that ensues from it, brings an end to the ego's body-based existence. In separating itself from the Great Mother, the ego also separates itself from the body, especially the underlying dynamic and instinctual regions. The body ceases being the locus of selfhood and is reduced to a mere object, an instrument for egoic purposes. The ego, no longer a body ego, now takes up residence in the psychic space associated with the head. It becomes a mental ego. The mental ego, which I shall discuss in chapter 4, is the ego of the latency period, adolescence, and early adulthood.

To this point we have considered the body ego's struggle with the Great Mother only in terms of the child's perception of the Great Mother, that is, only in terms of the child's primary object representation. The very same struggle, however, can be looked at in terms of the child's self-representation. For according to psychoanalytic object relations theory, the splitting of the primary object representation is at the same time a splitting of the self-representation. The splitting of the Great Mother into a Good Mother and a Terrible Mother is at the same time a splitting of the child's self-representation into a "good child" and a "terrible child." In perceiving the Great Mother as the Good Mother, the child perceives itself as a good child, as a lovable innocent worthy of the Good Mother's unconditional loving attentions; and in perceiving the Great Mother as the Terrible Mother, the child perceives itself as a terrible child, as a hateful being unworthy of love and deserving of reprimands and punishments.

This self-condemnation is a tragic dimension of the early childhood years. Owing to the splitting that inevitably occurs in the ego's perception of the Great Mother, the child is adversely affected in a way that the child can understand only as meaning that it is no longer unconditionally valuable, that it has a bad side if not an evil fundamental nature. The Great Mother has split into two primitive Manichaean goddesses, one of whom loves and nurtures a good child and the other of whom engulfs and punishes a terrible child. Operating on the prereflective assumption that the Great Mother's treatment of it is a statement of its inherent worthiness or unworthiness, the body ego at this point is subject to sudden shifts from self-love to self-hate. The emergence of the Terrible Mother as a powerful split-off "object" in the child's experience afflicts the child with a sense of negative self-value. The body ego, wanting desperately to be the good child, feels as though it must eliminate the terrible child. The good child and the terrible child, however, are two sides of the same body ego, just as the Good Mother and the Terrible Mother are two sides of the same Great Mother. The body ego's struggle to eliminate the terrible child, then, is a struggle against an integral part of itself.

Viewed from this child-centered perspective, the struggle between the body ego and the Terrible Mother shows itself also to be a struggle that the body ego wages against itself. And the act by which the body ego finally separates itself from the Terrible Mother shows itself also to be an act that the body ego—or rather the incipient mental ego—commits against itself. In alienating the outer, personal side of the Terrible Mother, the ego also commits an act of self-alienation; and in repressing the inner, physicodynamic side of the Terrible Mother, the ego also commits an act of self-repression. Primal repression is a bidirectional self-closing by which the child at once severs its internal relations with others and covers over the deepest Ground of its own being.

The ego, however, is unaware of the injury it has inflicted upon itself. In fact, the ego that has just resolved, or is in the process of resolving, the rapprochement crisis, experiences primal repression as "liberation" from overwhelming conflicts and inner storms. Interpersonally, the primary caregiver, now kept at a safe distance, no longer exerts an irresistible gravitational-solvent influence upon the ego and thereby ceases being experienced by the ego as a larger-than-life, split, desirable yet dangerous being. The primary caregiver, that is, ceases being the split Great Mother and is reduced to being simply the primary caregiver, a single and stable but "mere" human being. In psychoanalytic parlance, the ego in this way makes progress toward libidinal object constancy; its primary object ceases being split into radically fluctuating all-good and all-bad part objects and is gradually mended into a single object that, although imperfect, is stable, reliable, and fundamentally good.

Occurring simultaneously with this achievement of object constancy is an achievement of self-constancy. The child ceases splitting itself into all-good and all-bad "part selves" and, repressing the physicodynamic core of its being, strives to *become* good by adopting parental expectations as its own self-expectations, that is, by identifying with those expectations in the form of the superego. The superego, which begins to take form during the preoedipal period, is consolidated at the end of the oedipal period. The consolidation of the superego indicates that the rapprochement splitting of the self-representation has been completely mended.

In achieving interpersonal "liberation" from the gravitational-solvent influence of the primary caregiver, the ego also achieves intrapsychic "liberation" from the gravitational-solvent power of the Dynamic Ground. Primal repression puts this power safely to sleep at the base of the spine. Moreover, primal repression, as an embedded structure of the body, provides the ego, now located experientially in the region of the head, with a sense of standing on a firm foundation. The repression of the Dynamic Ground gives the ego a sense of having a solid ground, a secure basis that both supports the ego and insulates it from a hidden underlying "void" or "abyss," the dynamic unconscious. Accordingly, although primal repression inflicts a severe injury upon the psyche, this injury is one that is at first completely unevident to the ego, which experiences the effects of primal repression in a positive way. The ego experiences independence rather than loss of intimacy and self-control rather than loss of spontaneity. Only much later in life, if ever, does the ego's dualistic separation from others and from the nonegoic pole of the psyche give rise to seriously negative feelings. Only at midlife or later, typically, does the ego begin to experience its separation from others more as isolation than as independence and does it begin to experience its separation from the nonegoic pole more as incompleteness than as self-control.

Primal repression, although initially a response to the preoedipal rapprochement crisis, is not firmly consolidated until after the resolution of the Oedipus complex. In the next section, I shall follow the body ego's project to be an independent intimate of the Great Mother through the stages of psychosexual development up to the resolution of the Oedipus complex, when the project is finally brought to an end by the child's decisive commitment to the father.

THE BODY PROJECT, THE OEDIPUS COMPLEX, AND PRIMAL REPRESSION

In the body ego's interaction with the primary caregiver, the project to be an independent intimate of the Great Mother takes the form of the *body project*, which is the attempt on the part of the body ego to use its body as a means of achieving both closeness to and safe distance from the primary caregiver. The body project, I suggest, is an important aspect of psychosexual development during early childhood.

The stages of psychosexual development are rooted in bodily areas that bear a twofold relation to the Great Mother. On the one hand, these areas, as erotogenic zones, are avenues of access to original embedment. The mouth, anus, and genitals are made of sensitive tissue that has a capacity for a high energic charge. The stimulation of these zones, therefore, releases concentrated impulses of energy, potent outpourings that induce euphoria in the body ego and dissolve its self-boundaries, returning it to the bliss of original embedment. The body ego is polymorphously sensual, which means that it can be enraptured by means of any bodily surface or part. Nevertheless, the erotogenic zones are the points of the body that are most highly charged with ecstasy-producing energy. Stimulation of them effects an immediate melting of the body ego's boundaries.

The child, however, is not always allowed to enjoy the pleasures arising from the psychosexual zones, for these bodily areas are under the supervision of the primary caregiver. It is the primary caregiver who gives or refuses the breast, who stipulates the times and places for defecation, and who mandates that the genitals be covered and, in some instances, not touched. In short, it is the primary caregiver who guards the gates to original embedment. The child is allowed to dissolve itself in erotogenic bliss only when the primary caregiver allows.

The child's psychosexual situation, however, is more complex than this. For, as we know, the child is not only attracted to but also threatened by the self-dissolution that goes with reembedment. Therefore, the temptation to let go and give way to the energies released from the erotogenic zones is overlaid with anxiety. On the oral level, this anxiety of self-loss probably expresses itself as a fear of being swallowed or engulfed; on the anal level, as a fear of being emptied of self; and on the phallic level, as a fear of suffering some calamity—for the child quickly infers from the adult's concern that the genitals be covered that the genitals are taboo and dangerous in some way.

The psychosexual zones are, then, double-edged. And so too is the primary caregiver's supervision of them. From the point of view of the body ego, the primary caregiver uses these zones both to solicit approach and to bar access to original embedment. Accordingly, the body ego responds to the primary caregiver's enticements and injunctions with an inconsistency that expresses the ambivalences of its situation: it responds both obediently and defiantly. The young body ego in the first year and a half of life, not yet afflicted with rapprochement and oedipal complications, responds more often with obedience than defiance. Even the young body ego, however, experiences ambivalence toward the primary caregiver and original embedment—that is, toward the Great Mother—and therefore is prone not only to obedience but also to defiance. Oral aggression can in this way be seen as the other side of oral submission. Anal sadism can be seen as the other side of anal conformity. And phallic rebelliousness—for example, exhibition-ism, public urination—can be seen as the other side of phallic propriety. For the most part, the child tries to remain in the good graces of the primary caregiver, but the primary caregiver's threatening side prompts defensive-aggressive attacks. The body ego wants to be an independent intimate of the primary caregiver. Independence and intimacy, however, are incompatible for the body ego, and consequently the body ego tends to interact with the primary caregiver in contradictory ways, shifting dramatically between submission in the search of intimacy and defiance in defense of independence.

The body ego's fundamental project culminates in the oedipal conflict. It does so because, around the age of three or shortly thereafter, it dawns upon the body ego that there is someone who, it seems, enjoys just the sort of relationship with the mother for which the child impossibly strives: the father. The father is on intimate terms with the mother and yet is also a fully independent being. To the body ego, it seems that the father has what the body ego most deeply wants. Seeing the father in this way, the body ego understandably changes the focus of its fundamental project: the project to be an independent intimate of the Great Mother now becomes a project to replace the father in the father's relationship with the mother.[9] The body ego senses that if it could but assume the father's role *vis-à-vis* the mother, it could succeed in its desire to be at one with the mother without thereby suffering self-loss. Therefore a rivalry with the father ensues, or at least this is what happens in the eyes of the body ego.

This interpretation of the oedipal conflict implies that the child-caregiver relationship in the oedipal stage is not a relationship in which a *boy* child desires to experience *sexual* intimacy with the mother. It is rather a relationship in which a boy *or girl* child desires to *assume the father's role of independent intimate of the mother*. Boys and girls of course experience and seek to resolve the Oedipus complex in importantly different ways; nevertheless, boys and girls bring the same fundamental project into the oedipal period and begin pursuing this project in a new way within the distinctively triangular structure of the oedipal situation. Both boys and girls seek to be an independent intimate of the primary caregiver; and in entering the oedipal situation, they both begin to pursue this project by attempting to replace the father in his relationship with the mother.

Another implication of this interpretation of the Oedipus complex is that the child need harbor no fantasies of genital sexuality or fears of genital mutilation. The child need have no fixation on, or even any comprehension of, the mechanics of sexual intercourse. Nor need the child have any apprehensions about castration, much less, of course, clitoridectomy. Rather than being focused on sex, the child's fantasy focuses more generally on personal closeness with the primary caregiver. And rather that being focused on a particular organ, the child's fear is focused more generally on provoking the wrath of the father. The child perceives the father as a rival for the mother's affection. This perceived rivalry may or may not lead to a real antagonism with the father. In any case, however, given the father's virtual omnipotence in the child's eyes, the mere prospect of such an antagonism is sufficient to cause the child to fear for its life—however little the child might actually *understand* this fear.

In tendering this interpretation of the Oedipus complex, I am taking exception not only to the classical psychoanalytic view that the Oedipus complex is a sexual project but also to the existentialist view—advocated by Norman O. Brown (1959), by Ernest Becker (1973), and (in modified transpersonal form) by Ken Wilber (1980a)—according to which the desire for intimacy with the primary caregiver is a desire for godlike independence, the desire to be parent or cause of oneself, *ens causa sui*. This view is ingenious, but it suffers from insuperable difficulties. For example, it shares with the orthodox psychoanalytic view the problem of explaining how a child of such a young age can have knowledge of and desire for sexual-procreative activity. Moreover, this existentialist view badly misconceives the basic objective of the body ego, which does not aspire to the kind of independence that philosophers like Jean-Paul Sartre extol. True, the body ego does aspire to independence, but not unconditionally so, because it also longs for intimacy and support, closeness and reembedment. The body ego does not want absolute independence; rather, it wants to be an independent intimate of the primary caregiver. The existentialist perspective is seriously misapplied to the body ego. This perspective, however, does have a proper application: the mental ego. It is the mental ego that, having severed remaining ties of symbiotic union with the primary caregiver and having repressed the Dynamic Ground, is committed to the project of absolute independence. It is the mental ego that, as we shall see in chapter 4, strives to be *ens causa sui*.

To return now to the predicament of the child in the oedipal situation, it is evident that the child cannot win in its competition with the father; eventually, the child must capitulate. And the terms of surrender are clear: the child must relinquish all remaining hope of or claim to intimacy with the mother, who now belongs, in this way, to the father alone. In other words, the child at this point must concede half its fundamental project; it must forfeit intimacy and pursue independence as its exclusive goal. Now precisely this concession, we remember, is the outcome of the child's rapprochement struggle with the Great Mother. The capitulation to the father that resolves the Oedipus complex, then, finalizes a process already begun at the end of the rapprochement period. In capitulating to the oedipal father, the child completes the act of separating itself from the Great Mother. In surrendering to the father and in conceding to the father exclusive rights of intimacy with the mother, the child decisively closes the door to any further symbiotic participation in the Great Mother's being. In doing so, the child commits itself completely to primal repression as the structural basis of its being. Primal repression, therefore, at this point becomes a permanent psychic structure.

If the oedipal father is instrumental in finalizing the child's forfeiture of intimacy, he is also instrumental in finalizing the child's commitment to independence. For the oedipal father is, in the child's eyes, simultaneously a rival for intimacy with the mother and a model of worldly independence; as an independent intimate of the mother, he is everything the child wants to be. In surrendering to the oedipal father, then, the child not only submits to the father as rival for intimacy with the mother, thereby forfeiting intimacy in a final and decisive way, but the child also submits to the father as model of independence, thereby committing itself to independence in a final and decisive way. The father at this point becomes a being whom the child begins to emulate in earnest. The child, at last "weaned" from the Great Mother, begins now to follow the father's lead on the path of ego development and worldly independence.

The foregoing account of the Oedipus complex and its consequences is incomplete, because it does not address the crucial issue of gender differences in the oedipal period. This issue is fraught with difficulty and controversy. I have dealt with it at length in *Transpersonal Psychology in Psychoanalytic Perspective* and elsewhere (1994a) and therefore will not pursue it here. Suffice it here to say that, despite important gender differences, the Oedipus complex has a gender-common core: both girls and boys, I suggest, finalize their movement from intimacy to independence by making a double commitment to the oedipal father, a commitment that is at once a capitulation to the oedipal father as rival (for the intimacy to be relinquished) and an emulation of the oedipal father as model (of the independence to be achieved).[10]

CONCLUSION

The body-egoic period is bounded on one end by original embedment and on the other end by primal repression. The former boundary marks a condition of undifferentiated unity with the Great Mother, of blissful envelopment in the primary caregiver's embrace and blissful immersion in the Dynamic Ground. The latter boundary marks the point at which the ego finally disconnects itself from the Great Mother, winning independence by withdrawing from unitive intimacy with the primary caregiver and by divorcing itself from the Dynamic Ground. Original embedment is a condition of preegoic oneness with the Ground-caregiver Great Mother; primal repression in complete contrast is a condition of egoic alienation from the Ground-caregiver Great Mother. Focusing for the moment on the intrapsychic dimension, the two boundaries of the body-egoic period can, accordingly, be said to mark two diametrically opposed positions in the unfolding of the ego-Ground interaction. Original embedment marks the point at which the Ground is all and the ego nothing (in the sense of being merely potential), and primal repression marks the point at which the ego is all and the Ground nothing (in the sense of being submerged, sealed, unconscious).

The body-egoic period between original embedment and primal repression is a time during which the young child is torn between these extremes. The body ego has mixed feelings, wanting both intimacy with and independence from the Great Mother. It wants both to receive the Great Mother's blessings and to be its own, self-possessed self. These two desires, however, are in conflict with each other. The desire for intimacy conflicts with independence, for when the body ego comes into close contact with the Great Mother it suffers dissolution and reembedment. And the desire for independence conflicts with intimacy, for when the body ego makes a move of independence, it experiences a threatening separation from the principal reality of its world, a reality to which the body ego remains strongly attracted and attached. The body ego, pulled in these opposite directions by its two basic desires, is caught in a contradictory and, ultimately, untenable situation.

The conflict between the body ego's two basic desires becomes acute during the rapprochement subphase of the separation-individuation process. Upon entering this subphase, it becomes clear that one or the other of the body ego's two basic desires must be sacrificed. And in the interests of development, it is intimacy with the Great Mother— and, correspondingly, openness to nonegoic or physicodynamic life— that ends up being forfeited. In effect, the body ego is finally confronted with the choice of either regression or repression. There is no middle ground. The body ego can either yield to the Great Mother and thereby submit to continued reembedment and consequent loss of autonomy, responsibility, mind, and will, or it can separate itself from the Great Mother and thereby perpetrate a repression that forfeits intimacy, the body, dynamism, feeling, and creative imagination.

The child struggles with this fateful choice. Again and again it closes itself to the Great Mother only to be "enticed" back into her gravitational-solvent embrace. The child adopts the posture of primal repression (and primal alienation) only to relax its hold and give way once again to the lure of reembedment. At a certain juncture, however, the child finds that it cannot continue to waver. For the father eventually forces the child's hand, making the choice for or against the Great Mother at the same time a choice against or for the father. To continue to choose intimacy with the Great Mother is now also to incur the wrath of the father; and to choose independence from the Great Mother is now also to be accepted and affirmed by the father. Accordingly, the body ego decisively chooses against intimacy and for independence, against regression and for repression, against the Great Mother (and the non-egoic potentials she represents) and for the father (and the ego functions he represents). This choice is costly. It is, however, the only choice that is consistent with continued development.

This account of primal repression suggests an interpretation of the Christian doctrine of original sin. In particular, it suggests a way of answering three essential questions that vex the traditional account of this doctrine: (1) Why was humanity susceptible to sin? (2) In what respect can the act that was committed be considered sinful? and (3) In what sense can sin be said to be inherited?

Why were Adam and Eve moved to sin? We are told that they ate the fruit because they were tempted. But why would they have been tempted to reach for more than was already theirs in *paradise*? If they were really in paradise, they must have been completely happy and satisfied. If, however, they were tempted for something more, then it seems they must not have been in paradise after all.

The foregoing account of primal repression suggests that the paradisiacal conditions of Eden do not last and therefore that the act of sin is a response not to paradise but to the *loss* of paradise. Or in our terms, primal repression is a response not to the "blessed" state that obtains in the early body-egoic period, which is a time during which the negative side of the Great Mother's bivalence is as yet unpronounced, but is rather a response to the negative transformation of this state that occurs during the rapprochement and oedipal periods. If, as I have argued, the body ego comes to experience reembedment not only as a blissful release from self but also as a growth-obstructing loss of self, then sin, primal repression, can be understood to be an inevitable response to this unhappy change in the body ego's experience. On this interpretation, then, sin is not an act of gratuitous self-assertion but rather an act of necessary self-defense: the child really has no alternative but to choose independence over intimacy, repression over regression.

But if sin, so conceived, is an act of necessary self-defense, how can it be considered sin? Where is the wrong in self-defense? There is of course no wrong in self-defense. Therefore primal repression must be considered an innocent act, *at least initially*. But primal repression is not a momentary act; it is rather a posture that, consolidated at the end of the oedipal period, becomes a deeply embedded psychic structure. Solidified as such a structure, primal repression remains in place for most people throughout the rest of their lives. But this is simply to say that primal repression usually remains in place much longer than is developmentally necessary. For once the ego is strong and fully developed, it no longer needs to be separated from the Dynamic Ground. Hence, even though primal repression is at first a necessity to be regretted rather than a wrong to be condemned, it becomes, in time, an unnecessary and unwarranted obstacle to the ego's higher developmental destiny. In time, it becomes a way in which the ego is held back—or, rather, *holds itself back*—from meeting its ultimate spiritual Ground. In short, primal repression becomes a way in which the ego refuses God. It becomes sin.

Now we can address the question of how, if at all, sin can be said to be inherited. The problem here, of course, is that if sin is an individual act, it seems that, logically, it should be an individual guilt as well. Yet the traditional account of original sin does not accept this conclusion; rather, it holds that a collective, inherited sin arose from the acts of Adam and Eve. To avoid the logical oddity of this position (not to mention its self-evident unfairness), one suggestion has been that it is not sin per se that is inherited but rather only the predisposition to sin. This suggestion fits the account developed here, according to which we are born with a predisposition not only to close ourselves to the Dynamic Ground—a closing that, occurring in early childhood, is virtually inevitable and therefore innocent—but also to remain closed to the Dynamic Ground long after such a defensive posture has lost its developmental warrant. Sin, then, I suggest, emerges from our predisposition later in life to put off the day of reckoning and reconciliation, to shy back from the precipice of faith.

Some final questions: Is primal repression absolutely necessary? Granting that it is virtually inevitable, is it completely impossible to avoid? Could not, under exceptional circumstances, a child win independence without severing contact with the Ground, master ego functions without forfeiting physicodynamic potentials, and achieve self-possession without sacrificing deep interpersonal intimacy? Unfortunately, these questions have no easy answers. The possibility cannot be denied that a child of extraordinary ego strength blessed with parents of limitless understanding and love might be able to weather the contradictions of early childhood without succumbing to primal repression. Therefore, leaving this possibility open, the only warranted conclusion is that primal repression—along with the ego-Ground (mind-body, thought-feeling, will-spontaneity) and self-other splits based on primal repression—is an almost inescapable eventuality of early childhood development. Acknowledging the possibility of rare exceptions, it seems virtually unavoidable that the sins of the parents will be visited upon their children.

3

The Body Ego: Cognitive and Affective Development

HAVING IN THE LAST chapter treated the body ego's development from an intrapsychic and psychodynamic perspective, I shall in this chapter consider it as a process of unfolding stages of cognition and feeling. I shall follow out these stages up to the point of primal repression, which brings the period of the body ego to a close.

Consideration of the body ego's cognitive and affective life is important both for its own sake and because many of the aspects of this life, along with many of the aspects of the body ego's experience discussed in the last chapter, are early ("pre-") manifestations of nonegoic potentials that later (in their "trans-" form) become essential ingredients of integrated existence. These potentials enjoy a brief flowering during the body-egoic period only to be submerged and rendered dormant by primal repression. These potentials remain unconscious throughout the period of the mental ego's ascendancy. Then, once the ego, fully developed, embarks upon the transitional stages leading to integration, these potentials are derepressed, reactivated, and returned to consciousness. A reawakening of physicodynamic life occurs at this point, and the ego enters into an interaction with the nonegoic sphere that results, if it unfolds to culmination, in integration. The ensuing discussion of the cognitive and affective dimensions of the body ego's experience therefore is concerned not only with the preegoic stage of development but with the transegoic stage as well. In addition to reviewing essential elements of an early stage of development, the ensuing discussion will be previewing essential elements of the last and highest stage of development.

Drawing on both psychoanalytic and cognitive-developmental sources, I shall divide the period of the body ego into three principal stages of cognitive and affective growth: (1) the presymbolic stage (from birth to four or five months), (2) the referential-protosymbolic stage (from four or five months to approximately eighteen months), and (3) the symbolic-protoconceptual stage (from approximately eighteen months to four years).[1] This threefold division is based on stage transitions in the unfolding of the object concept in early childhood and corresponding stage transitions in the development of images.

The presymbolic stage is the initial stage of life prior to any understanding of object permanence and, therefore, prior to the development of images as symbolic designators of objects. Images may exist during this period, but, if they do, they do not yet refer to objects beyond themselves. The presymbolic stage is also a period during which affects, although rich and varied, have not yet acquired reference or meaning beyond the boundaries of the infant's experience.

The referential-protosymbolic stage is the period of infancy that begins with the initial understanding of object permanence and the corresponding development of images as designators of objects. Building on this initial form of object cognition and representation, the referential-protosymbolic stage is also the stage in which object attachment and feelings based on object attachment (e.g., affection, anger, separation anxiety) first emerge.

Finally, the symbolic-protoconceptual stage is the period that begins with the full development of the object concept and the corresponding development of images as symbols in the full sense of the term, that is, as representations that not only designate individual objects but also embody general meanings (protoconcepts). The symbolic-protoconceptual stage, based on a complete understanding of object independence and on an intitial grasp of general meanings, is also a stage in which the child begins to experience a wide range of new feelings made possible by these cognitive advances. As we shall see, the new feelings that emerge in this stage are markedly unstable ones. The cognitive advance marked by the move to the symbolic-protoconceptual stage awakens the child to a vastly larger and radically more unpredictable world, a world in which the child is subject to wild fluctuations and intense ambivalences in its feelings.

THE PRESYMBOLIC STAGE

The presymbolic stage begins at birth and extends to the age of four or five months. In Freud's account of early childhood development, the presymbolic stage corresponds to the period of primary narcissism and to much of the oral stage of psychosexual development. In Piaget's mapping of cognitive development, the presymbolic stage corresponds to the early substages of sensorimotor development. In Margaret Mahler's account of preoedipal development, the presymbolic stage corresponds to the neonatal phase and the ensuing symbiotic phase of development, which precede the separation-individuation process. And in the terms that have been introduced in our discussion, the presymbolic stage corresponds to the embedded condition in which the ego is only minimally differentiated from the Dynamic Ground.

It was long the accepted view that the consciousness of the newborn is a blank slate in the sense of being completely without discrimination or organization. This traditional view has been decisively overturned. Research on newborns in the last twenty-five years has revealed that newborns are much more cognitively discerning and structured than hitherto had been realized. Studies have shown that babies in the first months of life (1) give selective attention to the human face and to distinctive tonalities of human speech, (2) enter into complex social exchanges (e.g., subtle coordinations and synchronies with the primary caregiver), (3) discriminate among and have preferences for specific geometric patterns, colors, and sounds, (4) habituate to stimuli and therefore record stimuli in memory (recognition memory), and (5) learn from experience in the sense of recognizing that changes in one stimulus produce changes in another.[2] We now know that newborns are far from being cognitive blank slates and are in fact beings with sophisticated cognitive capabilities.

Although newborns are cognitively sophisticated in many ways, they seem to have no understanding of object permanence and therefore no ability to form mental representations of objects. Children in the first months of life discriminate among stimuli without showing evidence of recognizing that stimuli can be appearances of objects that exist when they are not being perceived. Accordingly, for newborns, as far as we can tell from observation, nothing has existence beyond the immediacy of experience; objects exist only as repeated, merely temporary stimuli. Newborns, it seems, lack an understanding of the independent existence of objects and therefore have no basis for producing object representations: object representations presuppose objects to be represented. If nothing exists beyond present experience, it follows that nothing is absent from experience that might need to be represented. In the presymbolic stage, the child's consciousness is discriminating and organized in many ways, but it is not yet a consciousness of enduring objects or, therefore, a consciousness that is capable of forming mental representations of objects.

If the presymbolic stage is without mental representations, is it for that reason also without mental images? Piaget answered this question in the affirmative. He argued (1951; Piaget and Inhelder 1971) that images arise only as object representations and, more specifically, only out of sensorimotor interaction with objects. For these reasons he held that images are not even possible until late in the first year (when, in his view, an initial understanding of object permanence is achieved) and in all likelihood play no significant role in the child's experience until midway into the second year (when the object concept is fully developed).

The classical psychoanalytic view on mental images differs markedly from this Piagetian view. According to Freud (1911a), images arise spontaneously and play a significant role in the child's experience almost from the outset of life. Soon after birth, Freud believed, the infant begins producing mental images in an attempt to satisfy unmet instinctual demands. This classical psychoanalytic view was taken up by many within the psychoanalytic community. Perhaps its strongest advocates were Melanie Klein (see Segal 1964, 1991) and the Kleinian Susan Isaacs (1943), who held that infants create images to satisfy instinctual demands even before those demands begin being frustrated. In contrast to this classical psychoanalytic view, Selma Fraiberg (1969), in an important paper, tried to bring psychoanalysis into agreement with Piaget's findings by arguing that the emergence of mental images should be dated to coincide with the achievement of an initial understanding of object permanence, which, according to Piaget, occurs around age eight or nine months.

It may be impossible to determine whether mental images exist in the first months of life as Freud, Klein, and Isaacs maintained. I shall not register an opinion on the matter. All that needs to be said here is that *if* mental images are present in the presymbolic stage, they are images that are *not* representations of objects. They are images that have the same status as all the other contents of the presymbolic infant's consciousness: they are stimuli among other stimuli. Presymbolic images, if they exist, therefore have the same status as percepts. Percepts at this point are not yet object presentations, and images, correspondingly, are not yet object representations. Both are merely temporary, appearing and disappearing, contents of the infant's consciousness. Given that presymbolic images, if they exist, have the same status as percepts, it is easy to see that they could, as Freud, Klein, and classical psychoanalysis more generally maintained, serve as substitutes for the objects of the instincts.

The presymbolic infant's cognition, then, is sophisticated in some respects and extremely rudimentary in others. While the presymbolic infant exhibits intelligence in its ability to discriminate among stimuli, record stimuli in memory (recognition memory), and learn from changes in stimulus configurations and stimulus sequences, this intelligence is still rudimentary in that the infant is not yet aware that some stimuli are externally derived and others internally generated. Although the presymbolic infant interacts significantly with objects, the objects with which it interacts are not objects in the strict sense of the term, because they have no existence apart from the infant's experience. Object relations in the presymbolic stage are more properly stimulus relations; the presymbolic infant knows no difference between its experience and the world. Accordingly, although some of the elements of the presymbolic infant's experience are cognitively more salient than others, all are ontologically on the same plane. All elements of the presymbolic infant's experience exist only *as experiences*.

The affective experience of the presymbolic infant is both as sophisticated and as rudimentary as its cognitive life. It is sophisticated in that the infant is capable of a wide variety of affective responses. Contrary to the traditional view of the newborn as a being that is not only cognitively unorganized but also affectively undifferentiated, recent studies indicate that the newborn is capable of a diverse array of feelings. Joseph Lichtenberg reviews recent studies and makes the following report:

> Infant research has demonstrated that an unexpectedly rich variety of affects are observable: interest, enjoyment, surprise, distress, anger, sadness, shame, disgust (Tomkins, 1962, 1963; Demos, 1982). Within ten days the infant can imitate affect expressions (Meltzoff and Moore, 1977) so that from very early in life the range of exchange of affective expressions between mother and infant is unexpectedly broad. Affect is from the beginning of life a component of all mental functions, amplifying the significance of all experience and contributing to the meaningfulness of all human exchanges. (1987, pp. 316–317)

The presymbolic infant gurgles, coos, beams, fusses, cries, and grimaces in response to internal and external stimuli. Its affective life is pronounced, subject to sudden shifts, and an integral part of the infant's moment-to-moment engagement of experience.

Among the affects characteristic of the presymbolic stage, one deserves special attention: blissful exuberance. The presymbolic infant gurgles, coos, and beams because it experiences upwelling, superabundant life. The presymbolic infant is radically open to the Dynamic Ground and is infused with and frequently blissfully dissolved by the power that rises from the Ground. The presymbolic infant is bathed in the water of life; ripples and waves of delicious energy move through the infant's body, filling it with delight. When its needs are satisfied and it is otherwise content, the presymbolic infant experiences a state of dynamic plenitude, blissful fullness.

Although the presymbolic infant is capable of diverse and highly significant feelings, its affective life is still extremely rudimentary. Because its cognition is not yet a cognition of enduring objects, its feelings are not yet affective responses to such objects. Rather, its feelings are either unprompted affective upwellings or affective responses to occurrent stimuli. To be sure, the presymbolic infant is intimately interactive with the primary caregiver. In responding to the caregiver, however, the infant is not responding to a being beyond itself. For the caregiver does not yet possess object permanence or, therefore, any degree of object independence. The caregiver, like everything else that is a part of the infant's experience, exists only *in* the infant's experience. The caregiver, too, then, is only a repeated stimulus pattern, and therefore the feelings that the presymbolic infant has for the caregiver are only temporary responses to elements of this pattern rather than lasting feelings for an enduring object.

THE REFERENTIAL-PROTOSYMBOLIC STAGE

Piaget (1954) held that the first major step toward understanding object permanence occurs at approximately eight or nine months of age, because children at this age begin to look for objects that they have observed being hidden from view. More recently, studies have shown that infants have a grasp of object permanence even before they are able to express it in motor behavior by searching for hidden objects. T. G. R. Bower (1982) reports studies that indicate a sense of object permanence as early as five months, and Renée Baillargeon (1987) has conducted experiments that reveal some grasp of object permanence even as early as three and a half months. In general, recent studies have shown that Piaget's perspective tying cognitive achievements to the motor skills that demonstrate them led him to date certain cognitive achievements later than they actually occur. Principal among the cognitive achievements that might have been misdated in this way are those pertaining to perceptual discrimination, object permanence, mental imagery, and initial forms of mental representation (see Mandler 1990). Following the more recent studies, I shall date the beginning of the referential-protosymbolic stage at about four or five months, the more likely date at which object permanence is first achieved. This date of course is only an estimate.

If mental images are not already present during the presymbolic stage, they emerge, I propose, during the referential-protosymbolic stage. Moreover, during this stage, mental images begin to serve as representations of objects. They do so, I suggest, because the achievement of object permanence is not only a precondition but also a sufficient cause of object representations. In addition to making object representations possible, the achievement of object permanence creates a *need* for object representations. This need arises because, in beginning to understand that things exist even when not perceived, the infant begins to understand as well that objects, and the primary caregiver in particular, can be absent from experience. The infant for this reason begins to experience a fear of object loss and a corresponding need to represent the primary caregiver during periods when the caregiver is absent. Cognition of object permanence is at the same time cognition of object absence and therefore of possible object loss. The fear of object loss, separation anxiety, first arises during the referential-protosymbolic stage, and this fear, I suggest, is the primary reason why mental images, if not already present earlier, emerge during this stage and begin serving as object representations.

The imaginal representations of the referential-protosymbolic stage are of the simplest type. They are exclusively denotative. They do not yet embody general meanings; they are simply substitutes for individual objects that, once within the field of experience, have disappeared from view. Referential-protosymbolic images therefore perform only the most basic semantic function: reference, designation. Because referential-protosymbolic images do not embody general meanings, they are not symbols in the full sense of the term. They are merely protosymbols or, to use Silvano Arieti's (1967) term, paleosymbols.

The mental images of the referential-protosymbolic stage, although images of absent objects, are still stimulus bound: they cannot be produced or sustained in mind without stimulus support. To be sure, given the initial achievement of object permanence, "out of sight" need no longer be "out of mind." Nevertheless, for the child to keep an object in mind, the child must be witness to a stimulus that can trigger an image of the object. For the referential-protosymbolic child possesses only recognition memory, not evocative memory—which, as Piaget (1954) showed, is not achieved until around age eighteen months. Memory of an absent object cannot be evoked at will but must be prompted by a stimulus that is in some way tied to the absent object.

This fact is exemplified in the phenomenon of the transitional object, which emerges at the outset of the referential-protosymbolic stage. The child's attachment to transitional objects such as stuffed animals or "good blankets" indicates that the child has a rudimentary grasp of the primary caregiver's existence as an enduring object that can exist beyond, and therefore be absent from, the child's immediate experience. The child holds onto the transitional object as a way of remembering the absent caregiver, as a way of keeping an image of the caregiver in mind. Without this object as a stimulus for memory, the child would not be able to form images of the caregiver. And even with the object, the images the child forms are probably only fleeting; they soon disappear, only to be reelicited by the stimulus of the transitional object.

The emergence of mental images as protosymbols occurs at a time when the child is making dramatic progress in sensorimotor cognition. As Piaget's classic studies have demonstrated, the child between four or five and eighteen months of age rapidly learns how its actions affect the environment. First the child learns specific action schemes that produce desired effects in the world. Next the child learns how to coordinate such schemes to produce more complex effects. And then the child begins to experiment with action schemes to discover what effects they produce. The referential-protosymbolic child is intensely interested in the world, which it explores by physically interacting with objects and observing the effects that ensue. The initial understanding of object permanence opens the world to the body ego. At first, this widening of horizons triggers a fear of object loss or separation anxiety and therefore causes the body ego to experience insecurity in relation to the primary caregiver. The body ego, however, soon overcomes this insecurity and begins to explore its new world. The fear of object loss subsides, and the body ego becomes a fearless investigator of the world, a little sensorimotor scientist who interacts with objects in a bodily way to see how they respond.

Feelings evolve in tandem with cognition. The achievement of object permanence and the corresponding emergence of mental images as object representations usher in feelings that are no longer just momentary responses to stimuli but are now ongoing affective engagements with enduring objects. Most importantly, these cognitive achievements introduce a new set of feelings in relation to the primary caregiver, who is now known to be a being who exists independently of the child's immediate experience. As we have seen, the initial grasping of the primary caregiver's independence—corresponding to the differentiation subphase of Mahler's separation-individuation process (from age four or five months to age eight months)—is fraught with anxiety. For the primary caregiver is here no longer a stimulus pattern existing wholly within the child's experience; she or he has become a being who can be absent from the child's experience, a being, therefore, whose nurturing presence is now uncertain. If, however, the infant begins at this point to experience separation anxiety in relation to the primary caregiver, that is only a negative indication that the infant has begun to experience *attachment* to the primary caregiver. Fear of object loss is the negative side of object attachment; both emerge with the first understanding of object permanence. Accordingly, the infant in the differentiation subphase experiences not only anxiety but also love (of the most primitive possible sort) in relation to a being other than itself. Such anxiety and love are the first object-related feelings in the strict sense of the term.

Differentiation from the caregiver and awareness of the caregiver's independence thus usher in both a fear of object loss and a feeling of loving object attachment. The fear of object loss attends the infant's initial awakening to the world beyond its own experience and thereafter tends to recede into the background as the child, in becoming a toddler, begins to experience an insatiable desire to investigate the world. After the initial shock of possible object loss, the body ego loses its fear and becomes a bold explorer. The cognitive assumptions that enable the child to overcome its fear of object loss at this stage will be explained shortly.

To use Mahler's terms, the child, having "hatched" from symbiosis and having overcome its fear of object loss, enters the *practicing* subphase of the preoedipal separation-individuation process. The practicing subphase is the period from the age of approximately eight to approximately fifteen months during which the child fearlessly explores the world, all the while assuming that the primary caregiver, when out of sight, is close by looking out for the child and accessible at any time as a refuge or "refueling" station. During the practicing subphase, the body ego experiences exhilarating feelings of discovery and skill mastery, feelings of frustration of the will, and feelings of both love and anger for the primary caregiver. The body ego's primary feeling for the caregiver remains loving attachment. However, because the caregiver at this point has to limit and discipline the body ego's exploratory behaviors, the caregiver also becomes an object toward which the body ego feels anger.

THE SYMBOLIC-PROTOCONCEPTUAL STAGE

Two cognitive advances occur around the middle of the second year that have profound effects on the child: (1) the full development of the object concept, which causes the child once again to experience fear of object loss, this time in the more serious form of abandonment anxiety, and (2) the development of mental images as symbols proper—that is, as bearers of general meanings—which causes the child's world to become radically unstable, subject to wild condensations and displacements of meaning. The net effect of these two changes is that the child becomes deeply insecure and struggles to achieve control of its environment and of the primary caregiver in particular. The child becomes intensely ambivalent. It is prone to split the primary caregiver (or the Great Mother) into "good" and "bad" objects, and it is subject to dramatic fluctuations in its experience from feelings of total helplessness to feelings of omnipotent mastery and control.

If the child achieves an understanding of object permanence around four or five months of age, that does not mean that the child at that age fully understands the independence of objects. For although the referential-protosymbolic child understands that objects continue to exist even when they are not perceived, it still assumes that objects are in some way tied to its field of experience. Studies by Piaget and others (see Bower 1982) show that children prior to sixteen or eighteen months assume that objects are tied to specific locations in space where they have previously been experienced by the child. For instance, from about six to about ten or twelve months of age, a child assumes that an object exists at the location where the object has repeatedly been experienced in the past. This assumption becomes conspicuously evident to an observer when the child, witnessing an object being hidden in a new location, still looks for the object in the old, familiar location.

By the time children are ten or twelve months old, they no longer make this mistake. Instead, they make a new mistake: rather than assuming that objects exist at the location at which they have been experienced most *regularly*, children begin assuming that objects exist at the location at which they have been experienced most *recently*. This new assumption is evident in children between ten or twelve and sixteen or eighteen months in a failure to understand invisible displacements of objects. For example, if a child in this age range sees an apple being placed under one of two cloths and then watches as the positions of the two cloths are transposed, the child will look for the apple under the cloth that has been shifted to the place where the apple was hidden. The child makes this mistake even though the cloth with the apple under it has a conspicuous lump in it, whereas the cloth that the child lifts is flat.

Children overcome this last mistake at about sixteen months. At this age children begin to undertake general searches for objects, searches no longer limited by the assumption that objects are tied to specific locations in space. This advance marks the full development of the object concept, because, with this advance, the child understands that objects have an existence that is completely independent of the child's experience. The child understands that objects, as entities that continue to exist when they are not perceived, exist unrestrictedly in objective space rather than only locally in experiential space. This understanding greatly enlarges the child's world. It also, however, as we shall see, renders the child deeply insecure.

Another indication that the object concept is fully developed around age sixteen months is that, according to Piaget, object representations can at this point be evoked at will in the absence of their objects. Objects can be recalled independently of triggering or supporting stimuli (such as transitional objects). The full development of the object concept involves not only an untying of objects from the child's experiential space but also a freeing of object representations from experiential cues.

In addition to the full development of the object concept, the other major cognitive advance signaling the beginning of the symbolic-proto-conceptual stage is the transformation of images from referential-proto-symbolic images into truly symbolic images, from images that perform a merely designative or referential function into images that serve as bearers of general meanings. Images may begin to assume such a truly symbolic function on their own, prior to the initial acquisition of language (see Hunt 1989). Nevertheless, the initial acquisition of language marks the point at which the transformation of images from individual object representations into bearers of general meanings occurs rapidly and pervasively. The symbolic-protoconceptual stage is the stage in which the child, in learning how to speak, begins to assimilate the conceptual framework of adult thought.

Symbolic-protoconceptual thought—or, in Piaget's terms, preconceptual or transductive thought—is, then, the first step in the process of concept acquisition. The child's task is to raise cognition from the level of particularity (individual object representations) to the level of generality or universality (representations of classes or kinds). The task is to move from the level of concretely given things to the level at which these concretely given things are comprehended as members of classes or instances of kinds. This task poses a challenge to which the child responds with zeal but, at first, with only partial success. The symbolic-protoconceptual stage therefore is a period in the child's cognitive development during which the child enters the adult's conceptual universe but is able to understand this universe only in an incomplete and inadequate way. Symbolic-protoconceptual thought is an important first step toward conceptual-inferential (i.e., operational, secondary-process) thinking; it is, however, a step that goes only partway toward this goal. Symbolic-protoconceptual thought is a transitional form of cognition that moves toward conceptual-inferential thinking but still suffers from limitations that preclude it from being an effective vehicle for this more mature form of thought.

Of these limitations, three are especially noteworthy. The first is that symbolic-protoconceptual thought is restricted to the medium of the imagination. In grasping a conceptual meaning, the symbolic-protoconceptual child does not formulate an abstract verbal definition. The child does not perform an inductive generalization on a variety of instances, abstracting common denominators and bracketing individual differences. Rather, the child relies on the imagination, on the autosymbolic process. And the autosymbolic process responds to the child's need with immensely creative assistance, spontaneously producing images in which dimensions of conceptual meaning are graphically depicted. The autosymbolic process is our chief creative faculty, and its creativity is here pressed into service in behalf of the young child, for whom it fashions concrete picture-meanings, which are the half-particular, half-universal forerunners of concepts proper. The autosymbolic process here produces symbolic protoconcepts, images that are no longer merely mental representations of individual objects but are instead concrete exemplars of kinds.

With the aid of the autosymbolic process, then, symbolic-protoconceptual thought takes a step toward the abstractly universal meanings of adult cognition. In taking this step, however, symbolic-protoconceptual thought remains a step short, because, operating exclusively in the medium of the imagination, symbolic-protoconceptual thought is unable to grasp general meanings except in concrete pictorial form. Symbolic-protoconceptual thought does not conceive general meanings as abstract universals; it fails to distinguish abstract concept from representative instance, essence from exemplar. This "half-abstract" character of symbolic-protoconceptual images is the reason why these images, although truly symbolic, are only *proto*conceptual. They are incomplete concepts, exemplary instances of concepts formed in the stead of the concepts themselves.

A second limitation of symbolic-protoconceptual thought is that the concepts that the child is expected to learn are not at first understood in terms of their core meanings but are rather understood in terms of accidental or local factors that happen to obtain in relation to those examples of the concepts to which the child is originally exposed. The child first learns a concept term as it is employed ostensively to designate items in the child's immediate environment. These items, in being the first instances of the concept with which the child becomes acquainted, are (mistakenly, but understandably) taken to be the paradigm instances of the concepts. What comes first in the order of the child's experience is taken by the child to be first in the order of meaning. The result is that the child burdens concepts with accidental accretions and extraneous relations deriving from the narrowness of the child's perspective.

The child, for example, might learn the word (and therefore concept) *dictionary* in relation to the particular volume that happens to be in the library of the child's house, which volume, let us suppose, is thumb indexed and quite large. It is entirely possible that the child, given this volume as the *de facto* defining instance of the concept, would incorporate such nonessential elements as "thumb indexed" and "large" into the meaning of the term *dictionary*. That is to say, in the child's mind a dictionary might be understood to be a large book with colored notches on the front edge of its pages. Such an understanding, it should be stressed, is a real cognitive achievement; it is definitely better than having no concept at all. Nevertheless, such an understanding falls considerably short of full comprehension. It is a real but only partial achievement. It is an achievement that not only allows the child to make many correct identifications (of dictionaries in this case) but also leads the child to make many incorrect identifications as well. Children at this stage of cognitive development operate with whole interlocking networks of such narrowly conceived and accident-laden concepts. No wonder they frequently tend to make bizarre associations and to ask what to adults seem like nonsensical questions.

A third limitation of symbolic-protoconceptual thought is that it does not yet grasp the substance-attribute distinction. This is not to say that symbolic-protoconceptual thought fails to grasp things as enduring objects, for object permanence is already achieved in the referential-protosymbolic stage. The enduring objects that are grasped, however, are not clearly conceived as substances possessing attributes,that is, as self-subsistent entities in which properties or qualities inhere. Because the distinction between substance and attribute has not been made with any degree of adequacy, the child, in being aware of objects, is in a sense aware only of groupings or constellations of qualities. I do not mean to suggest that the child has, as it were, decided to reify qualities and reduce substances to the status of mere collections of qualities. The point, rather, is that the child has not yet grasped the substance-attribute distinction and therefore is vague about the ontological status of objects. For the child, then, objects are in a sense both entities and qualities and in a sense neither entities nor qualities, because the distinction in question has not yet been completely made.

In the absence of an effective distinction between substance and attribute, the child—as E. Von Domarus (1944) was the first to realize[3]—frequently operates as if by a principle of predicate identity rather than subject identity. That is, the child frequently tends to understand by the expression *the same thing* not the same subject or substance but rather the same predicate(s) or attribute(s). The child is not clear about the difference between identity and similarity and consequently is liable to conflate what, from the adult point of view, are individually distinct entities. To return to the dictionary example, this means that the child who has learned the term *dictionary* in relation to a particular volume in the library of its house might be led to recognize a similar volume elsewhere not as another dictionary but as a reappearance of *the* dictionary. The reappearance of the same qualities would in this case be taken as a reappearance of the very same object.

A perplexing implication of predicate identity is that, because qualities are reproducible without regard to spatiotemporal restrictions, what the child takes to be a single thing can in principle exist in different locations at the same time. And so, to return again to our example, the child, it seems, is in effect committed to the possibility that the dictionary in the library of its house exists not only there but also in other locations, at one and the same time. Obviously, thought of this type can entangle the child in a thicket of contradictions.

A primary consequence of the predicate-identity principle is that objects, as concretely embodied general meanings, are subject to virtually limitless condensations and displacements. Psychoanalysis stresses the importance of condensation and displacement in relation to the primary process. The occurrence, indeed prevalence, of condensation and displacement in the symbolic-protoconceptual stage can be understood as a consequence of predicate identity because predicate identity, in treating similar things as manifestations of the same thing, allows both (1) that any instance of a concept or member of a class can stand for all the others, just as if it were the whole of the concept or class (condensation), and (2) that any instance of a concept or member of a class can be exchanged for any other, just as if it were a reappearance of rather than a substitute for the original (displacement). If similarity is reduced to identity, it follows that any representative of a type or kind can stand for all others or be substituted for any other. Cognition is free, vertically, to treat particulars as universals and, horizontally, to exchange particulars for particulars, virtually without restriction.

In sum, the symbolic-protoconceptual stage is a period of dramatic expansion, enrichment, and destabilization of thought. Thought is expanded to include a world of objects that are free to exist anywhere in space, irrespective of the location and needs of the child. Thought is enriched by the emergence of "concrete universals," images that, no longer merely designators of particular entities, are primitive bearers of conceptual meanings. And thought is destabilized because, in being raised halfway, but only halfway, to the level of universality, it becomes susceptible to sudden and wild shiftings between its particular and universal dimensions. The child entering the symbolic-protoconceptual stage, then, enters a world that is larger, more meaningful, and more labile than was the world of the referential-protosymbolic stage.

The affective experience of the symbolic-protoconceptual stage, based on the cognition of the stage, is distinguished by intensity and instability. The enlargement of the world brought about by the untying of objects from the child's experience causes the child to feel insecure and is a key factor in the acutely ambivalent rapprochement feelings discussed in the last chapter. And the emergence of half-particular, half-universal meanings leads to wild fluctuations of feelings that correspond to the condensations and displacements of symbolic-protoconceptual thought.

Let us recall that the body ego's initial understanding of object permanence at the beginning of the referential-protosymbolic stage triggered a fear of object loss. The infant is frightened to learn that the caregiver has an existence beyond the boundaries of the infant's immediate experience. Accordingly, the initial months of the referential-protosymbolic stage—corresponding to Mahler's differentiation subphase of the separation-individuation process—are characterized by separation anxiety and by a clinging to the primary caregiver or to a transitional object serving as substitute for the caregiver. This separation anxiety, however, is only a short-term difficulty, because, beginning around age eight months, the child overcomes the fear of object loss and begins to explore the world with curiosity and confidence, returning to the caregiver only for emotional "refueling." This change, in Mahler's terms, marks the transition from the differentiation to the practicing subphase of the separation-individuation process.

We are now in a position to explain why the child entering the practicing subphase is able to overcome the separation anxiety of the differentiation subphase. The explanation lies in the fact that the referential-protosymbolic thought of the practicing child still ties objects to the child's field of experience. The child entering the practicing subphase still harbors the assumption that the caregiver, although out of sight, is located at a place proximate to the child. The child therefore assumes that the caregiver is close by and always accessible in case of need. Accordingly, the separation anxiety experienced during the differentiation subphase soon subsides. The child entering the practicing subphase once again begins to take the caregiver for granted, assuming that the caregiver, although occasionally out of sight, is always easily within reach.

The child, however, is rudely disabused of this reassuring assumption once referential-protosymbolic thought is superseded by symbolic-protoconceptual thought. For the achievement of the full object concept carries with it an understanding that the primary caregiver is *not* tied to the child's experience. The caregiver, the child now realizes, in being absent from experience, could be anywhere, proximate or remote, accessible or inaccessible. This realization triggers a fear of object loss that is much more serious than the separation anxiety experienced by the child during the differentiation period. It causes the symbolic-protoconceptual child to experience *abandonment* anxiety, the fear that the primary caregiver may exit not only the child's immediate experience but also the child's known world.

In experiencing abandonment anxiety, the child loses its previous sense of confidence and begins to cling to the primary caregiver. This is why the beginning of the symbolic-protoconceptual stage coincides with the beginning of the rapprochement subphase of the separation-individuation process. *The achievement of the full object concept, I suggest, is the key factor responsible for the child's rapprochement insecurity and consequent contradictory (approach-avoidance, intimacy-independence) interactions with the primary caregiver.* In realizing that the primary caregiver is not tied to its experience, the rapprochement child tries desperately to keep the caregiver close by. Experiencing abandonment anxiety, the rapprochement child clings to the caregiver and tries desperately to be the center of the caregiver's attentions. In seeking this closeness with the caregiver, however, the child does not want to relinquish its hard-won independence, and consequently the child begins to experience the acute ambivalence toward the caregiver and the corresponding splitting of the primary object representation that are characteristic of the rapprochement crisis.

The achievement of the full object concept is, then, I propose, a primary factor behind the rapprochement child's contradictory feelings toward the primary caregiver. The discovery of the full independence of objects triggers abandonment anxiety, which, when combined with the child's continuing drive for independence, causes the child to experience both a strong desire for and a desperate need to separate itself from the primary caregiver. The intensity of this ambivalence, as we have seen, is sufficient to split the child's world in two. It splits the primary object representation, the Great Mother, into two seemingly independent and mutually exclusive realities: the Good Mother and the Terrible Mother. And, correspondingly, it splits the child's self-representation into disconnected good child and terrible child representations. The child's overall experience is in this way divided into opposing positive and negative sides—and the child's feelings are correspondingly divided into opposing feelings of object- and self-directed love and hate. These feelings are intense and in fundamental conflict; there is little neutral ground.

Abandonment anxiety is not the only cause of emotional instability during the symbolic-protoconceptual stage. Instability is also caused by the condensations and displacements allowed by symbolic-protoconceptual thought. These condensations and displacements, as psychoanalysis stresses, are dynamic as well as cognitive transformations. Psychic energy is allowed to move freely from object to object (displacement), each object being cathected to the maximum degree, as if it were the only object of its type (condensation). Responding to these dynamic transformations, the symbolic-protoconceptual child experiences suddenly changing, sharply punctuated, and highly charged feelings: in rapid succession, for example, the child is stunned, repulsed, terrified, enraged, overawed, enthralled, riveted, captivated, and delighted. The child's world has a highly charged atmosphere in which energy moves unrestrictedly and in dramatically changing ways, ways that cause the child to experience feelings that are both pronounced and short-lived. The symbolic-protoconceptual child's affective life is unstable not only because abandonment anxiety generates acute ambivalences but also because condensations and displacements of energy trigger powerful emotional fluctuations.

Arieti (1967) notes that condensation and displacement are evident in early-childhood feelings of magical power and vulnerability. The sense of power derives from the fact that, according to the principle of predicate identity, an action performed on one object automatically extends to all other objects bearing similar properties—for, if predicate identity prevails, these latter objects *are* the object on which the action is originally performed (displacement). The efficacy of actions therefore extends in principle as far as the most remote object possessing the properties or qualities that inhere in the object that is the proximate recipient of the child's deeds. So, for example, another person can be affected by manipulating an effigy or even by fantasizing action upon an image in mind. The reverse, however, also holds true. In experiencing a sense of magical omnipotence, young children also experience a sense of total vulnerability and defenselessness, for just as actions outgoing from the subject suffer no obstacles in the attainment of their ends, neither, it must be assumed, do actions incoming upon the subject. These, too, reach their goal without diminution or delay. The symbolic-protoconceptual child is as vulnerable with respect to the magical omnipotence of others as others are with respect to the magical omnipotence of the child. The symbolic-protoconceptual child is for this reason prone to omnipotence-vulnerability reversals. These reversals can happen at any time and in relation to any object. They occur most frequently, however, in relation to the primary caregiver (*qua* Terrible Mother). The child tends to shift back and forth between a sense of omnipotent independence from the caregiver and a sense of vulnerability before her irresistible and threatening power.

The acute conflicts, sudden reversals, and all-or-nothing intensity of the feelings of the symbolic-protoconceptual stage make life during this stage extremely difficult and ultimately impossible to sustain. The young ego must eventually find relief from the emotional upheavals to which it is subject if it is to gain any semblance of self-possession and self-control. Primal repression provides such relief. Primal repression severs the ego's remaining symbiotic ties with the Great Mother and, in doing so, quiets and stabilizes the ego's life, allowing the ego to reunify its world. Primal repression brings about both latency and object constancy, both a quieting of physicodynamic upheavals and a stabilizing of relationships with primary others. It provides the young ego with the calm that is needed for continued development.

CONCLUSION

Primal repression, in submerging nonegoic potentials, quiets not only dynamic and affective potentials but also the autosymbolic process, the source of the images that serve as the vehicle of cognition during most of the body-egoic period. We have just seen that primal repression plays a positive developmental role in quieting dynamic and affective potentials. The question therefore arises whether primal repression might also play a positive developmental role in quieting the autosymbolic process. This question, I believe, should be answered in the affirmative. Primal repression, I believe, may be a precondition of continued ego development not only because it brings an end to dynamic and affective upheavals but also, cognitively, because it weans the ego from reliance on the autosymbolic process.

The reason why it may be necessary to wean the ego from the autosymbolic process is that the autosymbolic process performs work for the ego that the ego must eventually do for itself. In producing symbolic-protoconceptual images, the autosymbolic process produces representations for the ego that, in their concrete particularity, happen to convey general meanings. Consequently, the autosymbolic process allows the ego to "get by," for most practical purposes, just as if it had grasped general meanings explicitly and in the abstract. The autosymbolic process may thus become a hindrance to continued cognitive development for the simple reason that it does its job so well. In creating images that have the character of concrete universals, the autosymbolic process elevates cognition halfway from mere particularity to full universality and at the same time does away with any pressing need to carry the process further.

Accordingly, if primal repression did not deprive the ego of autogenerated images, it is questionable whether an explicit set of verbally definable abstract concepts would ever come into existence. The repressive disconnection of the creative imagination may therefore play a positive developmental role. In weaning the ego from autosymbolic images, this disconnection may be the impetus that forces the ego to think for itself, to distinguish concept from concrete exemplar, and thereby to surmount the limitations inherent to symbolic-protoconceptual thought.

The transition from the body-egoic to the mental-egoic stage is two-sided. It involves a major loss of psychic resources, to be sure, because primal repression submerges the entire range of nonegoic potentials. This loss, however, is at the same time a gain, for the young ego needs to free itself from the influence of the nonegoic sphere in order to continue to develop. The ego needs to free itself from the influence of dynamic and affective potentials in order to achieve self-possession and stability in interpersonal relations. And, as we have just seen, the ego may also need to free itself from the influence of the autosymbolic process in order to complete the move to conceptual thinking.

The transition to the mental-egoic stage involves both losses and gains. The losses are great but are the necessary price to be paid for even greater gains. The transition to the mental-egoic stage is therefore a *net* developmental advance. Primal repression submerges nonegoic potentials, but in doing so it frees the ego to develop at an accelerated pace.

4

The Mental Ego

THE EGO THAT EMERGES after primal repression has been consolidated is no longer a polymorphously sensual body ego. It is no longer an ego identified with concrete somatic life; it is rather an ego that takes itself to be an entity that exists inside the body, an entity that exists somewhere in the region of the head and that commands the body from on high. This presumed inner entity is the mental ego.[1]

The mental ego that emerges during the latency period is by no means a full-fledged Cartesian ego. For the child of the latency period still thinks of itself in vaguely material terms; although no longer identified with the body, the latency child does not conceive of itself as a completely incorporeal mind. The latency child thinks of itself as something that exists at an inward location, but it does not yet think of itself as a completely disincarnate *res cogitans*. As John Broughton's studies (1978, 1980, 1982) have shown, children between about four and seven think of themselves in terms of a primitive head-body dualism. And children between about eight and eleven think of themselves in terms of a brain-body dualism. Not until adolescence does the mental ego begin to conceive of itself as a purely psychomental and therefore incorporeal subject.

I have treated the unfolding of the mental ego during the latency period in *Transpersonal Psychology in Psychoanalytic Perspective*. Accordingly, in this chapter I shall skip consideration of this initial stage of the mental ego and focus on the mental ego once it has become fully aware of itself as such, that is, as a Cartesian ego or *res cogitans*. This self-aware or Cartesian mental ego is the mental ego of adolescence and early and middle adulthood.

THE MENTAL EGO'S CRISIS OF AWAKENING IN ADOLESCENCE

Adolescence is a period of awakening in many senses. It is of course a period of sexual awakening and awakening to others as possible partners in sexually based intimacy. With the coming of puberty, the young person undergoes a dramatic bodily transformation and begins to experience strong new drives and sensations. And in undergoing these changes, the adolescent begins to experience compelling new feelings for and fantasies about others, feelings and fantasies that change the character of interpersonal relations in fundamental ways.

Adolescence is also a period of intellectual awakening in that, as Piaget (Inhelder and Piaget 1958; Piaget 1972) demonstrated, it is a period during which cognition undergoes a radical shift from concrete to formal operational thinking, from thinking still tied to concrete observable objects and circumstances to thinking conducted entirely in the abstract. Formal operational thinking is thinking that is able to perform operations on classes, concepts, and principles independently of any instances of those classes, concepts, and principles. During adolescence, cognition ceases depending on concrete exemplifications and begins being carried out purely in the medium of ideas: abstractly, hypothetically, universally, theoretically.

Additionally, adolescence is a period of moral awakening in that the achievement of formal operational thinking raises ethical understanding beyond the concrete level of *de facto* parental-social norms to the abstract level of universal moral principles and ideals. This raising of moral consciousness from the level of the particular to the level of the universal predisposes the adolescent to both cynical relativism and naive idealism. It predisposes the adolescent to cynical relativism because it allows the adolescent to look down on parental-social norms as "mere" conventions; and it predisposes the adolescent to naive idealism because it allows the adolescent to look up to abstract principles and ideals as offering perfect solutions to ethical difficulties. The adolescent does not yet appreciate the wisdom of experience stored in the particular or the vagueness and impracticality of the abstract and ideal.

Adolescence, then, is a time of sexual, interpersonal, intellectual, and moral awakening. It is a time during which the young person moves into a world that is alive with new drives and longings and that, intellectually and morally, is vastly larger and more complex than was the world of the latency period.

Concomitant with these dimensions of awakening is an awakening to self. The latency child, as we have seen, is an emerging mental ego that does not yet clearly conceive of itself as such. The latency child no longer identifies with the body and has begun to think of itself as an inner subject. In thinking of itself as an inner subject, however, the latency child is not yet able to think of itself as an incorporeal subject. Rather, it thinks of itself, vaguely and confusedly, as an inner subject that is at once psychomental and material in nature, as a subject that is located inside the head or that *is* the brain. Although the latency child, standing on primal repression, no longer identifies with the body as a whole, it continues, owing to the limitations of concrete operational cognition, to think of itself in concrete material terms. The latency child is no longer a body ego, but neither is it yet a full-fledged mental or Cartesian ego.

Only with the coming of adolescence does the mental ego truly become aware of itself as a mental ego. For the achievement of formal operational thinking means that the adolescent is no longer limited to thinking of itself in concrete material terms and can begin thinking of itself as a purely psychomental subject. Moreover, the adolescent, unlike the latency child, is given to introspection. Newly emerging feelings and fantasies draw the adolescent into the world of inner experience, which the adolescent explores with a fascination equal to the curiosity with which the latency child explores the outer world. By adolescence, then, the mental ego achieves Cartesian self-reflection, the *cogito*: it begins to turn its attention in upon itself and to think of itself in *exclusively* psychomental terms.

The adolescent's Cartesian self-reflection is initially a source of existential security, because it provides the adolescent with an immediate sense of existence. The adolescent, as a Cartesian, is able to say "I think, therefore I am." The mere fact of having inner experiences is taken as an incontrovertible indication of existing as an inner subject. This Cartesian self-reflection is reassuring to the adolescent. Despite the many doubts that plague the adolescent, the adolescent can always turn inward and enjoy a sense of self-certainty by means of the *cogito*.

If, however, Cartesian self-reflection is a source of existential security, it is also a source of existential anxiety; for the psychomental subject with which the adolescent is identified is never immediately present to itself within subjectivity. Unlike the body ego, which can see itself simply by looking in the mirror, the mental ego cannot perceive itself inwardly through introspection. Introspection, as many philosophers (from the Buddha to David Hume [1739] and Jean-Paul Sartre [1957]) have observed, reveals only psychomental contents (thoughts, feelings, images) and not the subject that is assumed to experience these contents. The psychomental subject is, then, inaccessible to introspection, and this inaccessibility—this absence?—is as disturbing to the adolescent as the self-certainty of *cogito* is reassuring. Cartesian self-reflection therefore tends to undermine its own self-certainty. The very psychomental self that is taken to be confirmed by Cartesian self-reflection is never experienced within this reflection, and consequently there is a gnawing worry that this self might really be only an empty self-reference, a merely presumed entity behind the scenes of consciousness. Cartesian self-reflection provides the adolescent with a sense of security only to stir an even deeper sense of apprehension, a fear that there might be no subject at the core of consciousness. This fear is the *anxiety of "nothingness."*

One way in which the adolescent's anxiety of nothingness is evident is in compulsive internal dialogue. If the mental ego cannot see itself through introspection, it can at least, or so it assumes, *hear* itself. Adolescent introspection is for this reason an introspective conversation carried out in a voice that is assumed to be the voice of the Cartesian subject. The "I think, therefore I am" is taken to be the mental ego speaking to itself. There is no inner mirror in which the mental ego can see a reflection of itself, and so the mental ego must rely on an inner echo to allay its ontological insecurities. Compulsive internal dialogue, as we shall see, is characteristic of the mental ego from adolescence on. What is characteristic of this dialogue during adolescence is that it arises in response to the anxiety of nothingness—and, as we shall see, a related anxiety of "guilt."

The anxiety of nothingness also plays an important role in the adolescent's concern with identity. As Erik Erikson (1950, 1956) has shown, adolescents are intensely focused on the question of ego identity. They are acutely conscious of how they present themselves to others and how they are perceived by others. Adolescents are concerned with these matters, I suggest, because identity recognition carries with it a sense of being. To have a recognized identity is to *be* something in the eyes of the world. Ontologically insecure, the adolescent not only engages in self-confirmatory internal dialogue but also is impelled to search for a sense of being from without. As Sartre (1956) says, turning Descartes around 180 degrees, "I am seen; therefore I am." Although the mental ego that awakens to itself in adolescence has no inner mirror in which to see itself, it enjoys a sense of being seen, and therefore of existing, when its projected identity is recognized by others. The adolescent seeks a being-for-others, an identity in the eyes of the world, to bolster an insecure sense of being-for-self.

Although adolescents try on a variety of identity possibilities, they do not really *forge* an identity. Adolescence, as Erikson explains, is a period of development protected by a "psychosocial moratorium."

Adolescents are allowed to experiment with many styles of dress, speech, thought, and behavior without having to make a firm commitment to any of them. For this reason whatever identity adolescents take on is only preliminary and tentative. The real work of forging an identity is the task of early adulthood, and it is an indication that adolescence is at an end when a person ceases identity experimentation and embarks upon a long-term identity project.

The adolescent suffers not only from an anxiety of nothingness and a corresponding drive to establish a sense of being but also from an anxiety of "guilt" and a corresponding drive to establish a sense of justification or value. The anxiety of guilt has both interpersonal and intrapsychic sources: interpersonally, it arises from the adolescent's struggle for independence from parents; and intrapsychically, it arises from the ego's struggle for independence from the (parentally defined) superego. These two causes are intimately interrelated. Indeed, the struggle for independence from the parents and the struggle for independence from the superego are really outer and inner, interpersonal and intrapsychic, sides of the same process.

Outwardly, the struggle for independence from parents produces a sense of guilt in the adolescent because it is an "unjustified" turning away from parents. To a degree, it involves a rejection of the people who have been the primary nurturers of the adolescent and who have embodied the ideals to which hitherto the adolescent had aspired. Adolescents, to a degree, withdraw from parents, cease looking up to them as authorities and role models, and even defy them and say hurtful things to them. In their attempt to break free from dependent emotional ties to parents, adolescents sometimes perceive and treat parents in exaggeratedly negative ways. Moreover, this rejection of parents occurs without having been provoked by any change on the part of the parents, who have done nothing to deserve this unkind treatment. The struggle for independence from parents, then, although developmentally necessary, involves a turning away from parents that is "unjustified" and, therefore, fraught with moral difficulties.

The turning away from parents is at the same time a turning of a deaf ear to the superego, which is not only the inner voice of conscience but also, for the adolescent, the inner voice of the parents. If adolescents cease looking up to parents as authorities and role models, they also cease accepting the superego as the standard of proper conduct. Adolescents struggle to free themselves from the internal power of the superego. This struggle is a moral struggle, a struggle against the inner moral law. It is therefore a struggle that, along with the struggle against parents, incurs a sense of guilt.

Edith Jacobson (1964) and Peter Blos (1962, 1972, 1974) have argued that the adolescent struggle with the superego causes the ego ideal to split off from the superego. Prior to adolescence, the superego defines the ego ideal; the latency child's attempt to meet the internalized expectations of the parents is at the same time an attempt by the child to achieve its own ideal self. For the latency child, the superego and the ego ideal coincide. This happy coincidence, however, comes to an end in adolescence. For in struggling against the superego, the adolescent at the same time struggles against the ego ideal implicit in the superego. The adolescent sees this superego-defined ideal self as only an immature, conformist, parent-sanctioned self. The adolescent is driven to break free from this old self, which means that the adolescent's projected ideal self must be defined in a new way, in terms other than those stipulated by the superego. This preliminary exploration of a new ego ideal is an exciting existential process. The adolescent enthusiastically elaborates scenarios of ideal selfhood. The abandonment of the superego, on the other hand, on which this process is based, is a cause of serious moral uneasiness.

Adolescents, then, are prone to experience a sense of guilt both because they commit an "unjustified" act of turning away from parents and because they divorce themselves from norms of selfhood implicit in the superego, the inner voice of conscience.[2] This sense of guilt is a strong driving force that impels adolescents to search or strive for distinctions that might confer warrant on their existence. Accordingly, adolescents are driven not only, in flight from "nothingness," to forge a sense of being but also, in flight from "guilt," to seek a justification for being.

Adolescents respond to their sense of guilt in the same ways they do to their sense of nothingness: internal dialogue and identity exploration. Internal dialogue is a means by which adolescents not only confirm their existence but also confirm their value as human beings. In seeking to confirm their value, adolescents, in their internal dialogue, tend to focus on such things as (1) their uniqueness as individuals ("I'm not like everyone else; they should appreciate me for who I am"); (2) present distinctions and accomplishments ("They invited *me* to the party"); and (3) projected scenarios of ideal selfhood ("Wait till they see me when . . ."). In talking to themselves in these ways, and in engaging in corresponding fantasy elaborations, adolescents seek to validate themselves as worthwhile persons. They talk to themselves about their specialness and value as a way of responding to the moral anxiety spawned by the break with parents and the superego.

Adolescents also seek to validate their self-worth by seeking confirmatory identity recognition. The quest for identity recognition is a quest not only for *être* but also for *raison d'être*. In attempting to be recognized as a "this" or a "that," adolescents attempt not only to *be* a "this" or a "that" but also to gain approval, and therefore to achieve a sense of value, for being a "this" or a "that." Adolescents usually seek this kind of recognition from peers rather than from parents. They seek to belong to a circle of supportive friends, a circle in which they can find not only recognition of the newly styled selves they are trying to be but also corresponding confirmation of their value.

Of course, not all adolescents belong to peer groups. Many are outsiders. Although being an outsider is painful, it does not necessarily mean that one has to suffer from a sense of being a "nobody"; a sense of being and value can be achieved during adolescence without belonging to an in-group. Indeed, a sense of being and value can even be achieved in being *rejected or condemned* by others. For being rejected or condemned confers an identity and a sense of specialness, even if only a negative one: one is labeled "a rebel," "different," "weird," or "bad" and therefore gains a sense of being and value in *not* being like others. Some teenagers cultivate negative identity recognition, seeking to be known as nonconformists, because, for some at least, having a negatively grounded sense of being and value is better than having no sense of being and value at all.

Because the identity experimentation of adolescence is provisional, an exploration of identity possibilities rather than a forging of a solid and secure identity, the anxieties of nothingness and guilt that motivate the adolescent's identity experimentation are by no means quieted during adolescence. If, then, young people are to gain relief from these anxieties, they must eventually quit their provisional identity experimentation and make a firm identity commitment, that is, a commitment to a long-term identity project. This transition from experimentation to commitment marks the transition from adolescence to early adulthood.

EARNING BEING AND VALUE IN EARLY ADULTHOOD

According to most accounts, two primary commitments mark the transition from adolescence to early adulthood: (1) a commitment to a primary other, and (2) a commitment to a primary social function, whether to a job or career in the public domain or to the function of nurturing and child rearing in the private domain, or both. The first of these commitments effects a shift of primary love investment from the parents, and from the mother in particular, to a new primary "object choice" and in doing so completes the process of emotional separation from parents. And the second commitment initiates a life activity by means of which a person develops capabilities and skills, makes a social contribution, and earns a worldly sense of being and value.

The adolescent's struggle for emotional independence from parents is a difficult and protracted process. Typically, the process requires most of the teenage years and is not complete until a commitment is made to another person as primary love object. This commitment, whether based on an explicit vow or on tacit understanding, rechannels a person's primary emotional investment into a new relationship and thereby facilitates the completion of the process of breaking free from parents. Commitment to a new primary love object is a decisive step in the direction of independence. With this commitment, the young adult is relieved of the deepest emotional ties to parents and is able to begin experiencing intimacy with a significant other on a peer basis, as a giver as well as receiver of nurture.

The commitment to a social function is for most people the most important step in the adult identity project. Young adults typically make a commitment to a job, career, or nurturing function and in doing so place themselves in a social role that gives definition and purpose to their existence. Commitment to a social function is of course only one component—albeit usually the principal one—of the identity project. The commitment to a new primary other is also an important component. This commitment clearly plays an important role in the identity project when it coincides with a primary commitment to a nurturing social function, for example, a commitment to support a partner working in the public domain or a commitment to raising children. The commitment to a new primary other, however, also plays an important role in the identity project even when it is unrelated to social function. For in making this commitment, one at the very least takes on an identity as a person with a partner, whether it be an identity as a wife, a husband, or, more generally, a person in relationship.

Along with the commitments to social function and relationship, many other commitments enter into the identity project as less basic elements. Young adults not only become accountants, carpenters, clerks, persons in relationships, mothers, fathers, and so forth; they also become representatives of life-styles, social classes, interest groups, political parties, and churches. These latter forms of participation in social life are important elements of the overall adult identity project. They are, however, elements that are less central than are the commitments to social function and relationship, which typically are the nuclear elements of the project.

The commitments making up the identity project have both negative and positive motivations. Initially, the motivations are to a significant extent negative: the young adult is still troubled by feelings of nothingness and guilt and seeks through the identity project to overcome these feelings by achieving a sense of worldly being and value. In becoming an accountant, carpenter, clerk, person in relationship, mother, father, socialist, Republican, Christian, Buddhist, and so forth, the young adult achieves a sense of being someone and a sense of making a legitimating contribution or statement in the world. The anxiety of nothingness motivates the identity project as an ontological project: a quest for being. And the anxiety of guilt motivates the identity project as a moral project: a quest for justification.

As strong as the negative motivations behind the identity project can be at the outset of the project, they tend to recede into the background as progress is made in the project. For the identity project is not just a way of overcoming feelings of nothingness and guilt by earning worldly being and value. It is also a way of engaging one's faculties, developing talents, learning how to meet the challenges of the world, giving expression to one's character, and, in general, growing in effective personhood. The identity project has its own rewards, and, assuming that progress is made in the project, these rewards gradually become the primary incentives of the project. The negative motivations behind the identity project never disappear entirely; in most cases, however, they move into the background. For most people, the identity project becomes increasingly positive in its primary motivations; it becomes less and less a flight from feelings of nothingness and guilt and becomes more and more a way of establishing and fulfilling oneself in the world. This movement away from the negative and toward the positive is characteristic of the period of early adulthood. (As we shall see later, the negative motivations behind the identity project tend to return to the fore at midlife).

One way in which the shift from negative to positive motivation manifests itself is in the mental ego's internal dialogue. The mental ego of early adulthood continues to talk to itself as a way of assuring itself of its existence and worth and thereby of avoiding feelings of nothingness and guilt. The mental ego in this period, however, also begins to talk to itself in a more positive and functional way, namely, in a way that carries out the actual work of *identity construction*.

An identity is a peculiar kind of "object." It is not an entity that exists apart from the mental ego that, as such, could be given to the mental ego to cognize. It is rather something that exists only in being conceived and in particular only in being processed through the mental ego's internal dialogue. The adult mental ego, for example, says to itself such things as "They accepted my manuscript; [therefore] I am a writer"; "I spent time with Jimmy; [therefore] I am a good father"; "They laughed; [therefore] I am clever"; "No one even noticed I was there; [therefore] I am not an interesting person." By means of internal conversations like these, the mental ego monitors how its actions play out in the world and how they bear upon what the mental ego is, that is, upon the mental ego's identity.

In talking to itself in these ways, the mental ego is actually constructing the very identity it is monitoring. The internal monitoring adds layers of confirmation or disconfirmation to the elements of the mental ego's identity, from its nuclear components to its more peripheral facets. Internal dialogue during early adulthood is the way in which the mental ego keeps track of how it is doing in the identity project and, therefore, of what its identity is. The identity constructed in this way is always in process; it exists as an ongoing, ever-revisable, never-finished product of the mental ego's self-monitoring efforts. In short, while internal dialogue during early adulthood continues to be a way of coping with feelings of nothingness and guilt, its primary function during this period is more positive. Internal dialogue during early adulthood plays an essential role in the identity project; it is the medium of identity construction.

Another way in which the shift from negative to positive is reflected is in the progressive reintegration of the superego and ego ideal. These two, which were split in antagonistic fashion during adolescence, are reunited by the demands of the identity project. The identity project, as a long-term commitment, requires both discipline and aspiration; it requires discipline to keep it on track and aspiration to keep it moving forward toward its goal. Discipline and aspiration, however, are precisely the functions, respectively, of the superego and ego ideal. In requiring discipline, then, the identity project stands in need of the superego, which is therefore reowned as the "propelling cause" of the project, that is, as the impetus that "pushes" the project from behind. And in requiring aspiration, the identity project stands in need of the ego ideal, which therefore is harnessed to the identity project as its "telic cause," that is, as the end that "pulls" the project from ahead.

Having already won independence from parents, the young adult no longer needs to struggle against parents or their internalized injunctions. In early adulthood, then, the superego is no longer charged with the same kinds of negative associations as it was during adolescence.

Moreover, we have just seen that in making the commitment to the identity project, the young adult creates a new need for the superego. For these reasons, the mental ego of early adulthood is able to reclaim the voice of the superego as its own voice, and in particular as the voice by which it exhorts itself to maintain its efforts in the identity project. The mental ego of early adulthood, that is, is able to reclaim the superego as the agency of self-discipline.

In making possible this reowning of the superego, the identity project at the same time makes possible a more realistic refocusing of the ego ideal. It does so by integrating the ego ideal within everyday life. Unlike the adolescent, who, in flight from the superego, tends to fantasize about grandiose possibilities of ideal selfhood, the young adult, in pursuit of the practical goals of the identity project, aspires to ideal possibilities that are realistic and down to earth. The young adult, for example, strives to be the *best* accountant, carpenter, clerk, partner, mother, father, daughter, son, Jew, Christian, or Buddhist that she or he can possibly be. The ego ideal as incorporated in the identity project remains ideal and therefore is not fully realizable. It becomes, however, an idealization of *realistic* possibilities.

The identity project, then, reunites the superego and ego ideal in positive ways. The superego becomes the "propelling cause" of the identity project, the ego ideal the "telic cause." The superego becomes the "stick" that keeps the young adult on the course of the identity project, and the ego ideal becomes the "carrot" that draws the young adult toward the ideal goal of the project. The superego and ego ideal are reunited as complementary motivating forces of the identity project. This reunion of the superego and ego ideal is another indication that the original negative motivations behind the identity project have given way and that the positive motivations of the project have come to the fore.

In growing in relationship with a primary other (and perhaps with children) and in making progress in the identity project, the mental ego gradually accomplishes the tasks of early adulthood. It learns how to experience intimacy within the confines of privacy and how to nurture as well as be nurtured. It learns how to meet the challenges of the world in the performance of a social function. In general, it develops both interpersonal and worldly skills. Moreover, as it grows in these ways, the mental ego achieves a sense of being and value: it *is* the identity that it has forged, and it has value and is justified by the contribution or statement that it has made in life. The mental ego making progress in the identity project in these ways is moving toward its ego ideal. It is headed in a direction that, it assumes, will lead to happiness. The emphasis, however, must be put on the word *assumes*.

THE MENTAL EGO AND COGNITION

As Piaget's vast work in the field of cognitive development has shown, cognitive development unfolds through a series of distinct stages: the sensorimotor stage (infancy), the preoperational stage (two to seven years of age), the concrete operational stage (seven to twelve years of age), and the formal operational stage (adolescence and beyond). Of these stages, the operational stages are most characteristic of the mental ego, although, as we shall see, the intuitive substage of preoperational thought is characteristic of the fledgling mental ego during early latency, and certain postformal modes of thought are characteristic of the mental ego during the later phases of its development in early and middle adulthood.

In our discussion of the spontaneous imaginal cognition of the body ego we learned that the creative source of this cognition, the auto-symbolic process, is repressed along with other nonegoic potentials in the transition from early childhood to latency. This repression of the autosymbolic process, we learned, has the consequence of eliminating from consciousness creatively produced images that serve as protocon-cepts and thereby of forcing the ego to begin thinking for itself, to begin distinguishing conceptual meanings from their concrete symbolic embodiments, logical relationships from relationships of fact. The beginning of latency, then, is the period during which the ego, as fledg-ling mental ego, begins thinking on its own in these ways.

The first stage of such independent thought is, following Piaget's account, the intuitive substage of the stage of preoperations. This stage lasts from about four to about seven years of age. The mental ego enter-ing this stage, no longer aided by the autosymbolic process, struggles to discern basic conceptual and class boundaries. In this early period of post-imaginal, post-autosymbolic thought, the mental ego is not yet able to perform cognitive operations; it is not yet able to demonstrate the logical relationships that obtain among things as instances of con-cepts or members of classes. All the mental ego is able to do at this point is recognize intuitively that things are instances of concepts or members of classes and discern intuitively that certain logical relationships obtain among things as such.

At about seven years of age, the child begins to be able to perform logical operations. The child becomes sufficiently familiar with conceptual boundaries and logical interconnections that it begins to be able to talk about them and to perform operations on things in terms of them. This improved understanding remains, however, on a concrete level: the child, although able to make proper class discriminations and to perform effective logical operations, is able to do so only in relation to particular things and events. The child is not yet able to conceive conceptual meanings or to perform logical operations in the abstract. The child's thought at this stage is for this reason described by Piaget as concrete operational thought. This concrete, object- or event-based mode of cognition is the type of thought that prevails throughout most of latency.

According to Piaget, concrete operational thinking lasts until adolescence, at which time thought advances to the abstract level of formal operational thinking. Beginning with adolescence, thought ceases being tied to concrete observable objects and situations and begins to reach toward abstract structures and hypothetical possibilities. Adolescence is a time during which the young person begins to manipulate not only things but also symbols of things, to do abstract thought-problems, to generate hypotheses about things not yet observed, and to engage in logical argument and purely theoretical explanation. All of these developments are characteristic of a formal, abstract-universal perspective.

The advance to formal operational cognition dramatically improves the range and power of thought. Formal operational thought is not limited to the particulars of the present situation and therefore is able to explore "what-if" alternatives. It can anticipate possibilities beyond given actuality. Formal operational thought, having climbed from the concrete to the abstract, is able to perform cognitive operations not only on particulars but also on the universals under which particulars fall. Formal operational thought is able to treat whole classes at once rather than being limited to treating members of classes one at a time. Formal operational thought is a powerful shorthand that traces patterns and relations that hold in general and therefore hold for all relevant particulars.

Formal operational cognition is the cognition that is most characteristic of the mental ego as mental ego. Piaget held that formal operational cognition, achieved during adolescence, is the last and highest form of cognition. In the last two decades, however, cognitive-developmental theorists have stepped forward to challenge Piaget's view by arguing that a distinct new level (or levels) of cognition emerges during adulthood. These theorists point to a number of ways in which formal operational cognition falls short of the cognition that is, or at least can be, achieved during adulthood. They argue, for example, that formal operational cognition is limited in being closed, static, detached, linear, uncreative, and absolutistic. Much of adult cognition in contrast, according to these theorists, transcends these limitations and is open, evolving, contextual, holistic, inventive, and pragmatic or "relativistic."

Klaus Riegel (1973) and Michael Basseches (1984a, 1984b), for example, have argued in favor of a dialectical conception of postformal cognition, suggesting that adult postformal thought proceeds through contradictions to higher syntheses. Francis Richards and Michael Commons (1984) have advanced a "meta-" conception of postformal thought, proposing that postformal thought is distinctive in moving, level by level, in the direction of increasing inclusiveness and unification. Patricia Arlin (1975, 1977, 1984, 1989) has proposed that postformal thought can best be understood as having an inventive character, as being a type of thought that is able not only to solve problems but also to discover them. Carol Gilligan and Michael Murphy (Gilligan and Murphy 1979; Murphy and Gilligan 1980) have argued that postformal thought is a cognition that is inherently tied to context and therefore is always perspectival and subject to ambiguities and uncertainties. And in a similar vein, Jan Sinnott (1981, 1984, 1989) has proposed that postformal cognition can be understood as a kind of relativistic thought in that, in her view, it is always based on a frame of reference and therefore always has a relative, a subject-focused or culture-centered, character.

No consensus has emerged on the nature of postformal thought, and some (e.g., Broughton 1984) have argued that the very idea of a fifth Piagetian stage is mistaken. A case can be made that all of the types of thought just described begin to emerge in the course of adult cognitive development. All of these types of thought, it seems, can be attributed to the mental ego as it moves toward middle adulthood. If, however, these types of thought are characteristic of the mature mental ego, they also, I suggest, point to cognitive possibilities that, in fully realized form, belong to stages of development beyond that of the mental ego. For the integrative, holistic, and inventive aspects of postformal cognition suggest that the ego is not only actively engaged in cognitive operations but also receptively open to the creative emergence of new patterns, models, and metaphors. These aspects of postformal cognition, that is, suggest not only that cognition continues to be centered in the ego but also that it has begun to draw upon nonegoic resources and in particular upon the autosymbolic process. The autosymbolic process, as we shall see, is an essential ingredient of transegoic cognition.

Because primal repression usually remains in place throughout the period of early adulthood, nonegoic potentials typically do not play a major role in cognition during this period. For those, however, whose cognition advances from formal operational to postformal modes of thought, some significant degree of egoic-nonegoic interactivity seems to have begun. If, then, the holistic and creative modes of postformal thought are to be grouped together as dimensions of a distinct cognitive stage, this stage should be recognized as a *transitional* stage. Ken Wilber (1980a, 1990) places forms of holistic-synthetic thought right at the transition between egoic and transegoic modes of cognition; I agree with him in this judgment.

THE MENTAL EGO'S DIFFICULTIES AT MIDLIFE

As the vehicle of the adult ego ideal, the identity project promises wholeness and enduring happiness. This promise is not fulfilled. It is not fulfilled, of course, if a person "fails" in the identity project. For if, for whatever reasons, a person does not meet with success in a primary social function, or in primary relationships, or in other important commitments of the identity project, it is understandable that that person would not experience the enduring happiness promised by the identity project. Such a person would feel incomplete and unsatisfied, as if he or she had missed out on essential life goods. Such a person would not in this case put the blame on the identity project itself; instead, he or she would point to situational or personal factors as the causes of the failure to succeed in the identity project and thereby to reap the primary goods of life.

The promise of the identity project, however, is not fulfilled even when a person succeeds in the project. For the happiness promised by the identity project cannot in fact be achieved by means of the identity project. It cannot be achieved because there is no way for the mental ego to feel complete and enduringly happy *as mental ego*. The mental ego, resting upon primal repression–primal alienation, is disconnected from the nonegoic pole of the psyche and from others. Owing to this double disconnection, the mental ego, *as mental ego*, cannot possibly achieve a sense of wholeness. Accordingly, no matter how successful the mental ego might be in the identity project and no matter how many reinforcing recognitions and rewards might be enjoyed as a consequence of such success, the mental ego has no real chance of achieving lasting fulfillment by pursuing the goals of the identity project.

We have seen that a person in the early and middle stages of the identity project typically tends to be less driven by the negative motivations behind the project and is increasingly moved by the positive incentives of the project. This shift from negative to positive, however, tends eventually to reverse itself. For if a person continues to be successful in the identity project but still fails to experience lasting fulfill-ment, that person will eventually begin to lose faith in the project itself. To succeed in the identity project and still not enjoy the fulfillment it promises is to be prone to the question "Is this all there is?"

Joan Borysenko reports the following case from her practice of psy-chotherapy:

> "Jack" was a patient of mine who came to therapy for just this reason. A tall, athletic man in his late forties, he was almost apologetic for taking up my time. "I'm not even sure why I'm here," he began. "I'm physically healthy, business is good, I've been married to a great lady for twenty-six years, and all the kids are out of the house and making a living." Jack paused to chuckle and reach for his wallet. . . . "How about this? I'm even a grandfather." Jack smiled as I bent over to admire the picture of his tiny new granddaughter.
>
> As Jack replaced the picture and put his wallet away, his smile faded. "I should be happy, huh?" He paused as he searched for words, shaking his head and focusing his eyes inward. "Something is wrong. Something has changed, Joan, and I don't think it's age. I'm not having a mid-life crisis, wor-rying about my gray hairs or chasing younger women. I'm con-tent with my life. I've got everything a guy could hope for. It's that, well . . . I used to like to get up in the morning. I looked forward to the day. Now, more and more, I wake up feeling, well," Jack searched for the right words again, "not exactly bored, but kind of empty. Kind of like, so what? Is this all there is? Is this all that life is about?" (1993, pp. 58–59)

Not only by "failing" in the identity project, then, but also by succeed-ing in it, one is liable at some point to sense that the promise implicit in the project cannot be fulfilled. Of course, in arriving at this point as a consequence of *succeeding* in the project, one is able to see that the prob-lem lies in the project rather than just in circumstances or in oneself. Nevertheless, the net result is the same: disillusionment in the identity project rather than fulfillment by means of it.

The emergence of disillusionment in the identity project can be gradual and can assume a variety of forms. In what follows I shall dis-cuss three ways in which disillusionment can express itself in its initial phases, prior to an explicit awareness that the identity project aims at something that, for the mental ego, is impossible to achieve.

RESTLESS DIVERSION

The question "Is this all there is?," whether articulated explicitly or merely felt implicitly, indicates that a person has begun to lose faith in the identity project and no longer feels the same drive to accomplish its goals. The question indicates that the positive motivations behind the project have begun to wane and that the negative motivations ("nothingness" and "guilt"), which had receded into the background, have begun to return to the fore. No longer wholeheartedly devoted to the goals of the identity project, a person here begins to be troubled by an inner sense of uneasiness and dissatisfaction with life, with a recurring sense of insecurity and lack. This sense of anxious insufficiency is not at first grasped as a cognitive insight. At first it is experienced only as a feeling of restlessness arising from a vague sense that something is missing and not right in one's life.

The sense of anxious insufficiency accompanying erosion of faith in the identity project can lead to activity just for the sake of activity, to activity just for the sake of not having to face what is troubling one within. Such activity is restless extraversion, which can properly be considered an existential difficulty of midlife. In an effort to escape from reemerging feelings of nothingness and guilt, the person undergoing midlife transition is frequently drawn to amusements, hobbies, escapades, and work just for the sake of work. These forms of activity keep attention tied to the external world and thereby keep the mental ego from having to face inner problems. Hobbies and work, of course, can keep the mental ego away from its inner self for long periods of time. And amusements and escapades, in their novelty, allow the mental ego temporary release from inner anxieties.

Although acts of restless extraversion can consume a good deal of time, they do not provide permanent relief from the anxieties that motivate them. Pauses in activity and periods of inactivity inevitably occur. And in any case the reemerging sense of uneasiness and dissatisfaction gnaws in a way that draws attention inward despite all efforts to remain outwardly focused. When the mental ego finds itself being drawn inward in this way, its primary recourse for avoiding facing its fears is internal dialogue. When outer forms of diversion are unavailable, the mental ego talks to itself as an inner form of diversion.

The function of internal dialogue at this juncture is similar to its function during adolescence, because, as in adolescence, internal dialogue is here used as a defensive response to the anxieties of nothingness and guilt. There is, however, this important difference: internal dialogue at this juncture has a retrospective focus; much of it is an attempt to rationalize the past. To be sure, much internal dialogue during midlife transition is just distracting chatter. A good deal of it, however, is also an attempt by the mental ego to convince itself that its life has not been as unsatisfactory as it now seems to be. The mental ego might mentally "pat itself on the back" by reviewing its accomplishments. Or it might reassure itself of its being and value by telling itself that it has done "what one is supposed to do."

In the "Death of Ivan Ilych," for example, Tolstoy has his protagonist, who is suffering from an illness at midlife, engage in the following internal dialogue: "'Maybe I did not live as I ought to have done,' it suddenly occurred to him. 'But how could that be, when I did everything properly?' he replied, and immediately dismissed from his mind this, the sole solution of all the riddles of life and death, as something quite impossible" (1886, p. 148). The mental ego at midlife is prone to talk about its past so that it will not have to face its present; it talks about its past accomplishments to try to convince itself that it *is* someone and that it *has* value. In talking to itself in this way, the mental ego is trying to overcome its reemerging doubts about itself. It is trying to convince itself of the very opposite of what it is coming to suspect about itself.

None of the mental ego's attempts to divert itself from its underlying problems solves those problems. For diversion, by definition, is a way of avoiding rather than addressing problems. The mental ego may lose itself in extraverted activities or indulge in rationalizing internal dialogue for considerable periods of time. The background anxieties that give rise to these diversions do not go away, however. On the contrary, they continue to grow.

NARCISSISM

The ontological and moral anxieties that accompany disillusionment can lead not only to restless diversion but also to narcissistic exaggeration in one's actions. If the identity project is not accomplishing what it promises, one response is to step up efforts in the project to make others take greater notice of one's being and value. This response is based on a hope that, by trying harder and thereby eliciting an increasing number of confirmatory responses from others, one will succeed in demonstrating beyond any further doubt one's existence and worth as a person. Pursuing this hope, some people at midlife put the identity project into narcissistic overdrive. They make greater and greater efforts to "succeed" so that others will shower them with more and more confirmation. The tacit hope is that this added confirmation will finally provide what is needed to quiet the reemerging anxieties of nothingness and guilt and therefore establish once and for all a solid and satisfying sense of being and value.

The narcissist is a person who needs to be the center of other people's attentions. For the narcissist, other people are, to use Heinz Kohut's (1971, 1977) term, *selfobjects*, that is, people whose purpose is to support the narcissist's sense of self. According to Kohut, a certain degree of narcissism is normal and healthy. Everyone relates to others as selfobjects and serves as selfobject for others in turn. People suffering narcissistic difficulties, however, relate to others almost exclusively as selfobjects and are unable for the most part to serve as selfobject for others. Whether one's narcissistic difficulties stem from insufficient mirroring and nurturing in early childhood (Kohut's view) or whether they emerge at midlife as a consequence of disillusionment in the identity project, the result is that a person becomes excessively self-centered and needy of being the center of other people's attentions.

The narcissist at midlife is, then, a person who makes exaggerated overtures to others as selfobjects in order to bolster a faltering sense of being and value. Such a person goes to others for this confirmation on the assumption that, if others can be convinced of the person's being and value, so, too, can the person herself or himself. The narcissist puts on an attention-getting performance for others in the hope that the praises of others will suffice to quiet reemerging ontological and moral self-doubts.

Narcissistic performances, however, cannot accomplish their aim. Success in the identity project, even spectacular success, can never permanently satisfy the negative motivations that drive the project. The reason is simple: the identity project, as a response to the anxieties of nothingness and guilt, is a form of *flight*. The identity project does not address the root cause of these anxieties (primal repression–primal alienation); rather, it seeks only to placate the anxieties by finding substitutes for what is really needed. What is really needed is a radical change that breaks through or dissolves primal repression–primal alienation and thereby leads to both intrapsychic and interpersonal integration, that is, to wholeness. But the mental ego at midlife is not yet ready for such a radical change, and therefore, rather than facing the anxieties of nothingness and guilt and attempting to eliminate their root cause, it instead takes flight from these anxieties by means of narcissistic performances on the stage of life.

Successful performances on the stage of life, however, provide no lasting peace, and in fact in the long run exacerbate the very anxieties they mask. For the anxieties of nothingness and guilt remain in the background and eventually reassert themselves. And when they do, the narcissist is led to conclude that, because prior successes have not been sufficient to bring an end to anxiety, even grander successes are necessary. Such narcissistic thinking involves a vicious feedback loop that can lead to increasingly exaggerated behaviors and, correspondingly, to growing frustrations.

DEPRESSION AND DESPAIR

Because restless diversion and narcissism do not solve the problems to which they are responses, they are frequently followed by periods of depression, periods during which the mental ego feels defeated and asks itself, "What is the use of trying?"

The mental ego becomes susceptible to depression when it first begins to lose faith in the identity project. The mental ego's best efforts have not made it happy. At first, when disillusionment is only dawning, the mental ego attributes its unhappiness to adverse circumstances or to its own inadequacies rather than to the identity project itself; the mental ego experiences temporary depressions as if they were due entirely to specific setbacks in life. These depressions run their course and the mental ego then picks itself up and resumes pursuit of the identity project, although perhaps without the same energy and faith it had before. Before long, however, another setback triggers another depression. The triggering event in this case may be more minor than the one before and the depression may take longer to overcome. Eventually, however, the mental ego picks itself up again and applies itself once more to the identity project. The mental ego's growing disillusionment and dissatisfaction, however, doom this effort in its turn. And so it goes: one depression follows another. The mental ego becomes increasingly susceptible to depression. Depressions tend to become more frequent, to last longer, and to occur in response to less important triggering "causes."

The mental ego may try to combat these depressions by seeking diversions or by making narcissistic overtures to others as confirming selfobjects. These measures, however, as we have seen, are only temporary expedients that allow if not help the underlying problems to grow. Accordingly, the mental ego is prone as time passes to become more persistently despondent about its life prospects. Depression tends to set in as a chronic malaise; it no longer needs a triggering event. It becomes a more or less permanent state expressing the mental ego's basic life outlook rather than a temporary response to affairs in the world. Depression of this sort is "pathological" in that it indicates that something is seriously wrong with the mental ego. What is wrong, however, has nothing to do with biology, life circumstances, or even, clinically speaking, psychology. Rather, the problem is *existential*; it stems from the impossibility of the mental ego's basic project in the world: the identity project.

Depression of this sort is very close to despair. For both of these states of mind are moods of hopelessness. The difference between them is that the disillusionment of despair is a disillusionment not only at the level of feeling but also at the level of thought. Existential depression indicates a *prereflective* loss of faith in the identity project, a loss of faith that is not yet aware of itself as such. Despair in contrast indicates a *reflective* loss of faith in the identity project, a loss of faith that not only senses the futility of further efforts in the identity project but that also understands the impossibility of the project itself. Persons subject to existential depression know that their actions are ineffective and frequently counterproductive as far as alleviating unhappiness is concerned. What they do not know is *why* their actions are futile. Persons suffering from despair have achieved understanding of this "why"; they have seen that the identity project is based on false assumptions. For persons suffering despair, the impossibility of achieving fulfillment through the identity project has been explicitly understood.

Because the identity project is the purpose of the adult mental ego's life, complete disillusionment in the project carries with it a loss of hope in life. The despairing mental ego has come to the end of the line. It has come to a point where it is unhappy and knows that it is incapable of doing anything to improve its situation. It has reached an existential impasse from which, it seems, no escape is possible. As we shall see in chapter 7, however, this impasse is really a crossroads. It is not only an end but also, potentially, a new beginning. It is a possible point of departure for life beyond the limits of the mental ego.

CONCLUSION

The mental-egoic stage of development is the stage that in the normal span of years is by far of the longest duration. The preegoic stage is brief and soon forgotten, and the transegoic stage is late in coming, when it comes at all. For most people, the mental-egoic stage is virtually coextensive with life itself. No wonder so few developmental theorists have looked upon the egoic stage *as a stage*, much less a stage that prepares the way for a higher transegoic stage of life.

We have seen that the mental-egoic stage has both positive and negative aspects; it is at once a stage of *ego development* and a stage of *dualism.* The mental-egoic stage is a stage of ego development because it is the stage during which the ego takes possession of itself, masters ego functions, enters into a primary relationship or relationships, and forges an identity in the world. The mental-egoic stage, however, is also a stage of dualism in that the accomplishments of the stage are based on primal repression–primal alienation. The mental ego is able to take possession of itself because it has divorced itself from the original sources of its being. And the mental ego is able to grow and commit itself to persons and goals in the world because it has reduced the power and scope of its own experience. The mental-egoic stage is dualistic because it is based on a disconnection of the ego from much of life. Precisely this disconnection, however, is what allows the ego, as mental ego, to take initial possession of itself and to grow and establish itself in the world.

The dualistic infrastructure of the mental-egoic stage is, then, initially a basis of ego independence and ego development. In time, however, as the ego matures, this infrastructure is transformed into a barrier by which the ego is held back from higher possibilities. The mature ego no longer needs for the sake of development to be protected from non-egoic potentials or from radical interpersonal intimacy. For the mature ego, then, primal repression–primal alienation loses its developmental warrant and becomes an obstacle to movement beyond the mental-egoic plane. This loss of warrant brings the negative side of the mental-egoic stage to the fore. The mental ego ceases feeling securely self-contained and protected from overwhelming influences and increasingly feels cut off and empty, out of touch with life. It ceases feeling self-possessed and independent and increasingly feels alienated and isolated. The very structures that hitherto had been conditions of ego development here become obstructions to ego transcendence. The mental-egoic stage is fundamentally two-sided; its positive side is evident throughout most of the stage, but the negative side becomes manifest as the stage approaches its end.

5

The Unconscious

HAVING SPOKEN BRIEFLY ABOUT the unconscious in earlier chapters, the time has now come to turn directly to the topic. In discussing the unconscious, table 5.1 will be our guide. I shall concentrate chiefly on the prepersonal and personal levels indicated in table 5.1, but I shall also have a few things to say about some of the transpersonal levels. These higher levels—manifesting themselves during the stages of regression in the service of transcendence, regeneration in spirit, and integration—are here discussed only briefly, because they are more properly the subjects of later chapters. The reason for considering them here is to show that, developmentally understood, the deepest core of the mental ego's unconscious—namely, the nonegoic pole of the psyche—is not only a lower, prepersonal realm (an id or archaic collective unconscious) but also, potentially, the source of higher, transpersonal forms of life.

Based as it is on table 5.1, the discussion in this chapter does not follow a narrative line or order of logical argument. It is organized, instead, like a reference manual. This format has stylistic drawbacks, but it will enable us to treat a large topic in a relatively short space.

The unconscious that is created by primal repression is the prepersonal collective unconscious, so called because this deepest realm of the unconscious is made up of species-wide powers, potentials, and predispositions that derive from the nonegoic or physicodynamic pole of the psyche as it is repressively organized in "pre-" form. The prepersonal unconscious has three principal levels. The first and most basic level is the *Dynamic Ground*, the source of psychic power: libido, energy, spirit. The second level of the prepersonal unconscious is the sphere of the *instinctual-archetypal* unconscious, which includes (1) the collective

TABLE 5.1

The Unconscious

		LEVEL OR EXPRESSION	POTENTIALS, STRUCTURES, MODES	TRIPHASIC STAGE
TRANSPERSONAL		Rootedness in Dynamic Ground as source and basis of life	Contemplative-creative cognition Blessedness, bliss Sacred embodiment Hallowed resplendence	Integration
		Emergence of the power of Ground as purgative-redemptive spirit	Healing, guiding images; vision Awe, ecstasy Return to polymorphous sensuality Reenchantment of the world	Regeneration in spirit
		Return of repressed; regression of re-pressor	Disturbing images; hallucination Alien feelings, dread Recrudescence of bodily life Strangeness; surreal atmosphere	Regression in the service of transcendence
		↑↑↑ Primal repression lifted; Dynamic Ground reopens		↑↑↑
PERSONAL		Personal embedded unconscious*	Filtering structures and operations COEX systems Autonomous complexes Ego identity Defense mechanisms	Mental ego
		Personal submerged unconscious*	Subthreshold signals Filtered stimuli Shadow Deeply repressed materials	
		↓↓↓ Primal repression (embedded*) ↓↓↓		
PREPERSONAL	SUBMERGED	Body Unconscious (repressed)	Autosymbolic-protoconceptual cognition: the primary process Full-bodied feelings Polymorphous sensuality Amplified experience Numinosity, enchantment	Body ego
		Instinctual-archetypal unconscious (repressed)	Ontogenetic instincts and archetypes Phylogenetic instincts and archetypes	
		Dynamic Ground (repressed)	Libido (power of Ground as restricted to sexual organization) Psychic energy (power of Ground as allowed to circulate freely)	

* Wilber's (1980a) term.

instincts and corresponding patterns of imaginal production that have been developed phylogenetically to deal with basic human needs and typical human situations, and (2) the universal patterns of imaginal production associated with the ontogenesis of the ego and its lifelong interaction with the Dynamic Ground. The former of these two subdivisions can be called the *phylogenetic* level of the instinctual-archetypal unconscious, the latter the *ontogenetic* level of the instinctual-archetypal unconscious. Finally, the third level of the prepersonal unconscious is the sphere of the *body unconscious*, which includes the remaining non-egoic potentials or modes of experience that, integral to the life of the body ego, disappear from consciousness when the ego repressively submerges the nonegoic pole of the psyche.

THE DYNAMIC GROUND

The Dynamic Ground is the seat of the nonegoic pole of the psyche and the source of psychic energy. As such, it is a necessary basis of all psychic life.

The most basic function of the power of the Ground is to serve as the fuel—that is, the activator and enhancer—of psychic processes. To use a term introduced by Stanislav Grof (1975) in a different context, the power of the Ground in its function as activator-enhancer can be said to be a *nonspecific amplifier* of experience. It is a magnifier of all dimensions of psychic life. When the power of the Ground flows, experience quickens, becoming alive and acute, if not tumultuous and overwhelmingly intense; when the power of the Ground ebbs, experience slows, becoming pale, distant, and dull. The presence of the power of the Ground potentiates experience across all dimensions; the absence of this power depotentiates experience.

In adopting the term *nonspecific amplifier*, I am proposing that the power of the Ground is an energizer of all psychic processes and systems and is not itself reducible to or exclusively expressive of any particular process or system. This perspective departs from the classical psychoanalytic conception of libido, according to which libidinal energy is a drive energy of an inherently sexual nature. If, however, the view I am proposing departs from the psychoanalytic view on the matter of whether psychic energy is *the same as* sexual energy, it still follows the psychoanalytic view to a certain extent in holding that psychic energy is *intimately linked* with the sexual system. For psychic energy, I suggest, as Wilhelm Reich (1942) surmised, arises from a source within the sexual system. Moreover, psychic energy is for most people—that is, as mental egos, operating under the constraints of primal repression—primarily contained within this point of origin. Primal repression seals the Ground and reduces the power of the Ground to a nearly dormant state within the sexual system. (The word *nearly* is used because the power of the Ground must remain active to some degree as the activator-enhancer of psychic processes.) Limited to this quiescent sexual organization, the power of the Ground is ordinarily activated and released from the sexual system only during sexual activity. For most people, then, I suggest, the power of the Dynamic Ground is *in effect* a sexual energy. Although it is a nonspecific energy, it is nonetheless experienced as a sexual energy because for most people it not only arises from a source within the sexual system but is also primarily concentrated in and expressed through the sexual system.

In light of these facts it is useful to retain the term *libido* and to use it in contrast to *psychic energy*. Accordingly, I shall employ *libido* nonreductively to designate the power of the Ground in its (mental-egoic) sexual organization, and I shall employ *psychic energy* to designate the power of the Ground in its role as nonspecific amplifier or fuel of psychic processes. Thus defined, *libido* and *psychic energy* designate two of the chief manifestations of the power of the Dynamic Ground. The other chief manifestation, to be discussed later, is spirit.

A second feature of the power of the Ground is that it is a force that is *gravitationally or magnetically attractive*, as is evident in the effect that cathexis objects have upon the ego. The ego is drawn to the power of the Ground and to anything upon which the power of the Ground is projected. Things cathected with the power of the Ground engage the ego's attention and are interesting, fascinating, or gripping to a degree that is directly proportional to the degree of their dynamic charge. Anything in which the power of the Ground is invested has a gravitational or magnetic effect upon the ego, and it has such an effect whether its manner of appearance to the ego is positive or negative. Negative attraction, for example, is evident in many neurotic fixations and in the morbid fascination that people have in things horrific, macabre, and demoniacal. In sum, the power of the Ground is a force that when invested in things draws the ego's attention to those things, whether pleasantly so (by rendering them inviting or enrapturing) or unpleasantly so (by rendering them gripping or hypnotically inescapable).

Owing to this gravitational or magnetic effect, the power of the Ground is able, if focused in sufficient concentration, not only to attract attention but also completely to command it—irrespective of whatever resistance might be mounted by the ego. The power of the Ground not only attracts the ego; it can also seize it. Stunning and gripping phenomena of all sorts exert their hold on attention by means of the power invested them. Many idioms describe this irresistible influence in remarkably insightful ways; for example, we say that one is held breathless or in suspense or that one is rendered speechless, petrified, riveted, and so on. All of these expressions connote *involuntary immobilization*. They indicate that a person, when in the presence of things highly charged with the power of the Ground, is vulnerable to being arrested or captivated.

In extreme cases the power of the Ground can even *absorb* or *dissolve* the ego. The power of the Ground has a gravitational-*solvent* effect upon the ego. The solvent effect of the power of the Ground is evident, for example, in entrancement and ecstasy. Entrancement involves not only a tethering of attention but also a mesmerizing absorption of awareness in a dynamically charged object or event. And ecstasy involves not only a euphoric infusion of the ego by the power of the Ground but also a dissolution of the ego's boundaries by this power. When in the field of influence of the power of the Ground, the ego is liable to be engulfed or swept away, absorbed or dissolved.

The power of the Ground therefore, from the ego's point of view, has potential dominion over the ego. It can command the ego's attention, halt ego functions, and even absorb or dissolve the ego. Moreover, the power of the Ground is able to do these things even if the ego is resistant and refuses to "let go." The ego therefore—or at least the mental ego[1]—is vulnerable in face of the power of the Ground.

This vulnerability, considered in conjunction with the ego's attraction to the power of the Ground, explains another basic feature of that power, namely, its bivalence—or, more accurately, its *seeming* bivalence, based on the ego's radical ambivalence toward it. The ego is both drawn to and apprehensive of the power of the Ground. For on the one hand this power is, to the ego, an alluring enlivener of awareness; yet on the other hand it is an uncontrollable and threatening force. It is a necessary condition of the ego's existence and operation; yet it is also a gravitational-solvent force that can seize, absorb, or dissolve the ego.

The bivalence of the power of the Ground is the source of perhaps the most basic problem of the ego's existence. This bivalence poses an insuperable problem for the body ego, which, after an initial period of blissful well-being, is subject to acute ambivalence and splitting in relation to the Ground-caregiver Great Mother. The problem of bivalence is hidden, but by no means solved, for the duration of the mental-egoic period, during which the Ground is submerged beneath primal repression and during which, therefore, the power of the Ground is able to manifest itself for the most part only through unconscious cathexes and projections. The problem of bivalence resurfaces with the onset of regression in the service of transcendence and continues to afflict the ego throughout this stage, and the stage of regeneration in spirit as well, because during these transitional periods the ego comes once again under the direct influence of the Ground and undergoes a death-rebirth transformation at the hands of the power of the Ground. As we shall see, the problem of bivalence is not overcome until regeneration in spirit culminates in integration proper. Only at this highest stage of development does the ego, at last harmoniously rooted in the Ground, cease being ambivalent toward the Ground and consequently cease being affected bivalently by the power of the Ground. Only at this point does the power of the Ground show itself to be a monovalent, wholly positive force.

Table 5.2 summarizes the major steps of the ego-Ground interaction in light of the ambivalence-bivalence phenomenon. Having already treated the steps up to primal repression earlier, I shall here briefly describe the remaining steps up to integration. This preview of ensuing developments is pertinent here not only as part of the inventory of the unconscious (in its higher transpersonal expressions) but also as a preparation for discussing the third of the three main expressions of the power of the Ground: spirit.

Primal repression radically alters the character of the ego-Ground interaction. It does so because, in submerging the Ground, it markedly restricts the expression of the power of the Ground. At this point, the transition to latency, the power of the Ground is reduced to a nearly dormant state within the sexual system. Except for what is released and utilized as psychic energy, the power of the Ground is here reduced to libido, the energy of the repressed-instinctual underside of life. Restricted in this manner, the power of the Ground ceases for the most part affecting the ego in direct and visible ways. It does, however, continue to affect the ego, although now primarily in indirect and invisible ways, through unconscious cathexes, projections, and transferences. The power of the Ground, unbeknownst to the mental ego, is invested in the objects of unconscious drives, archetypes, complexes, desires, and fears. These objects, charged with the power of the Ground, have a power over the mental ego, frequently riveting the mental ego's attention and sometimes drawing the mental ego into entrancements or absorptions—even though the mental ego may well be highly threatened by the objects to which, in these ways, it is drawn. These objects therefore become the foci of fixations, obsessions, and compulsions: the mental ego is driven to these objects and is sometimes taken captive by them for reasons it does not and cannot understand. These objects have an uncanny hold on the mental ego, and they consequently pose hidden limits to its self-possession and self-control.

Even when opposed by primal repression, the power of the Ground does on occasion "awaken" or break through to manifest itself directly within the field of the mental ego's experience. When such "ruptures of

TABLE 5.2

The Ambivalence-Bivalence Phenomenon

Stage	Disposition of Ego	Appearance of Ground
Integration	Ego is harmoniously rooted in Ground.	Power of Ground experienced in "pure" form as spirit, as the dynamic essence of enlightenment and love.
Regeneration in spirit	Ego yields to power of Ground.	Power of Ground experienced as purgative-redemptive spirit.
Regression in the service of transcendence	Ego is reopened to and fearful of Ground.	Power of Ground challenges the ego; return of the repressed; regression of the repressor.
Late mental-egoic stage: midlife transition	Ego's repressive self-possession begins to feel like alienation; ego fascinated by possibilities of ego transcendence.	Occasional incursions of power of Ground into consciousness; initial experiences of the numinous.
Mental-egoic stage: latency, adolescence, early adulthood.	Ego functions develop independently of physicodynamic influences.	Power of Ground, as energy of the unconscious, is dark and mysterious force that works invisibly through cathexes and projections.
Primal repression	Ego takes possession and control of itself by disconnecting itself from the Ground.	Dynamic Ground becomes seat of dynamic unconscious; power of Ground restricted to a primarily dormant instinctual organization (libido).
Late preegoic or body-egoic stage: the Oedipus complex	Ego's desire for intimacy with Great Mother is challenged by oedipal father.	Ground intermittently closed and reopened; negatively weighted bivalence of Ground-caregiver Great Mother.
Middle preegoic or body-egoic stage: the rapprochement crisis.	Ego is on course of independence but also aware of its dependence; acute ambivalence.	Maximum bivalence; splitting of Great Mother into disjoined opposing realities: the Good Mother and the Terrible Mother.
Early preegoic or body-egoic stage	Initial ego development; ego easily yields to reembedment.	Initial emergence of Great Mother as Ground-caregiver "object"; Great Mother appears primarily as Good Mother.
Original embedment	Ego is only minimally differentiated.	Womb of Great Mother; dynamic plenitude, bliss.

Time Line (vertical label along left side)

plane"[2] occur, the power of the Ground typically takes the form of what Rudolf Otto (1917) called the *numinous*. As described by Otto, the numinous is the *mysterium tremendum et fascinans*; it is a dynamic presence that is ineffable, overawing, and compellingly magnetic. Moreover, according to Otto, the numinous is dramatically bivalent in that it has both light and dark manifestations and engenders in the mental ego both ecstasies and agonies, both exaltations and abasements. Owing to the magnetic character of the power of the Ground, the mental ego is

irresistibly drawn to the numinous; owing to the captivating and solvent effects of the power, however, the mental ego is deeply apprehensive of the numinous, which it approaches full of "fear and trembling,"
afraid that it will be engulfed and destroyed. In sum, the power of the
Ground in its manifestation as the numinous is experienced by the mental ego as an incomprehensible, ego-eclipsing, entrancing, and discon-
certingly bivalent force. It presents itself as a reality that is daunting as
well as transporting, a source of engulfing gravity as well as uplifting
grace.

Once primal repression gives way and regression in the service of
transcendence commences, the ego begins to experience the power of
the Ground directly within consciousness. This opening of the ego to
the Ground has two chief consequences. First, because primal repression had submerged the Ground, the removal of primal repression triggers a dramatic awakening and resurgence of the power of the Ground,
which asserts itself within the ego's own domain. And second, because
primal repression had undergirded the mental ego, the removal of primal repression undermines the mental-egoic system and brings about a
regression of the mental ego into the underlying physicodynamic
sphere, that is, into the prepersonal unconscious, the nonegoic pole of
the psyche in its repressed organization. The interaction between the
ego and the Dynamic Ground that occurs during regression in the service of transcendence is therefore at once an upheaval and a "fall"; it is
at once a return of the repressed and a regression of the repressor. This
interaction is a collision between the two poles of the psyche, a confrontation between the ego and the power of the Ground.

The ego experiences the confrontation with the power of the
Ground as a challenge to its presumed sovereignty within the soul. The
ego, as mental ego, considers itself to be the exclusive owner and controller of psychic life. To the mental ego, the power of the Ground is an
alien intruder in the psyche, an intruder that threatens the mental ego's
authority. Accordingly, the ego responds to the encroachment of the
power of the Ground with all the resources at its command. It attempts
to banish the power of the Ground from consciousness, to shore up
egoic defenses, and thereby to reseal the Ground. These efforts, however, are unsuccessful, for the ego faces a power that is stronger than the
ego and is in fact the ego's own deeper and higher self. Hence, the confrontation between the ego and the Dynamic Ground eventually
reaches a turning point at which the ego realizes that its resistance to the
power of the Ground is futile and self-defeating. At this turning point
the ego finally understands that it cannot triumph over the power of the

Ground and should in fact yield to the power of the Ground. The ego here recognizes that the power of the Ground is *spirit*.

In arriving at this insight, the ego makes the turn to regeneration in spirit and enters into a new type of struggle. It ceases struggling against the power of the Ground and begins struggling against its own remaining resistances to the power of the Ground. This new struggle is therefore a battle of surrender to spiritual power. Here there occurs an uncompromising purging of everything remaining within the mental-egoic system that is closed or opposed to the spontaneous movement of spiritual power—for example, vestiges of primal repression, fears and defense mechanisms, and much of the identity-shadow complex. These impediments to the free expression of spiritual power are gradually dissolved so that the ego can become an unobstructed and completely faithful vehicle of spirit.

The turn to regeneration in spirit is, then, the point at which the ego reverses its stance toward the power of the Ground: the ego ceases opposing the power and begins cooperating with it instead. Correspondingly, the turn to regeneration in spirit is also the point at which there occurs a reversal in the manner in which the power of the Ground appears to the ego: threatening expressions of the power of the Ground begin to give way to healing expressions. The ego here begins to experience the power of the Ground as a redemptive force that heals rather than slays and that graces the ego with raptures and ecstasies. The ego continues to experience the power of the Ground in a bivalent manner throughout regeneration in spirit. As regeneration in spirit unfolds, however, the ego's experience of the power of the Ground is decreasingly negative and increasingly positive.

Once the ego has been purged of its last resistances to the infusive movement of the power of the Ground, it ceases experiencing the power of the Ground in a bivalent manner. No longer resistant to the power of the Ground, the ego is no longer treated violently by the power of the Ground. The power of the Ground is now gentle with and unconditionally supportive of the ego. The integrated stage that commences at this point is therefore one that is both powerfully infused and peacefully composed. It is a stage that transcends all darkness and violence. Even the positive experiences that highlighted the period of regeneration are transcended in this manner. These experiences continue to be every bit as luminous and powerful as before, but now, divested of all negative nuances, they lose their eruptive character and become smooth and serene. For example, rapture is transformed into contemplation, ecstasy into bliss.

Concomitant with these transformations, the power of the Ground begins to disclose itself in its innermost nature as the *dynamic essence of insight and affirmation of others*. To be sure, the power of the Ground continues here, as libido, to be released from the sexual system and, as psychic energy, to fuel psychic processes generally; moreover, it continues, as the numinous, to be an all-pervasive energy that imbues the world with an aura of hallowed resplendence. At this transition point, however, because it is liberated from exclusive association with the instincts and is disburdened of the resistance of the ego, the power of the Ground is able to reveal itself as well in its "pure" or pristine form: it is able to express itself as luminously intelligent and affirmatively outreaching life, as conscious light and love. That is, it is able to express itself as spirit.

The luminosity and outreachingness of spirit can be understood in terms of the foregoing account of the power of the Ground. They are, I suggest, the consciousness-amplifying and gravitational-magnetic aspects of the power of the ground when these aspects are manifested under conditions of dynamic freedom—that is, under conditions that allow the power of the Ground to express itself independently of specific psychic systems and without being opposed by psychodynamic resistances. When the power of the Ground, as psychic energy, is utilized to fuel specific psychic systems, it works as an amplifier of their distinctive modes of awareness. When it is not so channeled, however, and is instead allowed to express itself freely, it is experienced as pure luminous consciousness, either in the form of a powerful objectless contemplation (*asamprajnata samadhi, arupa jhana*) or in the form of an interior fluidic light. Daniel Brown (1986), in his cross-cultural study of contemplative experience, reports that at a certain stage of contemplative development "awareness opens up to the substratum of ordinary perception, namely, an incessant flow of light in the stream of awareness" (p. 240). The very energy that ordinarily functions invisibly as the medium of awareness, accentuating system-specific experiences and magnifying psychomental contents, here becomes the "object" of awareness, manifesting itself as luminous consciousness.

When the expression of the power of the Ground is opposed by the ego, its gravitational-magnetic effect is apparent only darkly or indirectly, either through fascinations and entrancements or, when the Ground is repressed, through unconscious cathexes and projections. Once the mature ego has become harmoniously integrated with the Ground, however, the power of the Ground, as liberated spirit, manifests its gravitational-magnetic character immediately and in an affirmative manner, namely, as spontaneous spiritual attraction, as the impulse to spiritual intimacy. Under these conditions the ego is completely at one with the life of spirit, which moves not only infusively, within the ego, but also outreachingly, from the ego, reaching out to bond with others, spirit to spirit. Under conditions of dynamic freedom, then, the power of the Ground is not only the light of wisdom but also the outflowing heart of compassion. It is the pure spiritual power that embraces and confirms others irrespective of their merits.

Of the many manifestations of the power of the Dynamic Ground, it is, I propose, spirit as expressed under conditions of dynamic freedom that alone displays the power's intrinsic character. Liberated spirit alone expresses the "essence" of the power of the Ground because it is only as liberated spirit that the power of the Ground reveals itself without either modulation or constraint. And as just explained, when the power of the Ground does reveal itself in this way, it shows itself to be luminous love, consciousness in search of communion. To be sure, the power of the Ground is rarely experienced in this "pure" form. For given that primal repression is the rule and dynamic freedom the exception, the power of the Ground is for the most part unconsciously organized as libido and is allowed to flow freely only as psychic energy, which is channeled and utilized without remainder by specific psychic systems. Only in those exceptional cases in which primal repression is lifted and the ego is harmoniously rooted in the Ground is the power of the Ground able to disclose itself as itself, not just as the numinous, but as the heightened consciousness and spontaneous love of spirit.

Contrary to the Freudian view, then, according to which spirit is only sublimated libido, the view I am proposing is that libido is repressed spirit.[3] Libido—and psychic energy too—is a limited form of spirit. In proposing this view, I am not suggesting that the reverse of Freudian reductionism is true. For whereas the Freudian view is that all psychic systems are ultimately subordinate to and expressive of sexuality, which is itself a psychic system, the view I am proposing holds that no psychic system has the privileged status of uniquely revealing the essential character of dynamic life. No psychic system is basic in this sense; rather, I suggest, the essential character of dynamic life is disclosed only when it manifests itself *independently* of all systemic expressions and organizations. Therefore, in saying that spirit is the essence of the power of the Ground, I am not proposing a reverse reductionism. Rather, all I am proposing is that the power of the Ground has a distinctive nature and that this nature is not fully evident in the sexual organization and expression of the power as libido, or in the system-specific utilization of the power as psychic energy, but rather only in the free expression of the power as spirit.

The power of the Ground, it must be stressed, is not merely a theoretical postulate. It is rather the very life of the soul. Although usually repressed and unconscious, the power of the Ground is something that is present within or that affects consciousness in many ways. As libido, it is a power that expresses itself dramatically through sexual arousal and orgasm. As psychic energy, it is a power that accentuates experience across all dimensions. And as spirit, it is a power that effects purgative-redemptive transformations of the ego, a numinous presence that hallows the world, and a dynamic essence that is inherent to both enlightenment and love. The power of the Ground is an actually existing dynamism that can be directly experienced by the ego.

Moreover, the power of the Ground is a force that, under certain conditions, is discernible not only subjectively but also physically. This fact is taken up in chapters 7 and 8, where I discuss the movement of the power of the Ground within the body that begins once primal repression is lifted. Suffice it here to say that the power of the Ground is something that affects the body as well as the mind and, therefore, is something that in principle is amenable to scientific study, including measurement by physical instruments. Science of course is not even remotely close to undertaking such a study. Discussion must first agree on the *existence* of something before it can begin to consider strategies for measurement. Admittedly, then, the foregoing account of the power of the Ground, although empirically meaningful, is not presently empirically verifiable except in a subjective and introspective way, and even then, really, only by those for whom the power of the Ground has become active as spirit.

A final observation is in order: in stressing the existence of the power of the Ground, I am not advancing an opinion on the ultimate ontological status of this power. Such a judgment would in any case be unwarranted. It would exceed the limits of human cognition. We simply cannot know—in this lifetime at least—whether the power of the Ground, in addition to being an intrapsychic phenomenon, is also an extrapsychic (metaphysical, cosmic) noumenon. Human experience suffices to affirm that the power of the Ground is a dynamic reality of extraegoic origin and numinous-sacred character, but it is not a sufficient basis from which either to affirm or deny the possibility that the power of the Ground is something that exists independently of the psyche. This position is *not* psychological reductionism; it is simply a confession of ignorance. Spirit may have its ultimate origin in a metaphysical source lying completely beyond the soul. As experienced by the ego, however, spirit is of necessity something that expresses itself within the boundaries of the soul. The ego can have no experience, and therefore no knowledge, of the power of the Ground as it may (or may not) exist beyond these boundaries.

THE INSTINCTUAL-ARCHETYPAL UNCONSCIOUS

The instinctual-archetypal unconscious consists of two levels, a phylogenetic and an ontogenetic level. The former of these levels was formed in response to environmental and social conditions affecting the species during the course of its evolution. The latter level, in contrast, derives from conditions governing the emergence of the individual organism or ego from the original sources of its existence. We shall begin by considering the ontogenetic level of the instinctual-archetypal unconscious.

THE ONTOGENETIC LEVEL OF THE
INSTINCTUAL-ARCHETYPAL UNCONSCIOUS

Ontogenetically, the dimension of the instinctual-archetypal unconscious that is of greatest archetypal significance is the interaction between the developing ego and the Great Mother. The ego-Great Mother relation is the source of many of the symbols that make up the collective unconscious. Since we have already treated this relation in chapter 2, the task here will be the limited one of describing the principal structural properties of the Great Mother system.[4]

The Dynamic Ground is the nascent ego's psychic womb and sustainer, and, as such, it constitutes the inner side of the *bidirectional* Great Mother system. The Great Mother is at once an outer and an inner source, support, and enveloping presence, at once the caregiving parent and the Dynamic Ground. To the body ego, however, these two dimensions of the Great Mother system are not separate in any way, and therefore the archetypal images through which the Great Mother is apprehended characteristically involve a degree of conflation of outer and inner, personal and depth-psychological, elements. For the body ego, then, the Great Mother is neither a fully personal (human) nor a merely impersonal (elemental) presence, but is rather a presence that combines these aspects in a mutually qualifying way.

To be sure, the Great Mother is at times depicted as a human being (reflecting the outer caregiver) and at times as prodigious elemental forces (reflecting the Dynamic Ground). More characteristically, however, the Great Mother is depicted in a way that reflects an intermediate position between these extremes. We have seen, for example, that she is depicted as nurturing or as dangerous animals, especially animals that

are either furry mammalian comforters (the Good Mother) or devouring monsters such as reptiles or wolves (the Terrible Mother). These
animals, in occupying a place below the human level and above the elemental level, are especially representative of the Great Mother system.
The Great Mother system, then, can be said to consist of images almost
all of which fall *between* the endpoints of an axis bounded on one end by
a completely human caregiver and on the other end by completely
impersonal elemental forces (waters, fires, and winds of either soothing
and nurturing or violent and destructive nature). Some of these images
no doubt fall closer to one endpoint of the axis and others fall closer to
the other endpoint, but in most cases, it seems likely, the images of the
Great Mother system reflect some degree of conflation of the outer and
inner dimensions.

The Great Mother system is *bivalent* as well as bidirectional. Owing
to the magnetic and nurturing nature of the Great Mother, the ego is
drawn to her and is prone to imagine her in positive ways (as a graceful
maiden, a furry mammalian comforter, or soothing elemental forces).
However, owing to the captivating and engulfing-consuming nature of
the Great Mother, the ego is also frightened of her and is prone to imagine her in negative ways (as an ugly witch, a devouring monster, or
dangerous elemental forces). The Great Mother system consequently
consists of images falling simultaneously on two axes, a bidirectional
and a bivalent axis. These two axes define the boundaries of the system
and therefore determine the field of possible images that can be
included within the system.

Figure 5.1 indicates that images of the Great Mother system fall on
markedly different points along the two axes of the system. We have
just noted that these images fall between, but rarely on, the endpoints
of the bidirectional axis, which means that neither a fully personal caregiver nor a completely impersonal Ground is representative of the
Great Mother system. The intermediate points on the bidirectional axis
are the ones that are most representative of the system, with the more
central points (representing nurturing or dangerous animals) being
more central to the system. In contrast, images of the Great Mother fall
near or at, but rarely between, the endpoints of the bivalent axis of the
system. That is to say, the Great Mother is virtually always conspicuously either positive or negative; the middle, neutral, ground of the
bivalent axis is rarely represented.

Images from the Great Mother system are an intrinsic and vividly
actual part of the body ego's conscious experience. The autosymbolic
process produces these images in response to the body ego's need to
understand the principal reality of its world. These images, which at

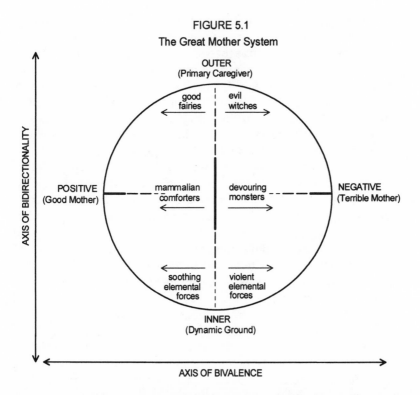

FIGURE 5.1

The Great Mother System

first are predominantly positive, undergo splitting along the bivalent axis during the rapprochement and oedipal periods of development and then disappear from consciousness altogether once primal repression is consolidated and latency begins. In psychoanalytic parlance, the point at which the images of the Great Mother system disappear from consciousness is the point at which libidinal object constancy is achieved. At this point the child's primary object representation ceases being split into two larger-than-life contrary opposites, the "good object" and the "bad object," and the caregiver begins being experienced as a single person who is imperfect but fundamentally good. The primary caregiver is no longer overlaid with images belonging to the Great Mother system.

With the onset of regression in the service of transcendence, the Dynamic Ground is reopened and many of the images of the Great Mother system are reactivated. Also triggered into activity at this point is an elaborate system of ontogenetic archetypes the images of which anticipate the forthcoming stages of transegoic experience. Among these images can be included all those that are signposts of the Way, the spiritual path, in both its positive and negative aspects: the myriad symbols of alienation, death, resurrection, purgation, transfiguration, hell, heaven, devils, angels, damnation, salvation, liberation, apotheosis, and so forth. Images such as these express in highly condensed fashion the possible spiritual itinerary of the mental ego: its "conversion" and withdrawal from the world, its awakening to spiritual power, its regression into the unconscious, its rebirth and regeneration in spirit, and its final integration and fulfillment. Images of this sort work to give the spiritual seeker a preview of the unknown territory that lies ahead in the highest stages of individuation or ontogenesis.

The archetypes of the Way, like the archetypes of the Great Mother system, belong to the collective unconscious. The archetypes of the Way, however, differ importantly from the archetypes of the Great Mother system in that, rather than being repressed archetypes of a period of development already over, they are, for most people, not yet activated archetypes of a period of development still in the future. Archetypes of the Way typically are not activated until the ego is mature and ready to move toward transegoic stages of development. Only at midlife or later, typically, do the archetypes of the Way begin projecting images that serve as guideposts for the spiritual journey. Whereas the archetypes of the Great Mother system belong to the mental ego's preegoic past, the archetypes of the Way belong to the mental ego's transegoic future. Accordingly, whereas the archetypes of the Great Mother system belong to the *prepersonal* collective unconscious, the signposts of the Way belong to the *transpersonal* collective unconscious.

THE PHYLOGENETIC LEVEL OF THE INSTINCTUAL-ARCHETYPAL UNCONSCIOUS

The phylogenetic level of the instinctual-archetypal unconscious consists of instincts and corresponding patterns of image production that, in the history of the species, have emerged in response either to the requirements of survival or to constantly recurring, universal human situations. Related to the demands of survival are, for example, the core id instincts of sex, child care, food acquisition, self-defense, and, perhaps, territoriality—together with their perceptual and imaginal correlates. And pertaining to universal human situations are, for example, archetypal patterns pertaining to such things as attainment of sexual and social maturity, gender differences (the archetypal *anima* and *animus*), old age, and death. These various constituents of the instinctual-archetypal unconscious are inherited from our evolutionary ancestors. They therefore belong to an archaic stratum of the unconscious.

According to classical psychoanalytic drive theory, the most basic of the instincts are sexuality and aggression.[5] These are powerful motivating forces that, as Freud stressed, can have a disruptive influence on the (repressive) foundations of "civilized" life. Developmentally, sexuality and aggression are conspicuously awakened at puberty. Although feelings analogous to sexuality and aggression exist prior to puberty, these feelings are only distant precursors of the hormonally based sexual and aggressive impulses that arise during puberty.[6] Because sexuality and aggression are present, if at all, only in incomplete forms during the period of the body ego, they play at most only a limited role in the childhood struggle leading to primal repression. Nevertheless, sexuality and aggression still must be counted as part of the repressed or submerged prepersonal unconscious, because, as nonegoic or physicodynamic potentials, they are inhibited by primal repression once they are activated. Sexuality and aggression are by no means completely contained by primal repression, but they are to a large extent restrained in their expression.

THE BODY UNCONSCIOUS

The body unconscious consists of many of the nonegoic potentials and modes of experience that are integral to the life of the body ego and that, after primal repression, are submerged into unconsciousness. Among these nonegoic potentials and modes of experience are (1) autosymbolic cognition (arrested at the symbolic-protoconceptual stage, the stage of the primary process), (2) concrete bodily feelings, (3) polymorphous sensuality, (4) amplified experience, and (5) numinosity or enchantment. Having already discussed the body ego's cognitive and affective experience in an earlier chapter, there is no need in this context to review the first two of these dimensions of the body unconscious. It should suffice to remind ourselves that spontaneous imaginal-symbolic cognition and concrete body feelings are among the potentials that belong to the body ego and therefore to the body unconscious as well. With this understood, the ensuing discussion of the body unconscious will be limited to considering polymorphous sensuality, amplified experience, and numinosity or enchantment.

POLYMORPHOUS SENSUALITY

Although psychic energy is, for the body ego, most highly concentrated in the erotogenic zones, it is not confined to those areas. It circulates freely throughout the whole of the body ego's physical being and, in doing so, enhances the arousal capacity of all bodily parts and regions. The body ego therefore is exceedingly sensitive to, and easily becomes engrossed in, tactile and other bodily stimulations. Tickling, caressing, and massaging, for example, delight the body ego and send it into somatic ecstasy. Experiences such as these are, for the body ego, intensely sensual. They are not, however, specifically sexual in nature. For the energy that empowers these experiences, although released from the sexual system, is not itself a specifically sexual energy. It is not yet libido in the sense that I am using that term, but is rather a nonspecific energy, an energy that empowers all modes of experience without being uniquely or inherently expressive of any one.

Primal repression closes off the Dynamic Ground and, in confining the power of the Ground to the sexual system (except for what is allowed to circulate freely as psychic energy), reorganizes the power of the Ground as libido. As a result, the body ceases being polymorphously sensual and becomes instead predominantly genital in its dynamic organization. Immediately following the consolidation of primal repression there begins the period of latency, which, with the arrival of puberty, is succeeded by mature genital sexuality. The adult mental ego is for the most part cerebrally aloof from immediate somatic experience, but it frequently descends from the upper mental regions to enjoy a genitally triggered discharge of libido. In sum, then, primal repression puts all of the body to "sleep" except the genito-pelvic region (and other intensely sensory-erotic areas). And in this sense polymorphous sensuality can be said to be rendered unconscious.

AMPLIFIED EXPERIENCE

The power of the Ground, as psychic energy, enhances every dimension of the body ego's life, including not just its somatic experiences but also its perceptions, feelings, and thoughts.

The body ego's perceptions are rich and vivid. Sensory qualities appear to the body ego with great vibrancy, endless variety, and exceptional definition and detail. In general, the body ego's perceptual experiences have the character of sensory displays; they are profusions of colors, sounds, odors, tastes, or textures.

Psychic energy also amplifies the body ego's feelings. These are passions that move powerfully throughout the body ego's being. They are strong emotive currents that run their course without inhibition or disguise. Unlike the mental ego, which tends to experience feelings in significantly attenuated form, the body ego experiences feelings in the fullness of their power.

And as for the body ego's cognition, although it may be lacking in logical rigor, it is in no way lacking in sheer force or vivacity. Given the supercharging effects of the power of the Ground, the concrete symbolic images that are the bearers of the body ego's thought tend to have a strong impact upon the mind. They are experienced as stunning realizations, insights of seemingly immense significance. For the body ego, the world is full of tantalizing secrets and beguiling mysteries, and when one of these secrets or mysteries is suddenly laid bare, the body ego is literally struck. It is stopped in its tracks, astounded, and filled with delight or dread.

Primal repression, in sealing the Dynamic Ground, has the effect of depotentiating experience across all dimensions. Perceptions are dulled; feelings are muted; and mental representations lose their power of impact. The superabundance of the body ego's experience is lost; it is put on hold and becomes a dormant possibility of the body unconscious.

NUMINOSITY OR ENCHANTMENT

The relatively unrestricted flow of the power of the Ground imbues the body ego's outer world with a sheen of numinosity. The world is accentuated with an aura that renders things superreal, both intense and gripping. The world is charged and magnetized. It is full of objects that possess heightened qualities and pulsate with magical power. The body ego therefore tends to be in awe of its world, which is enchanted. This enchantment, however, is not always a positive thing. For the numinous power that permeates the body ego's world can make things appear not only superreal and alluring but also strange and daunting. The body ego is therefore subject to sudden reversals in its experience. For example, the body ego may at one moment be rapt in a scene of great appeal only in the next moment to fall prey to bone-chilling dread and a sense of uncanniness. Whether positive or negative, however, the body ego's experience is extraordinary. The body ego lives in a world of marvel, mystery, and miracle.

Primal repression, in closing the Dynamic Ground, divests experience of its magic and leaves it without the power to astound. The power of the Ground is withdrawn from the world and returned to the deep unconscious, where it lies inactive, or "asleep," in the sexual system at the base of the spine.

PRIMAL REPRESSION

Primal repression, which disconnects the ego from the nonegoic pole of the psyche, is what first creates the prepersonal submerged unconscious. Primal repression, however, is not just a "cause" of the unconscious; it is—or soon becomes—a component or content of the unconscious. For it is a negative posture toward physicodynamic life that, once assumed, is soon petrified and forgotten. Primal repression is a deeply embedded *and invisible* infrastructure of the mental-egoic system.

Let us recall that primal repression is a psycho*physical* phenomenon. The mental ego rests upon a repressive foundation that possesses a definite physical dimension. The mental ego in effect uses the body as an instrument by which to separate itself from the Dynamic Ground. In the initial act of primal repression, the mental ego constricts the body in a layered way, beginning at the level of the anus (which adjoins the sexual system) and proceeding upward all the way to the base of the skull (which marks the beginning of the mental ego's sphere). These constrictions, which quickly solidify into permanent knots or body armorings, together form a hierarchy of barriers that contain the upward flow of the power of the Ground and that thereby protect the mental ego from the gravitational-solvent effects of that power.

In containing the Ground, the barriers constituting primal repression at the same time provide the mental ego with a firm underfooting, with a seemingly solid basis in being. Primal repression therefore works at once to submerge the Ground and to support the mental ego. It transforms the body from a supple and open vehicle for the free circulation of the power of the Ground into a rigid, impervious structure that at once caps the Ground and underprops the mental-egoic system.

This description of primal repression suggests the hydraulic model of repression, which is a model that has come under strong criticism. According to the hydraulic model, repression works by mobilizing a countercathexis, a counterpressure, that is equal to or greater than the energy of the repressed. Conceived as a hydraulic phenomenon, repression is a highly charged standoff of antagonistic energies, of containing energy versus expressive energy. The hydraulic model sees repression as a conflict in stasis, as a potentially explosive pocket of tension in the body-mind. The hydraulic model has been rightly criticized, because evidence does not support the existence of such pockets of tension.

Fortunately, the difficulties plaguing the hydraulic model of repression need not pose insuperable difficulties for the notion of repression per se. For repression need not work only in a hydraulic way.

As a countercathexis, repression might work not only by directly resisting the expression of the repressed but also, in doing this, by subduing or quieting the repressed and thereby rendering it dormant, or nearly so—similar to what happens when a cover is placed over a fire, leaving the fire to smolder rather than burn. If repression does work by this dual mode of causality, it would be able effectively to contain powerful forces without thereby creating a highly charged posture of containment. For the forces repressed would be reduced to dormancy or left to "smolder" and therefore would cease exerting a strong pressure against the containing countercathexis. The countercathexis, accordingly, would remain in place less to contain the repressed in hydraulic fashion than to keep the repressed in an inactive or nearly inactive state.

Primal repression, I suggest, works in this way. It not only constricts the body against the flow of the power of the Ground; it also, in doing this, deactivates the power of the Ground, leaving it to smolder. Primal repression, as a countercathectic "cap," allows only so much power to "combust" as is needed to fuel psychic processes and otherwise restricts the power of the Ground to a dormant sexual organization as libido. Like the genie in the magic lamp, the power of the Ground goes to sleep and lies in wait to be reawakened at a later time.

It follows from this analysis that primal repression is a countercathectic structure aimed against a potential rather than an actual force. Once primal repression is in place, the power of the Ground is for the most part deactivated and ceases challenging primal repression. Primal repression therefore remains in place, like the cap on the magic lamp, not so much, hydraulically, to contain an actual force as, preventively, to keep a dormant force from becoming active again. In this way, I suggest, primal repression exists as a deeply embedded and invisible infrastructure of the mental-egoic system.

As a physical structure, primal repression entails a chronic activation of the defensive posture of the body. Instead of being relaxed, erect, and open, the body is tensed, stooped, and closed. It is tensed in seeming readiness to respond to danger; it is stooped with a knotted anal sphincter and diaphragm and with hunched shoulders; and, braced in these ways, it is closed to what otherwise would be a free and continuous flow of psychic energy. This overall stance is functional in situations when the organism faces an external threat. So, for example, the body ego contracts in this manner when confronted with something frightening or dangerous. For the mental ego, however, this bodily stance has become permanent, indeed petrified, buried, and forgotten. In more or less exaggerated form, it has become an acquired structure of the body, which, as such, is unconscious. And the cause of this permanent defensive posture is not any external danger; it is rather a constant *inner* threat: the power of the Dynamic Ground. The mental ego is ossified in a closed defensive posture in response to the power of the Dynamic Ground.

Among the bodily defenses that can be included in the overall structure of primal repression are (1) a tight sphincter and diaphragm, (2) muscular contractions in the chest and upper arms, (3) a pelvis tilted forward with buttocks tucked in, (4) tension in the shoulders, which frequently are stooped or else drawn up into the neck, and (5) a zone of tightness at the back of the neck and base of the skull. These strata of rigidity are the focus of *hatha yoga* and other therapeutic approaches to the body, such as, for example, Reichian body work and the body therapies associated with such names as Alexander Lowen, F. Matthias Alexander, Moshe Feldenkrais, and Ida Rolf.[7]

Although all of these bodily defenses belong together as a group, some, it should be noted, are more forms of contraction from interpersonal intimacy (armored chest, hunched shoulders) than they are layers of resistance to the inner power of the Ground (tightened anal sphincter and diaphragm). The reason for this difference of focus is that primal repression, as we know, is at the same time primal alienation: the overall postural set by which the mental ego closes itself to the Dynamic Ground is at the same time the stance by which the mental ego retreats from others. Notwithstanding this bidirectionality, however, the postural set as a whole is a single defensive system. Although some of the structures of this system have more of an internal focus and others more of an external focus, all of the structures work together to defensively insulate the mental ego. They are all part of an overall stance of defensive containment (of inner energy) and retreat (from outer danger).

The physical infrastructure of primal repression assumes the character of an acquired structure of the body. As such, the layers of tension, constriction, and armoring making up this structure become part of the (prepersonal) *embedded unconscious*.[8] The defensive posture of the body is a constant of the mental ego's experience. The mental ego, therefore, is habituated to it and fails to notice it as a possible object for consciousness. Only in unusual circumstances is one or another aspect of this complex stance thrown into relief. For example, experiences of extreme relaxation can, by sheer contrast, reveal some of the ways in which the body is ordinarily rigid or tense, and experiences of exceptional physical resilience and buoyancy (such as occasionally occur during inspired performances in athletics or dance) can, also by contrast, reveal ways in which the body is ordinarily tight or locked. Also, as we shall see in chapter 7, the postural set of primal repression can be thrust into awareness during regression in the service of transcendence when the power of the Dynamic Ground, in reawakening, asserts itself against the repressive barriers that hitherto had contained and quieted it.

THE PERSONAL UNCONSCIOUS

The personal unconscious consists of a great number of different elements. The usual definition stipulates that the personal unconscious includes everything that, in being unconscious, is biographical or person specific, that is, is a consequence of or in some way reflects a person's individual history. This definition is useful but not entirely accurate, because in most accounts, including the one that follows, the personal unconscious includes as well cultural introjects and perhaps even inherited structures that are universal in scope. The usual definition, therefore, is not sufficiently broad.

Another definition is that the personal unconscious consists of all those things that, in being unconscious, are constitutive of the ego or the egoic system. This definition makes room for the social and inherited structures just alluded to, but it fails to include many unconscious materials that are merely individual or person specific in character, for example, subliminal stimuli and many complexes and highly charged systems of condensed experience (COEX systems, to be explained). This definition, then, is also too narrow.

Fortunately, the shortcomings of these two definitions can be overcome simply by combining them. Let us then define the personal unconscious as the class of all those materials (contents, structures, faculties, systems, operations) that, in being unconscious, are either (1) person specific or (2) constitutive of the ego or egoic system.

Proceeding on the basis of this definition, the personal unconscious can be divided into the *submerged* and the *embedded* personal unconscious.[9] The personal submerged unconscious encompasses all the materials that are repressed, screened, or otherwise made invisible by the limiting effects of egoic structures (operations, mechanisms). The personal embedded unconscious on the other hand consists of just these structures themselves. The distinction is a simple one: repressed contents require repressing mechanisms or barriers and screened materials require screening filters—and both sides of these parings are unconscious, though for different reasons. The repressed and screened materials are unconscious because they are barred from awareness by the exclusionary effects of repressing and screening structures. And these structures are themselves unconscious because they are (1) pre-

TABLE 5.3

The Personal Unconscious

Personal embedded unconscious*	Filtering structures and operations Autonomous complexes COEX systems Ego identity Defense mechanisms
Personal submerged unconscious*	Subthreshold signals Filtered stimuli Shadow Deeply repressed materials

* Wilber's (1980a) term.

supposed and therefore merely tacit structures that, in many cases, are (2) constitutive of the mental ego as subject of consciousness and therefore unavailable to it as objects of consciousness. The submerged unconscious and the embedded unconscious are correlatives. As a rule, one cannot be unconscious without the other also being unconscious; and on those occasions when one of the two, for whatever reason, is disclosed to awareness, the other, too, in principle becomes available to consciousness.

In treating the personal unconscious, I shall follow the order set forth in table 5.1, beginning with the personal embedded unconscious. The relevant section of table 5.1 is here reproduced as table 5.3.

THE PERSONAL EMBEDDED UNCONSCIOUS

Embedded structures (operations, mechanisms), as just noted, are unconscious because they are presupposed by consciousness. In being presupposed, embedded structures are invisible because they are in the background rather than foreground of consciousness. They are patterns or modes of experiencing that either have always been in the background of consciousness or have receded into the background because consciousness has habituated to them and therefore lost sight of them. As a rule, only new or unusual stimuli attract attention. In contrast, stimuli that are always or repeatedly present do not attract attention. They are merely implicit grounds. Embedded structures, I suggest, are just such implicit grounds—and so they must remain until such time, if ever, as their usual mode of expression is altered sufficiently to make them, in effect, new stimuli.

Many embedded structures are also unconscious because they are instruments of, rather than possible objects for, the mental ego's awareness. That is, they are structures *by means of which* the mental ego is conscious and therefore are not themselves things of which the mental ego might become aware. Ken Wilber makes this point. He says:

> At each level of development, one cannot totally see the seer. No observing structure can observe itself observing. One uses the structures of that level as something with which to perceive and translate the world—but one cannot perceive and translate those structures *themselves,* not totally. . . . The point is that each translation process sees but is not seen; it translates, but is not itself translated; *and it can repress* [or screen], *but is not itself repressed* [or screened]. (1980a, p.89)

In short, many embedded structures (operations, mechanisms) are forms *of* a subject and therefore cannot be objects *for* that subject.

Filtering structures. Embedded structures that filter or screen experience are of many types. Included among such structures are (1) acquired habits and dispositions of all sorts, (2) autonomous complexes and systems of condensed experience (COEX systems, to be discussed), (3) introjected cultural assumptions and values, and, perhaps, (4) certain inherited patterns governing language and cognition.

All of these types of embedded structures are examples of predetermined ways in which the mental ego, unbeknownst to itself, organizes or interprets experience. As such, they belong to the unconscious, specifically the personal embedded unconscious. All of these types of structures are similar not only in being embedded but also in having a selective focus or scope: they cue only on specific stimuli or specific ranges of stimuli. In having a selective focus or scope, these structures have a *limited* focus or scope, a focus or scope that excludes (screens, filters) as well as includes. The manner in which filtering structures exclude things from awareness and the specific types of materials that they exclude will be treated in the section on the personal submerged unconscious. The point to be made here is that filtering structures not only exclude things from awareness, relegating them to the personal submerged unconscious, but are themselves invisible to awareness—because they are presupposed by consciousness and, in some cases, because they are instruments rather than objects of consciousness.

Autonomous complexes. By autonomous complexes of the personal embedded unconscious I mean to designate ingrained patterns of response that have their origin usually either in a traumatic episode or in what might be called unfinished business (i.e., an abrupt halting of an important life experience or stage prior to closure or fulfillment). In the case of a trauma-induced complex, it frequently happens that both the exaggerated response routine that results from the trauma and the trauma itself are in large measure unconscious, the former because it is embedded, the latter because it is repressed. In the case of "unfinished business," in contrast, it is usually only the resulting complex that is unconscious—although, of course, the triggering episode (e.g., premature weaning or enforcement of rules of anal or genital propriety, imposition of a gender stereotype) may long since have been forgotten. Traumatic experiences typically cause negative fixations or blind spots and corresponding hostile or fearful, fight-or-flight reaction routines. "Unfinished business," in contrast, typically causes fixations on the satisfiers of unmet (usually infantile) needs and compulsive behavior with respect to those satisfiers or their adult surrogates. These fixations, blind spots, reactions, and compulsions are for the most part embedded and unconscious. Their more dramatic manifestations are of course quite evident, but most of their more subtle forms are completely invisible, at least to the person who suffers from them.

COEX systems. Stanislav Grof (1975) has introduced the highly useful notion of a COEX system, which is an abbreviation for *system of condensed experience.* A COEX system is a web of highly charged memories, meanings, and behaviors that are associated with a particular type of life experience. The key to the concept is that the first (or at least an early) instance of any type of experience, if it happens to be sufficiently impressive in a negative or positive way, tends to become the defining instance of all subsequent experiences of that type. Autonomous complexes can be considered examples of COEX systems, because the pattern of perception, feeling, and behavior distinctive of a complex is determined by the traumatic or unfinished character of the original experience from which the complex derives. Complexes, however, constitute only a small subclass of COEX systems. The notion of a COEX system has a wide extension; it includes all embedded structures that are products of a primary or core experience. No restrictions are placed on the nature or quality of the core experience, which can be negative or positive, unfinished or powerfully satisfying. The only character of the core experience that is required for it to be the ground of a COEX system is that it have a sufficient impact on a person to establish a highly defined preconception of and response to later experiences of the same kind.

Ego identity. Ego identity, or the self-concept, has already been treated in some detail. The reader is referred to the discussion in chapter 4 and to the discussion of the shadow in the section on the personal submerged unconscious, below.

Defense mechanisms. Examples of ego defense mechanisms are repression, projection, reaction formation, rationalization, intellectualization, and denial. All of these strategies of defense are employed unconsciously by the mental ego to ward off or transform thoughts or feelings that are threatening to it. Although many defense mechanisms are merely defensive, some are genuinely adaptive, as was originally suggested by Anna Freud in her classic *The Ego and the Mechanisms of Defense* (1936). Moreover, as Heinz Hartmann argued long ago, some of the ego's defensive strategies can, in their adaptive aspect, even assume a significant degree of independence from their original defensive function. Explaining this point, he says:

> An attitude which arose originally in the service of defense against an instinctual drive may, in the course of time, become an independent structure, in which case the instinctual drive merely triggers this automatized apparatus, but, as long as the automatization is not controverted, does not determine the details of its action. Such an apparatus may, as a relatively independent structure, come to serve other functions (adaptation, synthesis, etc.); it may also—and this is genetically of even broader significance—through a change of function turn from a means into a goal in its own right. (1939, p. 26)

Defense mechanisms, therefore, need not be merely defensive. They can also be coping mechanisms that are genuinely adaptive and, in some cases, at least partially independent of their initial defensive purpose.

The most important among the defense mechanisms are repression, projection, and sublimation. Each of these mechanisms can operate independently or in conjunction with one or more of the others. The mental ego, for example, might repress a shadow element, but perhaps not so completely as to keep it from being projected onto others and, to a certain extent, expressed in sublimated form within consciousness. For example, a person might be strongly identified with being independent. This identification could lead the person to repress the desire to be cared for by others—which desire, in being repressed, would be relegated to the shadow (discussed below). If the desire is repressed and relegated to the shadow, it would likely also be projected onto others, who would therefore be seen as weaker and more needy than they really are. In addition, the desire might be transformed or sublimated in some way that would render it compatible with the person's identity and therefore at least partially expressible within consciousness. The person might find a compartmentalized sphere of life in which to confess dependence and need of others while in all other spheres maintaining just the opposite stance. Religion is a possible sphere for such an outlet to occur. Perhaps the person would adopt a religious orientation stressing such elements as creaturely dependence, divine providence, and salvation through faith or grace.

THE PERSONAL SUBMERGED UNCONSCIOUS

The personal submerged unconscious consists of all of the materials excluded from awareness by embedded structures (operations, mechanisms). The personal submerged unconscious is the underside of the personal embedded unconscious. It consists of everything that is screened or repressed by filtering structures, autonomous complexes, COEX systems, features of ego identity, and defense mechanisms.

Subthreshold signals. Subthreshold signals, unlike all other contents of the personal submerged unconscious, are not excluded from awareness by embedded structures. They are, rather, excluded simply because they are too faint to impress themselves upon consciousness. Subthreshold signals are signals that arise and disappear without being detected either because they lie below the threshold of sensitivity of perceptual or cognitive "instruments" or because they are drowned out by the "noise" of ongoing psychomental activity.

Little need be said in support of the existence of subthreshold signals. The phenomenon of subliminal perception has been extensively researched, and its practical importance is quite obvious, especially to those who exploit it for purposes of advertising or propaganda. Subthreshold perception, however, is not the only type of subthreshold experience; also to be included under this description are internal bodily sensations and many contents of the psychomental flux or stream of consciousness. The body is constantly emitting signals, many of which are filtered or repressed by specific embedded structures, and some of which, it seems, are simply too faint to be noticed above the "noise" of usual egoic consciousness. Moreover, the ongoing stream of consciousness contains many elements that, owing to their low intensity, do not impress themselves upon the observing mind. It sounds paradoxical to say that there might be (unscreened, unrepressed) contents of mind that are not noticed by the mind. Paradoxical or not, however, this possibility seems actually to be the case—as is attested by many practitioners of meditation.[10] Practitioners of meditation report that during meditation consciousness becomes progressively more sensitive and begins to discern materials that before were present but undetected.

Filtered stimuli. Filtering structures, as we learned earlier, are structures that have a selective and therefore limited focus or scope. They are structures that not only include but exclude as well. For every stimulus that filtering structures select to be an object of awareness, there are many other stimuli that are rendered invisible or are barred from awareness. Filtering structures, therefore, are not only templates by which things are thrown into relief but also Procrustean beds by which things are excised from view. The major types of embedded filtering structures are, again, (1) acquired habits and dispositions of all sorts, (2) autonomous complexes and COEX systems, (3) introjected cultural assumptions and values, and, perhaps, (4) certain inherited patterns governing language and cognition.

Almost everyone is aware of how acquired habits and dispositions can work to narrow the range of experience. Acquired habits and dispositions are routines that regularly respond to the same stimuli in the same ways. Once such tendencies are triggered, everything that falls outside their established routines is ignored. This exclusion of "irrelevant" stimuli occurs not only in the case of conspicuous tendencies such as reflex emotional reactions and flagrant biases or prejudices but also in the case of very subtle tendencies of all kinds. In fact, subtle tendencies screen more pervasively than do conspicuous tendencies, because subtle tendencies are usually very global, whereas conspicuous tendencies are usually very specific in their foci and effects. For example, the proneness to pessimistic thinking, which is exceedingly subtle, cuts across the whole spectrum of experience, selecting negative cues and screening positive ones, whereas a more conspicuous habitual reaction such as stereotypical-prejudicial thinking of a particular sort (such as sexist or racist thinking) has a much narrower target, which it selects and screens in a highly defined way. In sum, acquired habits and dispositions are regularities by which experience is edited in an automatic manner that highlights (and sometimes exaggerates or fabricates) one dimension of experience while relegating other dimensions to obscurity or invisibility.

Cultural introjects such as basic social assumptions and values play an even larger role in editing experience. The socially transmitted worldview is a matrix of meanings that, in mediating between a person and the world, works to disclose certain aspects of experience and veil others. Alternative worldviews present alternative interpretations of experience, each one bringing certain aspects of things into focus while obscuring or excluding many other aspects. A socially acquired worldview is, then, a shared interpretive structure that gives shape and meaning to experience and that, in doing so, has the limiting consequence of restricting experience within definite boundaries. Or more accurately, a worldview is an interpretive structure that has this limiting consequence for all who are bound—that is, unconsciously committed—to it. From the perspective of an *embedded* worldview, then, the world as experienced *is* the world; the limits of the embedded unconscious are the limits of the world.

Some filtering structures may be inherited rather than acquired. The Jungian archetypes, for example, are inherited filtering structures—although they, deriving from the nonegoic pole of the psyche, are not part of the personal unconscious. Other possible examples of inherited filtering structures are (egoic-personal) structures governing language and conceptual-operational thought. The possibility of such structures has been debated throughout the history of philosophy and is strongly affirmed in the rationalist tradition in philosophy (Plato, Descartes, Leibniz, Kant, Chomsky). In recent decades the possibility of inherited cognitive structures has been explored by structuralist and cognitivist schools in anthropology, linguistics, and psychology. Also, psychoanalytic ego psychology holds that the ego is born with autonomous functions and "apparatuses" that allow it to test reality and effectively engage the world.

Unlike other filtering structures, inherited filtering structures, if such structures exist, are "hard wired": they are part of the human neurological apparatus and are therefore necessary rather than optional structures. They are structures to which human cognition is bound rather than structures that might be replaced by other structures that would provide an alternative organization or interpretation of experience. Accordingly, whatever might be screened by inherited filtering structures is irretrievably beyond the reach of human cognitive capacity. To use Kant's (1787) expression, things screened by inherited filtering structures are "things in themselves" (*Dinge an sich*), things inherently undetectable by human cognition. Acquired habits and dispositions and embedded cultural assumptions and values can be disembedded and replaced by other structures, thereby bringing into relief aspects of the world that otherwise would go unrecognized. Such a possibility, however, does not exist in the case of inherited structures. For although it is possible in principle to disembed and disengage inherited structures, it is not possible, given their "hard-wired" status, to replace them. The only possible alternative to organizing or interpreting experience according to inherited structures is not to organize or interpret experience at all. The only possible alternative is to abandon all attempts to bring order and meaning to experience and to open the mind in a wholly (but also merely) receptive manner. Many people have suggested that just such a receptively open state is at the basis of mystical experience, given the suspension of thought and the transcendence of the subject-object division that are characteristic of that experience.

The shadow. The shadow is the negative underside of the mental ego's identity or self-concept. The mental ego has a vested interest in seeing itself in a certain way, namely, as possessing those features that enter into its identity project. The mental ego's sense of being and value is based on the features of its identity. Accordingly, the mental ego is prone to dissociate itself from everything about itself that is incompatible with its identity. The elements of the mental ego's larger self that are alienated in this way coalesce as the shadow, the unconscious psychic subsystem containing the dark and disowned dimensions of the personality.

Although virtually all of the features of a person's identity are a product of an intersection of that person's unique personality with society's common roles and categories, some features owe more to the individual person than to society and others owe more to society than to the individual person. That is, some features are more nearly specific to the person, whereas others approach being stereotypical, reflective of dominant cultural patterns. And what is true in this way of identity is true also of the shadow, because the contents of the shadow are determined by the features of identity. The shadow therefore also contains some elements that are more distinctive of the individual person and others that are more representative of the larger culture.

Among those contents of the identity-shadow system that represent cultural patterns, two in particular deserve comment, namely, those that derive from the cultural paradigms of maturity and gender.

Every society has an implicit definition of maturity. Every society operates with a set of expectations that are imposed upon children to make them "shape up" and act as adult members of the society are "supposed to act." A certain set of attitudes and behaviors is prescribed as a condition of being accepted as a full member of the group. Identification with this set of attitudes and behaviors naturally results; the set is introjected and becomes a part of a person's ego identity or self-concept. Such an adoption of the social definition of maturity has two primary consequences: on the one hand, it promotes what a society considers to be responsible behavior; on the other hand, however, it requires that people repress those parts of themselves that are deemed immature according to the prevailing standard. These parts of the personality, in being repressed, are relegated to the shadow. In Gestalt therapy these dissociated elements are referred to as the "Underdog." As a group, they include all the "childish" impulses that importune the mental ego, whining at it and tempting it to drop its responsibilities and pursue such courses as those of pleasure, laziness, rebellion, and the like.

The cultural norms governing gender also play a large role in the formation of identity and therefore in the formation of the shadow. Males, in identifying with the cultural definition of masculinity, at the same time alienate those parts of themselves that, according to that definition, are feminine. And women, in identifying with the cultural definition of femininity, at the same time alienate those parts of themselves that, according to that definition, are masculine. Masculine identities beget feminine shadows; feminine identities beget masculine shadows. Men and women, then, typically have a contrasexual component to their (personal) unconscious.

I added the parenthetical qualification because the contrasexual elements of the shadow should be distinguished from the archetypal *anima* and *animus*, which we referred to earlier in the discussion of the instinctual-archetypal unconscious. The archetypal *anima* and *animus*, as Jung explained, are *inherited* structures that govern our sense of what it means to be a woman or a man.[11] These archetypal structures no doubt determine to a significant extent the character of cultural norms of masculinity and femininity. The fact remains, however, that cultural norms governing gender differ significantly from society to society and in their turn have a formative influence on the psyche. Accordingly, I think it is best to distinguish between the archetypal *anima* and *animus*, which are innate, and the contrasexual elements of the shadow, which are culturally acquired. The former belong to the archetypal-instinctual unconscious, the latter to the personal submerged unconscious.

"Immature" impulses and contrasexual elements of the personality are but two types of elements belonging to the shadow. The shadow also contains many other elements, some of which are more stereotypical and others of which are more distinctive of the individual. The shadow is a highly complex mental-egoic subsystem; it includes a vast number of personality fragments, half-formed alter egos, each of which in an unguarded moment is capable of rising up and taking possession of the whole person.

Despite its threatening aspect, the shadow is not inherently negative or evil. Many of its elements, although contraconventional, are intrinsically positive. For example, the contrasexual elements of the shadow, as Jung has shown, are essential ingredients of human wholeness; and some of the "immature" impulses belonging to the shadow are refreshingly childlike rather than merely childish. The shadow, then, contains many elements that are potentially positive. Many of its elements, although proscribed by the mental ego, would, if integrated, enlarge and enrich the conscious personality.

In being disowned, the elements of the shadow are projected upon others. The mental ego for this reason tends to exaggerate those features in others that correspond to parts of its own shadow. These features function as threatening stimuli to the mental ego, which fixates on them and reacts to them in excessive fashion. The mental ego is prone to see things in a selective and exaggerated way, because its shadow is a distorting lens through which it apprehends the world. The shadow stands between the mental ego and the world. Wherever the mental ego goes, the shadow is always projected one step ahead; and whomever the mental ego meets, it is in some ways meeting only the other side of itself.

No clear line separates the more strongly repressed parts of the shadow and deeper, prepersonal levels of the unconscious. For all of the prepersonal unconscious falls outside the scope of the mental ego's identity or self-concept and therefore lies within the farthest reach of the shadow. The shadow, then, although belonging to the personal unconscious, extends beyond the personal unconscious into prepersonal realms.

Deeply repressed materials. The most deeply buried materials of the personal submerged unconscious are those that have their origin in serious abuse or trauma during early childhood. Physical, sexual, or emotional abuse and terrifying experiences such as being abandoned cause grave psychic injury. To survive, the child must cover over the wound in its soul and attempt to deny the reality of its experience. The child must cut itself off from much of itself and live in a dissociated fantasy realm. The consequence of this survival strategy is that powerful feelings and memories are lost to consciousness. They are buried at the very bottom of the personal submerged unconscious.

CONCLUSION

The unconscious has a complex structure. It has prepersonal, personal, and transpersonal levels and submerged and embedded dimensions. The prepersonal unconscious, in its submerged dimension, consists of the Dynamic Ground, the instinctual-archetypal unconscious, and the body unconscious. These levels of the unconscious are prepersonal because they represent the nonegoic pole of the psyche as it was repressed and disjoined from consciousness during early childhood. These levels represent the lost experience of the body ego. Also, these levels, in being prepersonal, are more specifically part of the prepersonal *submerged* unconscious because they are buried beneath consciousness by primal repression—which itself belongs to the prepersonal *embedded* unconscious.

The personal unconscious consists of innumerable embedded structures and corresponding submerged contents: filtering structures (habitual patterns of thought and perception, complexes, COEX systems, cultural introjects) and corresponding filtered stimuli, features of ego identity and corresponding shadow elements, defense mechanisms and corresponding threatening materials. Most of the personal unconscious is biographical or acquired; most of the personal unconscious is laid down or submerged during a person's lifetime. Some structures of the personal embedded unconscious, however, may be inherited, for example, basic cognitive structures and ego functions.

The transpersonal levels of the unconscious are possibilities of experience that come into play only after primal repression has been lifted and the potentials of the nonegoic pole of the psyche have been liberated from their prepersonal submerged organization. The lifting of primal repression reawakens nonegoic potentials, including most importantly the power of the Dynamic Ground. The ego begins to experience the upwelling of nonegoic life directly within the sphere of consciousness. At first, the ego is seriously disturbed by the resurgence of nonegoic potentials. Eventually, however, the ego is purged of its resistances to nonegoic life and begins to experience nonegoic potentials in their "trans-" character. In particular, the ego begins to experience the power of the Ground as a spiritual power that redemptively transforms the ego and enriches all dimensions of its experience. The nonegoic pole of the psyche remains unfathomable and unpredictable even after primal repression has been lifted. Once primal repression has been eliminated and integration achieved, however, the nonegoic pole becomes a wellspring of higher life rather than a dark and threatening submerged realm. It ceases being the deep unconscious and becomes the fertile void.

6

Meditation: The Royal Road to the Unconscious

FREUD, AS IS WELL known, spoke of dreams as the royal road (*via regia*) to the unconscious. Long before Freud, Patanjali spoke of meditation as the royal yoga (*raja yoga*), the royal road to union with the higher self.[1] Both dreams and meditation are pathways to the unconscious and thereby, ultimately, to integration. In this chapter, I shall consider the case of meditation and try to explain why it can be an effective means of self-exploration and self-transformation.

A DEFINITION OF MEDITATION

In Eastern spiritual traditions, two main types of meditation are widely practiced, whether separately or in conjunction. These are, first, receptive mindfulness leading to insight and, second, concentrative practices leading to absorption. The primary example of the first of these types is the insight (*vipassana*) meditation of Buddhism, and the primary example of the second type is the yoga meditation of Patanjali's *Yoga Sutras*. For our purposes, I shall refer to the former of these types as receptive meditation (RM for short) and the latter type as concentrative meditation (CM for short).

RM is the practice of sustained nonselective alertness. In practicing RM, the meditator maintains the stance of an open and unmoving witness. Whatever emerges in or before the mind is observed with alert attention but not in any way acted upon or reacted to. The images, feelings, and thoughts that present themselves to consciousness are witnessed uninterruptedly and with full consciousness but without in any way being engaged or pursued. In RM, the meditator emulates the character of a polished mirror, which reflects objects clearly and without becoming involved with them. Contents of consciousness are allowed to arise and disappear without any interference from the meditator, who remains a clear and steadfast witness, and *only* a witness. In addition to the mindfulness-insight meditation of Buddhism, an important example of RM is found in the "just-sitting" (*shikantaza*) form of meditation (*zazen*) in Zen.

CM is in one respect the complete opposite of RM. For whereas RM, as "mirror consciousness," is completely nonselective in focus, CM maintains a singularity of focus. CM selects a specific object, image, idea, or other reference point and focuses undivided attention upon it. According to Patanjali, whose *Yoga Sutras* (Aranya 1983; Feuerstein 1979) is the classic text on CM, CM practice can be divided into three stages: *dharana* (concentration), *dhyana* (meditation), and *samadhi* (absorption). *Dharana* is the attempt on the part of the meditator to maintain alert attention upon the chosen object, and, as such, it involves a struggle against tendencies toward distraction and drowsiness. *Dhyana* is achieved when these two problems are surmounted; it consists of a steady, easy flowing of consciousness to the chosen object. Finally, *samadhi* occurs when, after sustained practice, subject-object separation disappears and the subject becomes absorbed in the object. The subject at this point becomes totally immersed in the object and is therefore completely unselfconscious. Phenomenologically, all that exists at this point is the object as illumined by and revealed to consciousness. Also, although *samadhi* is initially achieved with an object, the possibility exists of achieving and maintaining the state without a supporting object (*asamprajnata samadhi*). Such an objectless *samadhi* is still a state of illumined absorption, but it is one that, in addition to being selfless (i.e., unselfconscious), is objectless as well. In addition to Patanjali's *raja yoga*, major examples of CM are the *jhana* (absorption) meditations of original Buddhism, the elaborate visualization meditations of Tibetan Buddhism, and the *koan* exercises of Zen.

In addition to differing in having either an open or a fixed focus, RM and CM differ in that CM leads to absorbed states whereas, according to most accounts, RM does not.[2] RM and CM no doubt differ in other ways as well. Despite their differences, however, RM and CM share a common nature in that both are forms of attention that, held fast, do not act upon or adopt any stance or posture toward experience. RM—to follow a description provided by Zen master Yasutani-roshi (Kapleau 1967, p. 53)—requires that the meditator be as openly alert as a swordsman in battle while at the same time being as still as Mount Fuji. And CM requires that the meditator focus a pure beam of consciousness upon the chosen object, alertly witnessing the object without in any way manipulating it or bringing preestablished structures or meanings to bear upon it. In both RM and CM the mind is supposed to be both stationary and free of all mediating sets, postures, lenses, and filters. Given that RM and CM are alike in these ways, meditation can be defined as the practice of *unmoving and unmediated attention*.

MEDITATION AND PRAYER

Although meditation and prayer are frequently contrasted in a sharp way, they clearly have much in common. Indeed, prayer can be considered a type of meditation, because it satisfies the definition of meditation just set forth. Prayer requires both stillness and complete presence and is therefore a type of unmoving and unmediated attention. Accordingly, rather than ask how prayer differs from meditation, it may be more appropriate to ask how it differs from other *types* of meditation. And the answer to this question, it seems, is that prayer is distinctive (1) in assuming the existence of a superior reality to which prayer is ultimately addressed, a reality that is somehow responsive to prayer, and (2) in adopting an attitude of reverent entreaty or surrender toward this reality. Prayer, then, I suggest, is a species of meditation that stands apart from other species by virtue of the ontological assumptions that underlie it and the affective or attitudinal posture that pervades it.

The fact that prayer is addressed to a higher reality does not mean that all types of prayer are therefore types of CM. For the superior reality to which prayer is addressed, although the ultimate goal of prayer, is rarely the immediate "object" of prayer. Most people who pray are religious *seekers*, people for whom the divine is less a discernible presence upon which consciousness might focus than it is an absence that needs to be filled, an unknown "not-there" to be beckoned through an attitude of supplication or surrender. Despite having the divine as its ultimate "object," then, prayer is not necessarily a concentrative exercise. Prayer can take the form of either RM or CM. Either of these two forms of meditation can be used as a way of beckoning the divine.

Types of prayer that can be considered RM practices are all those that, in adopting the attitude of reverent supplication or surrender, do not thereby attach themselves to any particular image or idea of divine reality. No form or figure of a god or god-representative, nor any divine attribute, nor any particular motif or datum of religion (e.g., a verse, symbol, icon) is specifically addressed. Rather, the person practicing this kind of prayer remains choicelessly aware of all that enters experience, whether this person is situated in the arena of action or in anchoritic isolation. The person practicing RM prayer makes no effort to keep anything in mind or to banish anything from mind; all effort is devoted exclusively to awaiting the "presencing" of the divine. This kind of prayer is therefore altogether without position taking and object preference; nothing is singled out as a matter of primary regard or avoidance. Rather, everything is witnessed equally and disinterestedly; each thing is allowed to come and go as it will. The only constant is the posture of supplicatory, surrendered openness.

A prime example of such receptive prayer in the Roman Catholic tradition is the prayer of recollection. Described by St. Teresa of Avila in *The Interior Castle* and *The Way of Perfection*, the prayer of recollection is a sustained posture of nondiscursive receptivity to the Holy Spirit.[3] It consists of a state of inner poise and quiet in which, typically without attention being given to any particular figure or form, the person in prayer waits, vigilantly and without interruption, to be touched by spiritual power. It consists of a naked receptivity of the soul, an empty openness that invites the influx of the Holy Spirit. Teresa at times speaks of recollection as a state achieved by the meditator (later called *acquired recollection*) and at times speaks of it as a state into which the meditator is drawn by divine power (later called *infused recollection*). Whichever of these interpretations is followed, it is clear that the prayer of recollection is a state that no longer (like *dharana* or beginning mindfulness) struggles against drowsiness or distraction. Recollection is a state of gathered, poised openness to spiritual power.

Prayers that can be counted as instances of CM are all those that focus devotional attention on a theme or object of religious significance, for example, a scriptural reading, mantra, icon, symbol, theological idea, or thought or visualization of a deity, savior, or saint. All such practices typically observe the three stages that are characteristic of CM generally: *dharana, dhyana,* and *samadhi.*

For example, according to the Roman Catholic tradition, the path to contemplation begins with discursive meditation, which is similar to Patanjali's *dharana.* Discursive meditation differs from *dharana* in that it probes the meaning of the theme or symbol to which the meditation is addressed. Discursive meditation, however, is otherwise like *dharana* in that it keeps attention tethered to a specific point of reference and, in doing so, frequently must struggle against drowsiness or distraction. Following discursive meditation, the second stage of contemplative practice is the prayer of recollection. Although this prayer is typically a form of RM, it can also be practiced in the manner of CM. The gathered receptivity characteristic of recollection can be either a wide-aperture receptivity after the fashion of RM or a focused receptivity—a dwelling upon an object that embodies or channels spiritual power—after the fashion of CM. When practiced in this latter way, the prayer of recollection is similar in important respects to Patanjali's *dhyana*, because, like *dhyana*, it is a form of easily sustained and smoothly flowing focused consciousness that no longer struggles against drowsiness or distraction. Finally, the third stage of contemplative practice—which is the stage of contemplation proper—is the stage of infused contemplation. This stage corresponds to Patanjali's *samadhi*, because, like *samadhi*, infused contemplation transcends the subject-object division. In both infused contemplation and *samadhi*, the meditating subject becomes unselfconsciously immersed in experience. The first two stages of CM prayer include both a subject and an object; the subject beckons the divine by giving undivided attention to a sacred object. Infused contemplation, however, like *samadhi*, no longer involves a subject attending to an object. For the subject, in being infused, becomes absorbed, either in the object of prayer or in spiritual power itself.

I have given special attention to prayer as a form of meditation for two primary reasons. The first is to combat the sharp distinction between Eastern meditation and Western prayer that has been drawn by many Western churches since the influx of Eastern spiritual practices into the West during the 1960s and 1970s. Many Western churches have gone out of their way to stress the differences between Eastern meditation and Western prayer, sometimes going so far as to claim that forms of Eastern meditation are not forms of spiritual practice at all. This stress on difference has not been helpful. According to the foregoing account, meditation and prayer are sibling species of a single genus. They are both practices of unmoving and unmediated attention, and they both unfold through the same basic sequence of stages. Moreover, as we shall see, they both have similar effects upon the psyche, accessing the unconscious in much the same way.

The second reason why I have given special attention to prayer is that different transpersonal paradigms have different implications about the types of spiritual practices to be pursued. Take for example the two paradigms discussed in chapter 1, the dynamic-dialectical paradigm, on which this book is based, and the structural-hierarchical paradigm as formulated by Ken Wilber. Of these two paradigms, the dynamic-dialectical paradigm is clearly the one that would more likely recommend that meditation be practiced in the form of prayer. The dynamic-dialectical paradigm leans in this direction because, in placing

the ego in relation to the Dynamic Ground, this paradigm sees meditation, whether RM or CM, as a practice by which the ego opens itself and
ultimately reunites itself with a superior reality. That is to say, for the
dynamic-dialectical paradigm, meditation is in a basic sense understood as prayer. In saying this, I of course am not suggesting that prayer
is the only viable or effective (much less morally proper) form of meditation for people whose spirituality is based on the dynamic-dialectical
paradigm. Nor am I suggesting that any specific creedal themes or
images are or are not appropriate in the practice of prayer. My point,
rather, is simply that the dynamic-dialectical paradigm, in placing the
ego in relation to a superior Dynamic Ground, sees meditation as having many of the same relational dynamics as prayer.

The structural-hierarchical paradigm, in contrast, while in no way
excluding prayer, does not so evidently point in the direction of prayer.
Given its conception of the psyche as a hierarchy of structural levels, the
structural-hierarchical paradigm sees meditation as a practice that facilitates a level-by-level ascent through the structural hierarchy. According to Wilber's (1980a, 1990) account, meditation accomplishes this
ascent by loosening the identification that consciousness has with the
current structural level and thereby rendering consciousness receptive
to the influence of the next higher level. For the structural-hierarchical
paradigm, then, meditation is not conceived relationally as an interaction between the ego and a higher spiritual power; it is rather conceived
hierarchically as a process by which consciousness climbs to a higher
structural level. Nothing in the paradigm corresponds to or specifically
suggests the relational presuppositions of prayer.

MEDITATION AND THE UNCONSCIOUS

As is well known, Jung believed that Westerners should avoid Eastern
spiritual practices, including meditation. He felt that these practices,
having evolved in cultures very different from those of the West, are
not suited to Westerners and even pose definite risks to the Western
psyche.[4] In particular, he felt that meditative practices like those of
Indian yoga are inappropriate for Westerners because, in his view, such
practices remain exclusively within the sphere of consciousness and
therefore do not access the unconscious—which, according to Jung, is
the first item on the Westerner's spiritual agenda. For example, speaking of Indian yoga, Jung said:

Yoga technique applies itself exclusively to the conscious mind and will. Such an undertaking promises success only when the unconscious has no potential worth mentioning, that is to say, when it does not contain large portions of the personality. If it does, then all conscious effort remains futile, and what comes out of this cramped condition of mind is a caricature or even the exact opposite of the intended result. (1936, p. 535; CW, 11, par. 871)

According to Jung, meditation is an exercise of the conscious ego that works to strengthen the ego and thereby to increase the "cramp" in the conscious mind.

For Jung, then, meditation is *not* an avenue of access to the unconscious. On the contrary, it is a practice that increases the ego's hold on consciousness. Meditation therefore leads to just the opposite of what Westerners need, Jung believed. Westerners do not need stronger egos; they need to relax their egos and thereby open themselves to the unconscious. Accordingly, in place of meditation, Jung recommended *active imagination* for his Western clients. Active imagination is the practice of allowing images to arise spontaneously from the unconscious. It is a practice that draws upon the autosymbolic process by inviting it to produce images that give symbolic expression to the unconscious. Rather than exercising the ego, as does meditation in Jung's opinion, active imagination opens the ego to creative manifestations from the nonegoic sphere.

Jung's assessment of meditation is, I believe, seriously mistaken. Jung is correct in saying that meditation is an exercise of the conscious ego. Undeniably, the ego is active in taking up the practice of meditation and, in the initial stages of meditation at least, in working hard to achieve unmoving and unmediated attention. If, however, Jung is correct in holding that the ego is active in these ways, he is mistaken, I believe, in proceeding from this fact to the conclusion that meditation works to increase the ego's hold on consciousness. For the conclusion simply does not follow. Logically speaking, other conclusions—even the opposite conclusion—are equally possible. Indeed, I propose, the opposite conclusion is in fact true. In taking up meditation, I suggest, the ego embarks upon a practice that works precisely to *decrease* its hold on consciousness and thereby to open it to the unconscious—completely contrary to what Jung believed.

Meditation works to decrease the ego's hold on consciousness because, as the practice of *unmoving* attention, it has the effect of bringing a halt to the ego's activities and, as the practice of *unmediated* attention, it has the effect of disengaging the ego's embedded structures. Meditation, then, although an act on the part of the ego, is an act of "not-doing" and "undoing" rather than of "doing." In attempting to be an unmoving and unmediated witness, the ego undertakes to cease its activities and to suspend or release its ingrained patterns of relating to experience. Rather than acting upon experience or bringing any structure to bear upon experience, the meditating ego undertakes fully but also *merely* to attend, whether with mirrorlike attention (RM) or laser-like attention (CM). Meditation, then, is not a way in which the ego takes consciousness more firmly in its grasp. On the contrary, it is a way in which the ego releases consciousness from its grasp. Meditation *is* an act on the part of the ego, but it is a negative act. It is the act of *discontinuing* ongoing activities and *letting go* embedded mediating structures. It is therefore an act that "uncramps" rather than "cramps" consciousness, an act, consequently, that opens rather than closes the ego to the unconscious.

The specific way in which meditation reveals the unconscious can be described as follows. Meditation, as an act of "not-doing" and "undoing," inhibits egoic activities and loosens embedded structures; consequently, it (1) draws attention to those activities and structures, thereby exposing them to consciousness, and (2) arrests or disengages those activities and structures, thereby opening consciousness to materials they had excluded from awareness. Hence, meditation, as an act of "not-doing" and "undoing," works both to throw light on egoic activities and embedded structures and, in time, to uncover materials filtered or repressed by them.[5]

This accessing of the unconscious typically unfolds in an ordered sequential manner. First, meditation applies a brake to the ego's ongoing activities (operational cognition, active volition, internal dialogue), thus bringing those activities into clearer focus and exposing to view elements of experience that those activities otherwise obscure. Second, meditation progressively disengages layers of the embedded unconscious (ingrained sets and stances, preestablished cognitive programs and filters, ego armors and defense mechanisms), thus throwing those layers into relief and eventually unscreening or derepressing the corresponding elements of the personal submerged unconscious. And third, meditation progressively loosens primal repression, thus drawing attention to that deep psychosomatic structure and preparing the way for a return of the submerged prepersonal unconscious.

In beginning meditation, whether RM or CM, the first thing the meditator becomes aware of is the virtually incessant activity of the mind. In attempting to "not-do," the meditator becomes aware of how active the mind is and how mental activities go on all by themselves, despite the meditator's attempt to be an unmoving witness. The activity that becomes most conspicuous at this point is the mental ego's internal dialogue. The mental ego, as we know, talks to itself in an effort to establish a sense of being, whether its inner talk is a way of monitoring the identity project or just a way of assuring itself of its existence as the subject of consciousness. Given this existential-ontological significance of internal dialogue, the mental ego finds silence threatening and therefore is compulsive in its inner talk. Internal dialogue is always in the background of the mental ego's consciousness. It is so much a part of the mental ego's moment-to-moment experience that much of it goes unnoticed by the mental ego. When, however, the mental ego begins meditating and attempts merely to witness rather than "do," this constant background chatter becomes frustratingly evident. In attempting to be a silent witness, the mental ego realizes what a nonstop talker it is.

Internal dialogue—together with accompanying fantasy ("inner cinema")—is a serious distraction for the beginning meditator. A good deal of practice is required before the meditator becomes able to sustain attention for significant periods without succumbing to the temptation to talk inwardly. With continued effort, however, the meditator makes progress in quieting internal dialogue. The continued practice of unmoving attention gradually lowers the volume of inner speech and renders it less commanding of the meditator's attention. In both RM and CM, the meditator eventually arrives at a point at which internal dialogue ceases being a serious distraction. In RM, this point is reached when the posture of alert openness becomes stable and can be sustained without effort. In CM, this point is reached when *dharana* is superseded by *dhyana*.

As one continues the practice of meditation, one becomes aware not only of egoic activities, and internal dialogue in particular, but also of innumerable ingrained patterns of relating to experience: sets, stances, programs, filters, defenses. These ingrained patterns are deeply embedded forms of experience that, as such, are normally unconscious. Usually, they are part of the personal embedded unconscious. Now, however, in being "undone" by meditation, these ingrained patterns begin being uncovered. In attempting simply to attend, the meditator becomes aware of the many ways in which he or she is already engaged in or resistant to experience. That is to say, in trying *and failing* simply to attend, the meditator becomes aware of the mediating structures belonging to the personal embedded unconscious.

By practicing meditative "undoing," then, the personal embedded unconscious is gradually brought into view (see table 6.1). This process of disclosure usually unfolds from less to more subtle layers of the personal embedded unconscious. Accordingly, behavioral tendencies and petrified physical postures are usually the first layers to be made conscious. After these, superficial psychological masks and affections may be exposed. Many filtering structures may be next, followed, in the most likely sequence, by deep-seated complexes and COEX systems, nuclear elements of ego identity, and the most deeply embedded mechanisms and postures of defense. In principle, the whole of the personal embedded unconscious can be brought to light by the practice of meditative "undoing." The personal embedded unconscious, which had been an invisible infrastructure of the mental ego's experience, is in this way revealed to consciousness.

A qualification is needed here: the account just given of how the personal embedded unconscious is rendered conscious applies better to RM than CM. It applies better to RM because RM is an open form of awareness that registers stimuli as they occur. Accordingly, in RM, the meditator becomes aware of the embedded unconscious *during* the course of meditation. The practice of meditative "undoing" loosens or disengages embedded structures, thereby throwing them into relief and bringing them to the meditator's *immediate* attention. In RM, of course, the meditator does not pay any special attention to these structures as they are brought to light; the meditator is aware of them as she or he is aware of any other content of consciousness. Layers of the embedded unconscious, in being disclosed, are merely registered; the contents of consciousness accompanying their disclosure are observed

TABLE 6.1

The Personal Unconscious

Personal embedded unconscious*	Filtering structures and operations Autonomous complexes COEX systems Ego identity Defense mechanisms
Personal submerged unconscious*	Subthreshold signals Filtered stimuli Shadow Deeply repressed materials

* Wilber's (1980a) term.

and allowed to pass away like all other contents that come before mirrorlike RM consciousness.

The manner in which CM discloses the personal embedded unconscious is a bit different. For CM's exclusive devotion to a focal object restricts the field of attention and closes awareness to stimuli other than the focal object itself. This exclusivity of focus is the goal of the initial stage of concentrative practice (*dharana*) and is fully established once the meditator, in achieving the second stage (*dhyana*), is no longer vulnerable to distractions. If, however, CM disallows awareness of the embedded unconscious during the course of meditation, it nonetheless readies the meditator for encounter with the embedded unconscious after meditation is concluded and the focal object is dropped. CM has this delayed effect because, after concluding the practice of CM, the meditator reenters the field of activity in a relatively relaxed and disengaged condition. It takes time for embedded structures, disengaged by CM, to be reengaged. After CM, then, when stimuli evoke embedded structures, the meditator is able to observe these structures being brought back into play. This process is in a sense the reverse of what happens in RM. For whereas RM allows the meditator to witness the gradual disengagement of the embedded unconscious, CM, once finished, allows the meditator to witness the gradual reengagement of the embedded unconscious. The basic causality is the same; nevertheless, the timing (during or after meditation) and the direction of the process are different.

Before discussing the uncovering of the personal submerged unconscious, I should stress that it is not the purpose of meditative "undoing" to dismantle or deconstruct the embedded unconscious. Most embedded structures perform vital functions, and meditation would deserve no credit if its only effect were to obstruct such functions. Accordingly, although meditation *does* disengage the embedded unconscious, its purpose in doing so is not to eliminate embedded structures. The purpose is rather to loosen embedded structures sufficiently to "uncramp" the conscious mind and thereby, as we shall see in a moment, to regain access to submerged resources that are essential ingredients of personhood.

Meditation, in disclosing the personal embedded unconscious, also works to disclose the personal submerged unconscious (see table 6.1). It does not have this latter effect immediately, because submerged materials are less easily uncovered than the embedded structures that screen or repress them. For example, the object of an unconscious resistance is less easily disclosed than the embedded resistance itself; we frequently learn *that* we are resistant before we know *what* it is that we resist. A lag-time normally separates the disclosure of a layer of the personal embedded unconscious from the disclosure of the corresponding content of the personal submerged unconscious. Meditation typically brings attention to embedded structures before it disengages them sufficiently to overcome their exclusionary (screening, repressing) effects. Nevertheless, if meditation is continued, the point is reached at which exclusionary effects are overcome and, therefore, at which submerged materials are allowed conscious expression. Meditative "undoing" thus works not only to cast light on the personal embedded unconscious but also, eventually, to uncover the personal submerged unconscious.

The order in which the personal submerged unconscious is uncovered is variable, but a typical sequence would be as follows: subthreshold signals would be uncovered first, followed by filtered stimuli of various sorts, followed by the shadow, followed finally by more deeply repressed elements of the (egoic) personality. I shall speak briefly to each of these levels of the personal submerged unconscious.

Subthreshold signals, in belonging to the personal submerged unconscious, are excluded from awareness more by the "noise" of the mental ego's internal dialogue than by the screening or repressing effects of the personal embedded unconscious. The mental ego's inner talk is loud enough to drown out more subtle elements of experience. As we saw earlier, however, meditative "not-doing" gradually quiets internal dialogue. Accordingly, meditation creates inner conditions that are conducive to the emergence of subthreshold materials. Meditation quiets consciousness and thereby makes it possible to detect not only faint somatic signals but also subtle affective currents and tiny bursts of ideation. Robert Ornstein (1972) describes this effect by comparing it to the emergence of the stars brought about by the setting of the sun. Just as the setting of the sun allows the stars to be seen, so the quieting of internal dialogue allows low-intensity sensations, feelings, and thoughts to be discerned.

Filtered stimuli are of many types. We have seen that they include everything screened by acquired habits and dispositions, autonomous complexes and COEX systems, introjected cultural assumptions and values, and, perhaps, inherited patterns governing language and cognition. Here we need make only the general point that filtered stimuli, like all elements of the personal submerged unconscious, are returned to consciousness as a consequence of the loosening and disengaging effect that meditation has on the personal embedded unconscious. Not only are embedded filters brought to consciousness in this way, but so too, given the progressive "uncramping" of consciousness, are the stimuli submerged by them.

The uncovering of filtered stimuli is usually followed by the derepression and disclosure of the shadow. Consisting as it does of those parts of the personality that are repressed because they are incompatible with ego identity, the shadow remains repressed so long as the mental ego continues to *be* its identity, that is, so long as the mental ego continues to hold onto its identity as to its very self. Now because the practice of meditation involves a progressive "undoing" or "letting go," it has the effect of loosening the mental ego's hold on its identity and therefore of opening the ego to the possible disclosure of the shadow. Meditation detaches the mental ego from its identity, and in doing so it not only brings the identity itself into view but also creates the conditions under which the shadow can be released from concealment. Meditation is frequently described as a relaxation technique to calm the mind. This description is not false, but it is misleading. For although meditation quiets the mind, it also, in leading toward a release of the shadow, can lead to acute distress. Experiencing the derepression of the shadow, as Jung observed, requires considerable courage.

The derepression of the shadow is not the only challenge the meditator faces from the personal submerged unconscious. For the practice of meditative "undoing" eventually loosens all repressions, starting at more superficial levels and proceeding to ever-greater depths. As repressions are "undone" in this way, the ego is opened to progressively more hidden repressed materials, passing beyond the shadow to, ultimately, a person's most deeply buried wounds and traumatic memories. The continued practice of meditation, then, can lead not only to an anguishing disclosure of the shadow but also to extremely disturbing recollections and accompanying feelings and fantasy elaborations.

The full airing of the personal submerged unconscious completes the meditative journey through the personal unconscious. Most people who take up meditation do not get this far. Many discontinue meditation soon after beginning practice because they lose interest in "just sitting" without "doing" anything. Others discontinue meditation when it enters difficult areas of the personal submerged unconscious; they lose their nerve when it comes to facing the shadow or other repressed materials. Moreover, of those who do persevere to the end of the journey through the personal unconscious, only a few go any further. For once the exploration of the personal unconscious is complete, the meditator hits a "wall." This "wall" is primal repression, the barrier that separates the ego from the nonegoic pole of the psyche. Great perseverance may be required to work though this deepest repressive barrier. For those, however, who do cross the threshold of primal repression, the nature of the meditative experience changes profoundly.

MEDITATION BEFORE AND AFTER CROSSING
THE THRESHOLD OF PRIMAL REPRESSION

In crossing the threshold of primal repression, the meditator comes into contact with the *numinosum:* the Dynamic Ground is unsealed and the numinous power of the Ground begins to reenter consciousness. Simultaneously, potentials belonging to the body unconscious and the instinctual-archetypal unconscious are reactivated and begin expressing themselves within consciousness. The meditator comes under the influence of the power of the Dynamic Ground and begins to undergo a spontaneous psychospiritual transformation. Meditation, which up to this point had been an exercise of will or an action on the part of the ego—the negative action of "not-doing" and "undoing"—now becomes a process that the ego undergoes.

Meditation changes in many ways once one has crossed the threshold of primal repression. The general atmosphere of meditative consciousness is transformed by the presence of the power of the Ground and other reactivated nonegoic potentials. Moreover, specific experiences of an extraordinary nature may occur, including, for example, experiences of light and sound, awe and devotion, fear and love, dread and bliss, trance and rapture, and, in some cases, inner vision and audition.

In the Buddhist tradition based on RM (*vipassana* meditation), extraordinary experiences like the ones just mentioned are called the "ten corruptions" and are said to arise after insight has become sufficiently refined to discern the impersonality (*anatta*) and impermanence (*anicca*) of all mental contents.[6] The reason for calling these experiences "corruptions" is that, as sudden and dramatic occurrences, they have the power to divert attention and to lead one to believe that one has achieved *nirvana* when in fact one has only begun the "journey to the other side" (of the prepersonal unconscious).

Similar experiences in the Zen tradition are called *makyo* ("diabolical phenomena"). This term is used because extraordinary psychic experiences can ensnare the meditator and lead her or him away from the proper path of practice. The occurrence of *makyo* or of the "ten corruptions" is evidence of the opening of the prepersonal unconscious and the tapping of its physicodynamic potentials. Experience becomes supercharged and strange, and on occasion the autosymbolic process, heretofore active only in dreams, brings forth images of visionary quality. Quite literally, the meditator's experience at this point can take on the character of a dream.

Progress in RM from this point involves both a deepening and an anchoring of insight. Disorienting experiences such as the "ten corruptions" or *makyo* gradually wane and the meditator becomes increasingly better able to maintain keen witnessing consciousness within what is now a dynamically awakened field of experience. Experience remains supercharged with the power of the Ground and open to the full range of nonegoic spontaneities. The meditator, however, is increasingly able to observe the play of spontaneities without getting caught up or carried away. The meditator, that is, is increasingly able to return to the equipoise of RM within the domain of dynamically active consciousness. Peaks and valleys are still experienced; nevertheless, the direction of RM at this point is toward increasing lucidity and steadiness or "calm abiding" in the midst of superabundant, spontaneously upwelling life.

When RM is practiced as prayer, crossing the threshold of primal repression is conceived as the opening of the psyche to the transformative action of spiritual power. In the Roman Catholic contemplative tradition, for example, passing over this threshold is understood as a transition leading from the prayer of recollection to contemplative states marked by the discernible presence of the Holy Spirit. Infused by the Holy Spirit, the person in prayer is here led through numinous and transforming experiences: agonies and ecstasies, terrors and transports, dark nights and dawning illuminations, ruthless purgations and redemptive influxes of grace. This opening to the Holy Spirit is the point of transition from active (ego-initiated) to passive purgation. It is the beginning of infused contemplative experience.

In other terms used in the Roman Catholic tradition, this opening to the Holy Spirit is the beginning of the "illuminative way," which is the initial period of spiritual awakening that leads through periods of purgative-redemptive transformation to the "spiritual espousal" and, finally, the "spiritual wedding" of the self with the divine. In her *Interior Castle* St. Teresa of Avila explains that dramatic experiences such as agonies and ecstasies, terrors and transports gradually disappear as the spiritually awakened person moves toward the ultimate goal of spiritual union or the "spiritual wedding."[7] Similar to Buddhist *vipassana* meditation, which becomes progressively more lucid and steady after initial awakening, contemplative prayer, according to Teresa, becomes progressively more discerning and composed.

Turning to CM, crossing the threshold of primal repression has the distinctive effect of raising the meditative state from "mere" unmoving one-pointedness to full absorption or, to use Mircea Eliade's (1969) apt term, *enstasy.* In Patanjali's system, this breakthrough to a higher plane is what lifts the meditator from *dharana* (wavering one-pointedness) and *dhyana* (effortless one-pointedness) to *samadhi* (absorption, enstasy). Crossing the threshold of primal repression leads to *samadhi*, I suggest, because the awakened power of the Ground is now invested in the meditation object, which therefore becomes a powerful cathexis object that draws the meditator into an object-based absorption. The focusing of attention on an object now has the effect of directing the power of the Ground to that object, which becomes a power-object exerting a gravitational-solvent influence on the meditator. The meditator is drawn to the object and is then absorbed in it. *Samadhi*, that is, is a consciously achieved mobilization of energy leading to enstasy; the ego consciously creates the dynamic conditions for its own absorption.

Patanjali (Aranya 1983; Feuerstein 1979) presents an elaborate classification of *samadhi* states. Initial *samadhi* achievements are unstable and "gross." The ego, as it were, is "sucked" into an object-based absorption that is astir with spontaneously arising images, ideations, and corresponding affects. Such initial *samadhi* achievements Patanjali calls *savitarka* and *savichara samadhis*, absorptions that are cognitively and affectively active in ways triggered by the object. As progress is made in *samadhi*, according to Patanjali, absorptive experiences of greater clarity and calm emerge. Eventually, the meditator is even able to dispense with objects or "supports" for the absorptive experience and achieve states of pure objectless absorption (*asamprajnata samadhi*). Paralleling the unfolding of RM and contemplative prayer after initial awakening, the unfolding of CM proceeds from more turbulent states to states that are transparent and still in their potency and spontaneity.

BEYOND MEDITATION

The character of meditation changes profoundly after the meditator crosses the threshold of primal repression and thereby comes into direct contact with the power of the Dynamic Ground. Prior to this point, meditation is like drilling for oil. Whether RM or CM, meditation is a process that loosens layer after layer of the embedded unconscious until it arrives finally at the deepest layer: primal repression. Meditation then begins to loosen this layer. As noted earlier, this phase of the meditative process can last a long time. Some people may be developmentally ready to move quickly and easily across the threshold of primal repression. For most people, however, perseverance is required, and even then there is no guarantee that primal repression will eventually give way. In those cases when this happens, however, the meditator "strikes oil": the power of the Dynamic Ground. The power of the Ground begins to flow into consciousness, and the meditative process is henceforth radically transformed.

Besides the extraordinary phenomena that sometimes accompany initial awakening, there now occurs a fundamental change in what it means to practice meditation. Specifically, meditation ceases being a practice of steadfast "not-doing" and "undoing" and becomes a practice of "going with the flow" of dynamically awakened experience. To mix metaphors, the ego no longer "drills for oil" and now begins to "ride the waves" of power emanating from the nonegoic sphere. The ego is sometimes deluged and sometimes borne wildly aloft by the forces now acting upon it. The ego undergoes purgative agonies and redemptive ecstasies. As the transformative process unfolds, however, these violent ups and downs gradually give way to a new equilibrium. As the ego approaches integration, it is able more and more easily to remain calm and clear in the midst of awakened experience. It is increasingly empowered and decreasingly overpowered by the dynamic spontaneities of nonegoic life.

CONCLUSION

A final point should be made before leaving the topic of meditation: because primal repression is an embedded psycho*physical* structure, the purpose of meditation can be assisted by physical exercises. Among the practices that are effective in this regard, the best known are the postures of *hatha yoga*.[8] Yoga postures (*asanas*) work to unblock the body so that energy latent in the body can be awakened and flow freely. The manner in which yoga postures accomplish this unblocking is essentially the same as the manner in which meditation accomplishes the opening of the unconscious: steadfast "not-doing" and "undoing." Yoga postures are positions that, if held fast, arrest bodily movement and loosen bodily rigidities and constrictions, including those belonging to the overall posture of primal repression. Yoga postures have much the same effect on the physical level that meditation has on the psychic level. *Hatha yoga* can therefore be practiced as a supportive adjunct to meditation.

7

Regression in the Service of Transcendence

VIRTUALLY EVERY RELIGIOUS TRADITION acknowledges periods of severe difficulty that sometimes precede or follow spiritual awakening. These periods are variously described as the dark night of the soul, the spiritual desert or wilderness, the state of self-accusing (Islam), the great doubt (Zen), the ordeal of dying to the world, encounter with temptation or with diabolical phenomena (the "ten corruptions" of Buddhism, the *makyo* of Zen), Zen sickness, the descent into the underworld or into hell, and the death of the self.[1]

All of these descriptions capture one or another aspect of the period during which the ego undergoes a withdrawal from the world and a return to the Dynamic Ground. As a process that disengages the ego from worldly involvements and submits the ego, beyond its knowledge and will, to the underlying physicodynamic sphere of the psyche, this "dark night" must be considered a type of regression. Because the physicodynamic pole of the psyche is originally lost via repression, it can be restored only via regression. However, if the dark night is a type of regression, it is not a regression in any usual sense of the term. The dark night is not a regression in the strict sense, for it is not a merely retrograde movement to earlier or more primitive modes of functioning. Nor is the dark night a regression in the service of the ego, for it does not serve in the long run to consolidate the ego in a position of supremacy within the field of consciousness. On the contrary, the dark night radically undermines the (mental) ego and submits the ego to the Ground, making the ego, eventually, a servant of spirit. The dark night is, then,

171

more a regression in the service of spirit than it is a regression in the service of the ego—or more precisely still, it is a *regression in the service of transcendence.*

Up to this point I have described regression in the service of transcendence as a process that begins with the lifting of primal repression and the consequent opening of the ego to the prepersonal unconscious. Here I shall adopt a wider view and include in the notion of regression in the service of transcendence not only the ego's encounter with the prepersonal unconscious that occurs after the lifting of primal repression but also a period of withdrawal or "dying to the world" that occurs prior to the lifting of primal repression and that itself leads to this lifting. Both of these stages are part of the dark night of the soul according to St. John of the Cross, the preliminary stage of withdrawal corresponding to what he calls the night of the senses and the stage of encounter with the prepersonal unconscious corresponding to what he calls the night of spirit. Regression in the service of transcendence, as I shall treat it here, then, is a two-stage process, consisting of a preliminary stage of withdrawal and an ensuing stage of regression proper.[2]

The first stage of regression in the service of transcendence consists of a set of interrelated difficulties that have been made famous in the writings of the existentialists, included among which are such states of mind or feeling as alienation, meaninglessness, nothingness, guilt, anxiety, and despair. During this period, the world loses its meaning, life loses its purpose, and the mental ego loses its presumed substance and justification. The period is one of disillusionment and alienation from the world. Worldly engagements are suspended, and worldly being and value are lost. The process leads, its seems, nowhere and to nothing—except to existential exile and despair. In fact, however, the first stage leads to an acknowledgment of "nothingness" and "guilt" and from there in some instances to an inner conversion that loosens primal repression and reopens the Dynamic Ground.

The second stage, much rarer than the first, is the period of encounter with the prepersonal unconscious that follows the opening of the Dynamic Ground. During this stage, the ego comes into contact with the physicodynamic potentials of the nonegoic sphere and is affected by these potentials in dramatic and disconcerting ways. Accordingly, the second stage of regression in the service of transcendence consists of a variety of highly unusual phenomena that for the most part are described only in works dealing with either psychopathology or mysticism. This stage sometimes begins with the sudden occurrence, triggered by the reopening of the Dynamic Ground, of extraordinary experiences such as transports, raptures, deep intuitive insights, and visions. These experiences accompanying spiritual awakening, when they occur, are highly impressive and can mislead the ego into thinking that it has achieved enlightenment or spiritual fulfillment. For this reason they are called "temptations," "corruptions" (Buddhism), or "diabolical phenomena" (*makyo*, Zen). The fact of the matter is that a radically new realm of experience has been opened up, but not exactly the realm that the ego had hoped and prayed for. The ego has indeed been opened to the Dynamic Ground, the source of spiritual life. The ego, however, which is still predominantly a mental ego, is far from being ready to live harmoniously with the power of the Ground (or with physicodynamic potentials generally). Accordingly, following the "honeymoon" of initial awakening, the ego begins to enter extremely difficult developmental territory. The opening of ego to the Dynamic Ground leads at first not to the final goal of *moksha, nirvana,* or salvation but rather, typically, to a long and dangerous encounter with the prepersonal unconscious.

The prepersonal unconscious is the sea upon which the second stage of regression in the service of transcendence unfolds. This sea is vast, and the far side of the sea is reached, usually, only after many trials have been endured. Among the difficulties that can be encountered on the way to the far shore are (1) disconcerting feelings; (2) strange bodily phenomena; (3) dread and a sense that the world has become strange; (4) disturbances to cognitive processes; and (5) recurrence of the ego-Ground conflict accompanied by fear of ego death.

The experiences belonging to the two stages of regression in the service of transcendence, and especially those that occur during the second stage, are difficult to comprehend in terms of established social, psychological, and spiritual categories. Considered individually or from a nontranspersonal perspective, these experiences do not fit into a coherent pattern. It is little wonder that they are usually considered symptoms of psychopathology.

For example, experiences belonging to the first stage of regression in the service of transcendence have been grouped together as symptoms of "existential vacuum," "existential neurosis," or "existential sickness" (Frankl 1962, 1969; Maddi 1967, 1970; Yalom 1980) or as symptoms of a schizoid or "divided self" (Fairbairn 1940; Guntrip 1952, 1961, 1969; Laing 1960). And experiences belonging to the second stage have as a rule been considered symptoms of one or another of the psychoses, usually either schizophrenia or bipolar psychosis. In many if not most instances it may be correct to categorize experiences like those belonging to the stages of regression in the service of transcendence as pathological phenomena. In some instances, however, a different interpretation is in order. For in some instances, I propose, the experiences in question have a redemptive rather than pathological significance and, therefore, are properly understood as part of a process of transcendence rather than as symptoms of mental illness. The experiences belonging to the two stages of regression in the service of transcendence can, we shall see, be arranged into a coherent pattern if they are viewed from a transpersonal perspective; viewed in this way, they can be seen to be natural expressions of human development as it moves beyond the level of the mental ego.

I shall proceed here, as in earlier chapters, by presenting what I take to be the ideal-typical case. This "pure" model of regression in the service of transcendence is not meant to describe anyone's actual experience; actual experience usually diverges significantly from the idealized pattern. In particular, most actual cases probably do not involve all or even most of the experiences that will be discussed here. Nor do they usually observe the strict division between the two stages: in most actual cases, it seems likely, the Dynamic Ground, if it opens at all, probably opens before the first stage has unfolded all the way to the end. Also, most actual cases are not as severe as the case I have constructed. This point needs to be stressed as strongly as possible. The ensuing account, then, in presenting the ideal-typical case, does not present a representative case; rather, it presents an *exaggerated* case. The ideal-typical case overstates actual experience, but it is precisely in doing this that it renders actual experience intelligible in its underlying logic and causality.

STAGE ONE: WITHDRAWAL FROM THE WORLD

The first stage of regression in the service of transcendence commences when the mental ego begins to suffer disillusionment in and with the world, that is, when the mental ego begins to realize that its deepest desires cannot be fulfilled by the world. When this disillusionment initially arises, the mental ego does not understand what it most deeply desires: being and value. Nor does the mental ego understand that its inability to satisfy its deepest desires is due to no fault of the world but rather to impossibilities inherent to its own fundamental project in the world: the identity project. Nor, of course, does the mental ego understand the existential insecurities that motivate its quest for being and value: the anxieties of nothingness and guilt. Nor, finally, does the mental ego understand why the identity project is ultimately impossible: because no amount of worldly accomplishment and recognition can eliminate the anxieties of nothingness and guilt so long as their ultimate cause, primal repression–primal alienation, remains in place. Upon first suffering disillusionment, all the mental ego understands is that what it most wants from the world, the world cannot possibly provide. Initially, the mental ego's disillusionment consists of no more than a profound disappointment in the world, which is seen (distortedly) as being deficient in certain fundamental regards.

Disillusionment leads to alienation. Disabused of hope of finding fulfillment in the world, the mental ego begins to withdraw from the world; it suffers alienation. This alienation is two-sided: it is at once something that happens to the mental ego and something that happens to the mental ego's world. On the side of the mental ego, alienation consists of a gradual loss of interest, drive, and capacity for engagement. And on the side of the world (as seen by the mental ego), alienation consists of a gradual loss of "realness" and meaning. The mental ego becomes apathetic, confused, and cut off; simultaneously, the world becomes barren, purposeless, and out of reach. Alienation is a condition that pervades the entire realm of the mental ego's existence. The mental ego, in a sense, loses its life, as it dies to the world. In turn, the world ceases any longer to be a world in the full sense of the term, as it is reduced to a mere stage or setting, a flat, lifeless backdrop.

Alienation is not a voluntary process. Alienation follows upon disillusionment as an effect follows upon a cause, not as a decision follows upon an insight. It is therefore a process that the mental ego suffers and is powerless to reverse. Once the process is under way, the rift between the mental ego and the world widens, despite whatever efforts the mental ego might make to renew its interest and involvement in the world. Alienation is not renunciation. The mental ego does not give up the world; rather, the world simply slips away, becoming distant and unreal.

Alienation, by withdrawing the mental ego from the world, relieves the mental ego of continued futile strivings after being and value. It suspends the identity project. Far from being a blessing, however, this suspension of the identity project actually increases the mental ego's problems. For the identity project was the means by which the mental ego quieted the anxieties of nothingness and guilt, and therefore the abandonment of the project allows these anxieties to reemerge. Alienation, by withdrawing the mental ego from the world, returns the mental ego, most unwillingly, to its deepest fears about itself.

The process of alienation causes the mental ego considerable distress, for it sweeps away all of the mental ego's moorings in, and reasons for, being. The mental ego loses its foothold in the world and is deprived of its earned sense of being and value. The whole of the mental ego's worldly existence is undermined, and for this reason the mental ego experiences anxiety, "fear and trembling." Moreover, in time the mental ego begins to suffer despair, "sickness unto death." For without relief from its alienated condition, the mental ego eventually begins to feel as if it were permanently cut off and bereft, as if it were without hope of ever finding its way back to a meaningful existence in a real world.

Although a seemingly lifeless state of mind, despair is potentially explosive, because it has the power to make the unthinkable thinkable. It is a state of mind that, because it is unendurable and yet inescapable within the system of known possibilities, impels the sufferer at last to embrace what hitherto would have been impossible. For the alienated mental ego, the unthinkable that despair prompts it to think, the impossible that despair drives it finally to embrace, is precisely its "nothingness" and "guilt." Despair, it turns out, is worse than the mental ego's worst fears about itself. Despair therefore pushes the mental ego to the brink, from which it jumps. That is to say, the mental ego does what, for it, is impossible: it accepts its "nothingness" and "guilt" and takes the leap of faith. In taking this leap, the mental ego "lets go" at the deepest level of its being and thereby loosens primal repression and reopens the Dynamic Ground. This reopening of the Dynamic Ground marks the beginning of the second stage of regression in the service of transcendence.

Let us now look more closely at the steps or substages that lead from disillusionment to despair and from despair to the reopening of the Dynamic Ground.

FROM DISILLUSIONMENT TO ALIENATION

Disillusionment usually occurs at first only vaguely and on the level of feeling: the mental ego merely senses that its efforts are somehow pointless. Then disillusionment grows into conscious insight: the mental ego eventually *sees* that its deepest desires cannot be satisfied by anything the world has to offer. Perhaps the mental ego comes to this insight by failing in a worldly goal. Or perhaps it arrives at this insight by succeeding in a worldly goal only to discover that restlessness and dissatisfaction continue. Or perhaps it is brought to this insight by means of self-analysis or philosophical reflection. Whichever of these avenues might produce the insight, however, the meaning is the same: complete fulfillment is not possible through the identity project, through worldly accomplishments, distinctions, and rewards. To understand this fact in a thoroughgoing way is to be fully disillusioned. To be fully disillusioned is to be on the verge of alienation.

Knowing that it cannot find fulfillment in the world, the mental ego gradually loses interest in the world and begins to withdraw from the outer arena of life. In ever-increasing measure, the mental ego begins to exhibit the classic signs of alienation: lack of motivation, disorientation, and a sense of being out of touch with things and out of step with the rhythm of events. The mental ego suffers from flagging interest in the world and decreasing desire to pursue old aims. It also suffers from confusion, or anomie, as old principles and priorities no longer make sense. And compounding these problems, the mental ego senses that even if old motivations and meanings were to return, they could not be translated into action, because somehow it, the mental ego, is cut off from the world and unable to enter the flow of life. Alienation disables the mental ego; it saps the mental ego's drive, obscures its purposes, and throws it out of gear. Alienation renders the mental ego listless, aimless, and unable to act. To be sure, the alienated mental ego, panicked by its disconnected condition, might try very hard to achieve engagement and to act effectively in the world. But these efforts are not likely to succeed. More often than not, such efforts yield only contrived behaviors, caricatures of real actions.

This disabling of the mental ego is, however, only one side of a two-sided process. For alienation is an affliction that affects the mental ego's world as well as the mental ego itself; it is not only a process by which the mental ego secedes from the world but also a process by which the world becomes lost to the mental ego. Generally stated, the world during the process of alienation undergoes *derealization*.[3] It loses its substance and meaning, its credibility and compellingness. It loses its familiarity, aliveness, and sense and becomes distant, dead, and "absurd." It is reduced to an arid and meaningless landscape, a wasteland. These changes in the world are of course merely apparent; they occur in perception rather than in reality. Nevertheless, these changes seem entirely real to the alienated mental ego. From the point of view of the mental ego, the world seems to be undergoing an actual mind-independent transformation. Moreover, not only does the mental ego see the world as undergoing such a transformation, it also typically sees its own predicament as being an effect of this transformation, even though, of course, the causality really works just the other way around. The mental ego takes its own dissociation and disorientation to be responses to the world's destitution. To the alienated mental ego, then, it seems as if the world were undergoing a completely objective derealization, and it seems also as if it were this derealization of the world that is the cause of the mental ego's deteriorating relationship with the world.

The reason for the ostensible change in the world is that the world, as a realm alive with meanings and values, is a subjective interpretation or construction. Hence, the withdrawal of the mental ego from the world is at the same time a "deinterpretation" or deconstruction of the world. This insight is to be credited to phenomenology.[4] A world, according to phenomenologists, is always a world *for* a subject; it is an experiential field that is not only objectively given but also subjectively construed and colored. Or, in a phrase, a world is a *setting lived by a subject*. As a setting—an outer context, stage, or landscape—a world exists independently of any subject, as a completely objective framework of things and events; phenomenologists, even transcendental phenomenologists, are metaphysical realists rather than idealists. If, however, the world exists independently of the subject, it has meaning and value only in relation to a subject. As an objective setting, a world is not a world in the full sense of the term, for it is not lived in, and thereby enlivened by, a subject. A setting becomes a world in the full sense only when it is understood by a subject's intentional (interpretive or meaning-bestowing) acts and is animated by a subject's cathexes. And, to return to the main point, the opposite is also true: a world ceases being a world in the full sense, and is reduced to a mere setting, when it is deserted, and consequently "disintended" and decathected, by its subject—which is just what happens in the case of alienation.

Viewed from a phenomenological perspective, then, alienation can be said to be a process by which the mental ego "unworlds" itself and, in doing so, causes the world to lose its "world-ness" and become thereby a mere setting. Because the world's loss of world-ness is an effect of the mental ego's "unworlding" (appearances to the contrary notwithstanding), it follows that aspects and phases of the mental ego's alienation have objective correlates—that is, that aspects and phases of the mental ego's unworlding are reflected in the world as losses of features of its world-ness. Accordingly, a direct correspondence obtains between the symptoms of the mental ego's alienation and the dimensions of the world's derealization. The mental ego's secession from the world, for example, is reflected objectively in a recession of the world from the mental ego. The mental ego's apathy is reflected in the world's aridity, the mental ego's isolation in the world's remoteness, the mental ego's anomie in the world's meaninglessness, the mental ego's anxiety in the world's unreality, and so forth. Because, phenomenologically, the world *is* the world as it is lived by a subject, the steps of the mental ego's alienation from the world are registered in changes in the world itself—

which, again, are in turn incorrectly taken by the mental ego to be the causes of its alienation.

If any one idea or image by itself captures the essence of alienation in its effect upon the world, it is that of *flatness*. Alienation affects the mental ego's world by leveling it, by throwing it out of relief, by divesting it of the dimension of lived depth. Alienation has this effect because it involves the withdrawal of intentional acts and cathexes, and it is precisely the outreach of these projections that creates the dimension of lived depth. Depth is a consequence of a subject intersecting with a setting by sending forth vectors of thought and feeling. Thought vectors (intentional acts) deepen a setting with layers of meaning; feeling vectors (cathexes) deepen a setting with attractive or repellent values. When, therefore, a subject withdraws these vectors from the world, the result is that the dimension of depth is lost. The world goes flat; its horizons disappear and it collapses into a two-dimensional setting. In just this way, I suggest, alienation has the general effect upon the mental ego's world of divesting it of all modes and gradations of lived depth. It works to conflate all differences between figure and ground, intimacy and distance, urgency and unimportance. The world of the alienated mental ego, therefore, is one in which, progressively, nothing stands out and in which there are no hidden recesses. It is a world in which everything is shallow, neutral, uniform, and gray.

More concretely, the world of the alienated mental ego is a world without peaks or valleys, challenges or disappointments, profundities or banalities, heroes or fools. It is a world in which no action is any more exigent than any other, no person any deeper or more mysterious than any other, and no discourse any more meaningful than any other. It is a world in which everything is "equal." Actions are equal because they have all been reduced to mere motions. Persons are equal because they have all been reduced to mere personas. And all discourse is equal because it has all been reduced to mere words. The world of the alienated mental ego is flat throughout, for, in withdrawing from the world, the mental ego has ceased intersecting in depth with the world.

A perfect example of what it is like for the world to go flat is available from the domain of the cinema. Everyone is familiar with what happens when one is suddenly drawn out of the action of a film. Let us consider one such possible scenario: A man and a woman are viewing a mystery-suspense film. The woman is totally absorbed. The world of the film is, for the present, her world. She identifies with or responds to the characters and is caught up in the action. The man in contrast, having already seen the film on a previous occasion, is not absorbed, and let us suppose that, out of boredom and impatience, he reveals the conclusion to the woman—which conclusion, let us also suppose, the woman finds disappointing. Given such a situation, we can reasonably assume that the woman would suffer disillusionment and would lose interest in the film. That is to say, she would become alienated from the *world* of the film. Simultaneously the film itself would go flat; without the depth factor provided by outreaching thought and feeling, the film would cease being a self-contained world, a reality unto itself, and would become instead only a film, a fiction. The characters would be reduced to mere actors saying lines, and what was a compelling drama would be reduced to a mere plot or story line. The world of the film would no longer be engaged, and so it would cease being an engaging reality. It would become only a setting, a sequence of scenes.

The experience of the mental ego as it suffers disillusionment and then alienation is virtually identical with that of the moviegoer. Prior to disillusionment, the mental ego, like the moviegoer, is absorbed in the world, which is experienced as completely real and alive. But upon suffering disillusionment, the mental ego's world, like that of the moviegoer, undergoes derealization; it is divested of sense and seriousness. It goes flat. What were meaningful deeds now become only idle motions or empty roles; what were real people now become only surface characters; what were living histories and institutions now become only documents and buildings. The experience of the mental ego parallels that of the moviegoer in all of these ways. The mental ego's experience, however, differs from the moviegoer's in one crucial respect: the world that the mental ego loses is not an optional world of fantasy but rather the given world of material and social reality. Consequently, whereas the moviegoer loses a few hours and a few dollars sitting through a film that does not attract her or his involvement, the alienated mental ego is in danger of losing its life. It is in danger of becoming an exile from the world.

Disillusionment undeniably liberates the mental ego from the futility of attempting to achieve fulfillment through the identity project. This "liberation," however, is not experienced as a positive development, for in making the mental ego no longer *of* the world, disillusionment has the consequence of disallowing the mental ego any longer to live *in* the world. The mental ego is forced into existential exile, condemned to wander in a desert without end. The Dynamic Ground is at this point still closed, so there are no oases in this desert, no upwellings of numinous power to quench the mental ego's thirst for life. Disillusionment therefore is a double-edged sword: in cutting through the illusions that bind the mental ego to the identity project, it simultaneously severs the only tethers by which the mental ego is anchored in the world.

THE DEANIMATION OF EGO IDENTITY

The loss of the world entails the loss of the mental ego's identity, for identity is founded upon the world and is inextricably a part of it. Ego identity, or the self-concept, is selfhood *in the world*. It is the mental ego's self as defined and justified in terms of worldly categories. Hence, when alienation renders the world remote and unreal, it does the same to ego identity. The mental ego's withdrawal from the world initiates a process of disidentification from its being-in-the-world; in other words, the derealization of the world is at the same time a deanimation of ego identity.[5]

The deanimation of its identity brings the mental ego to perceive itself in the same way it perceives others: just as it perceives everyone and everything else in its derealized world as flat and dead, so the mental ego sees itself as flat and dead. The mental ego senses that it is no longer a real person in a real world but is rather only an assemblage of traits, habits, routines, and roles that are played out on a lifeless stage. Just as the mental ego now sees other people only as facades without foundations, so, too, it sees itself as only a set of poses. It therefore ceases to believe in itself, to take itself seriously, for it has become only a mask, a persona, a disguise.

The mental ego, in coming to perceive itself in this way, gains self-knowledge that it did not possess before. The core features of ego identity are usually unknown; as we learned in chapter 5, they are usually part of the personal embedded unconscious. They become evident, as a rule, only when special efforts are made such as those involved in psychotherapy, meditation, and other forms of disciplined self-reflection or when exceptional circumstances obtain such as those involved in developmental transition, change in basic life roles or lifestyle, *and alienation*.

The reason why alienation works to reveal the mental ego's identity is that, in derealizing the world, it inhibits the expression of identity and thereby draws attention to identity. Actions expressive of identity are unable to find engagement and therefore are dishabituated and thrown into relief. Such actions, in being deprived of the world as context for their expression, tend either to fall dead or to become awkward caricatures of themselves. They become wooden or unwieldy, and consequently they also become glaringly evident. Alienation disallows the mental ego any longer to *live* its identity, and its identity is therefore disembedded and brought into view. As Hegel observed, "The owl of Minerva spreads its wings only with the falling of dusk" (1952, p. 13). So long as the mental ego lives its identity, it does not know its identity. However, as soon as the mental ego, in dying to the world, begins also to die to its selfhood in the world, then, too late, it attains self-knowledge.

The alienated mental ego's heightened self-knowledge (combined with its total ineffectiveness in action) is the source of a thoroughgoing ambivalence, which the mental ego directs toward both itself and others. The alienated mental ego takes pride in its lucid self-knowledge, and yet it also despises itself for its utter uselessness to the world. And as for others, the alienated mental ego holds them in contempt for their blindness, their lack of reflective self-awareness, and yet it also envies them for their engagement and effectiveness in the world. As Dosto-evski's underground man puts it, the worldly person is stupid but strong, whereas he, the underground (alienated) man, is wise but abjectly weak. The alienated mental ego is privy to a wicked disjunc-tion, which it takes to be an inescapable truth: "Those who do, do not know; those who know cannot do."

The alienated mental ego experiences the loss of identity as self-loss: the mental ego's sense of being derives from its identity, and there-fore the loss of identity carries with it the feeling of loss of being, that is, of death. The alienated mental ego feels as if it were undergoing an inexorable process of dispossession leading in the direction of complete paralysis (inability to act) and death (inability to be). The alienated per-son, as Kierkegaard puts it, suffers from a "sickness unto death."

ENCOUNTER WITH THE SHADOW

So long as the mental ego lives its identity, the shadow remains securely repressed as part of the personal submerged unconscious. When alien-ation sets in and the mental ego's identity is deanimated, however, the shadow is derepressed—and it rises into consciousness, subjecting the mental ego to a host of unwelcome self-insights.

The alienated mental ego, accordingly, is afflicted with much gnashing of teeth and many stings of conscience. It sees through its rationalizations and deceptions and confronts the hidden, dark side of its personality. Having already been disillusioned with the world, the mental ego is now disabused of its illusions about itself. It is jolted into a rude awakening and brought to what must seem the worst possible self-reckoning—although, alas, more difficult reckonings lie ahead. It is brought to the position of seeing *through* the illusions of the world and selfhood in the world *to* what seems like the exclusive reality of the shadow. The mental ego now encounters those features of the person-ality it had shunned. And without its identity to fall back on, it cannot help thinking that these shadow elements constitute its real and true self. Having been dispossessed of the self to which it was attached (ego identity), the mental ego is now forced to own, entirely and exclusively, the self that it has not wanted to be (the shadow). To say the least, this acceptance of the shadow is a difficult experience for the mental ego.

The experience does not last long, however. For the shadow, as the negative underside of the mental ego's worldly identity, is also tied to the world. The derealization of the world that is part of the alienation process consequently entails an eventual deanimation not only of identity but of the shadow as well. The shadow, however, must be derepressed before its deanimation can begin. The typical sequence, then, is (1) derealization of world and concomitant deanimation of identity, (2) derepression of the shadow, and (3) deanimation of the shadow.

Ironically, the mental ego, after being shocked and anguished upon first witnessing the shadow, sometimes begins to cling to the shadow when it begins to undergo deanimation. The mental ego, it turns out, would sometimes rather be something that in its own eyes is humiliating or reprehensible than not be anything at all. Dostoesvski's underground man gives forceful expression to this frame of mind:

> Oh, if I had done nothing simply from laziness! Heavens how I should have respected myself . . . because I should at least have been capable of being lazy; there would at least have been one quality, as it were, positive in me, in which I could have believed myself. Question: What is he? Answer: A sluggard; how very pleasant it would have been to hear that of oneself! It would mean that I was positively defined, it would mean that there was something to say about me. "Sluggard"—why, it is a calling and vocation, it is a career. (Kaufmann 1956, p. 66)

This curious attachment to the shadow indicates that the mental ego, given no other alternatives, will sometimes, and perhaps even typically, choose *being* over *value*. The mental ego, after suffering the loss of its identity, is frequently willing to sacrifice all sense of value and justification just to preserve some vestige of being-in-the-world. Being the shadow is better than not being at all. But being the shadow is not a long-term possibility. For the shadow, too, is in time deanimated by the process of alienation.

ALIENATION AND ANXIETY

The existentialists have made the point that anxiety is the basic mood of the alienated condition. The alienated mental ego experiences chronic anxiety, for reasons that we shall now consider.

First and foremost, of course, the alienated mental ego experiences the loss of the world and, even more, the deanimation-death of its worldly identity with great alarm, even panic. No matter how hard the mental ego tries to reestablish contact with the world and to resuscitate its worldly self, it cannot, and therefore it is subject to repeated and intense bouts of anxiety. Speaking of the alienated person, Waltraut Stein says: "And in a very real sense he is dying, as he feels less and less like a real person. This sense of dying can come upon him slowly or suddenly. In either case, panic is possible at any time, should he catch a glimpse of complete dispossession, of death. Then he feels totally disorganized and runs 'every which way'" (1967, p. 270). The alienated mental ego has been cut off from the world and is in the process of losing its footing in being. It is in a deeply unsettling, indeed terrifying, predicament.

Occurring in conjunction with the mental ego's anxiety over loss of being is an anxiety over loss of justification. These go hand in hand: because the mental ego's identity is the basis of both its being and its value, the deanimation of worldly identity deprives the mental ego not only of its being but also of its reason or justification for being. And to add insult to injury, the emergence of the shadow, which follows upon the deanimation of identity, finally dashes all of the mental ego's airs of specialness and worth. The mental ego is forced to confront the rejected parts of its personality and consequently is decisively relieved of its pretensions of distinction, if not grandeur. In sum, the mental ego is dispossessed of both being and justification, and it is highly anxious over both of these losses—although it is frequently if not typically most anxious over the loss of being.

The mental ego's situation, however, is even more complicated than this account indicates. For lurking behind the anxiety over loss of being is the more basic anxiety of nothingness, and lurking behind the anxiety over loss of value is the more basic anxiety of guilt. In each of these pairs of related anxieties, the first anxiety is in fact the mental ego's fear of losing that which shields it from the second. That is, the anxiety over loss of being is the mental ego's fear of losing the sense of being based on identity (and secondarily on the shadow), which, if totally lost, would leave the mental ego completely exposed to its "nothingness." And the anxiety over loss of value is the mental ego's fear of losing the sense of justification based on identity, which, if totally lost, would leave the mental ego completely exposed to its "guilt." The process of alienation undermines the mental ego's confidence in its being and value and, in doing so, exposes the mental ego to its "nothingness" and "guilt."

The process of alienation, in short, leads inexorably toward "nothingness" and "guilt." At first it does so through a withdrawal from the world, carrying with it a concurrent erosion of worldly being and value. During this phase of the process, the mental ego as it were backs its way toward "nothingness" and "guilt" without acknowledging them directly. Still unheedful of its deepest fears, the mental ego here remains focused on the world and the loss of worldly being and value. This outward focus, however, can be maintained only up to a point. For the withdrawal from the world eventually runs out of ground. A point is reached at which ego identity (and even the shadow) is completely beyond resuscitation, leaving the mental ego without a vestige of worldly being or value to cling to. At this point the mental ego can no longer postpone the inevitable, and so it begins anxiously to make an about-face. It begins the uneasy process of looking forthrightly at itself, of facing its "nothingness" and "guilt."

The anxieties caused by loss of being and value together with the anxieties of nothingness and guilt are perhaps the anxieties most basic and central to the alienated condition. These anxieties, however, are not the only anxieties inherent to the alienated condition. For example, the mental ego's encounter with the shadow must be counted as an anxious, or anguishing, ordeal, because the mental ego is forced to see, and then accept, all manner of unwelcome truths about itself. It is stung repeatedly by negative self-insights, and it shudders in view of what it now reluctantly acknowledges as its true self.

The alienated mental ego also suffers from an anxiety over freedom—or at least it does so during the early stages of its withdrawal. Sartre (1956) calls this species of anxiety *vertigo of possibilities* because it is the experience of being dizzied by the radical open-endedness of life, the unlimitedness of one's choices and chances. The alienated mental ego is prone to being dizzied in this way because the process of alienation, in separating the mental ego from its identity, reveals to the mental ego that its nature is not fixed but is rather an overwhelmingly vast set of possibilities. The mental ego is not in a position from which it might boldly reenter the world, pursuing new purposes and forging a new sense of being and value. Cut off from the world, it is unable to achieve the sustained engagement that would be necessary to pursue new possibilities in an effective manner. Its actions, intermittent and inconsistent at best, are more fitful attempts at acting than engaged, goal-achieving deeds. Moreover, the mental ego's awareness of new possibilities usually coincides with the derepression of the shadow, which colors the perception of new possibilities in a negative and frightening way. The mental ego's newfound possibilities therefore do not appear to it as inviting opportunities among which to choose, but rather as possibilities for the exercise of "absurd" freedom, possibilities for doing "anything," no matter how out of character, no matter how inappropriate, no matter how reprehensible. The mental ego is for this reason afraid of its newfound possibilities. It is assailed and daunted by them. The discovery of radical freedom is not, then, for the alienated mental ego, a cause for celebration; it is rather a cause of vertiginous anxiety.

Accompanying this anxiety of freedom is a corresponding anxiety of responsibility—for freedom and responsibility are correlative notions. The magnitude of responsibility is a function of the scope of freedom: the wider the freedom, the greater the responsibility. And the character of responsibility—whether it is experienced as something positive or something negative—is a function of the character of freedom: a happy freedom is a welcome responsibility, a dreaded freedom a burdensome responsibility. Accordingly, because the freedom of the alienated mental ego is suddenly widened without limit and because the character of this expanded freedom is negative, the alienated mental ego experiences its responsibility as being at once great and oppressive. More specifically, the alienated mental ego relates to its responsibility as to a burden from which there is no relief. Like Sisyphus—a favorite figure among existentialist writers—the alienated mental ego feels as if it were condemned to bear a heavy weight without any chance of recess or remission. Fully cognizant of its present actualities and future possibilities and utterly disabused of all rationalizations and self-deceptions, the alienated mental ego has no excuses for what it is and does. It alone shoulders the responsibility for its existence, even for its world (in the phenomenological sense of the term). And it trembles under the weight.

DESPAIR

The mental ego's inability to stem the tide of alienation deprives it of hope and brings it finally to despair. Despair signals that all recourse within the mental-egoic system has been exhausted. It signals that the world is irretrievably lost and that ego identity (and the shadow) is completely defunct, beyond all possibility of reanimation. It signals that the mental ego has been totally dispossessed. Despair, that is, indicates that alienation has run full course and that the mental ego has arrived at its nadir. This nadir—at which there is no world and no self—I shall call *zero point*.[6] Despair, then, is the state of mind of the mental ego at zero point.

Having lost the last vestige of its worldly being and value, the mental ego at zero point is on the verge of encountering its "nothingness" and "guilt." It avoids this encounter as long as possible; it tries again and again to repossess the world and to reenliven its identity, even long after it knows that such efforts are in vain. The encounter with "nothingness" and "guilt," however, cannot be postponed indefinitely. The simple fact is that despair is unendurable. Consequently, the mental ego is eventually led to try *anything* that might relieve it of its condition, even to face its worst fears about itself. Despair is relentless; it pushes the mental ego ever closer to the brink, from which, finally, the mental ego leaps: it concedes its "nothingness" and "guilt" and opens itself to the beyond.

"NOTHINGNESS" AND "GUILT"

The only hope for the mental ego at zero point, then, lies in accepting its "nothingness" and "guilt," where by acceptance is meant not just a cognitive avowal but a complete assimilation or working through. Such acceptance, however, is understandably extremely difficult for the mental ego. Just how difficult is indicated by the fact that the mental ego sometimes refuses to accept its "nothingness" and "guilt" not only (1) after learning that the world and identity in the world cannot be repossessed but even (2) after being repeatedly exposed to the fact of "nothingness" and "guilt" and even (3) after coming to realize that only the acceptance of this fact can possibly bring an end to despair. The mental ego, as it were, sometimes continues to float new loans on its existence even after it knows full well that it is bankrupt, and even after it knows that only a confession of bankruptcy can save it from disaster.

Taking denial to these lengths is, of course, utterly perverse. It is also, probably, rare. Nevertheless, as Kierkegaard (1849) has shown, such perverse denial—which he terms demoniacal defiance—is a last-ditch move on the part of the mental ego that is sometimes a precursor to a leap of faith. It sometimes happens that the mental ego chooses to spite itself rather than save itself just to continue to be itself. What a curious thing the mental ego is!

But despair is unremitting. It gradually wears the mental ego down until, finally, the mental ego has no energy left with which to avoid the truth. Reaching this juncture, the mental ego at last quits its denials and submits itself to the inevitable: it accepts its "nothingness" and "guilt." In doing so, the mental ego undergoes a deep inner opening: it relinquishes its last defense and bares itself to powers from beyond. Or in our terms, it lets go the false support of primal repression and thereby opens itself to the Dynamic Ground. This inner opening, if and when it occurs, marks the end of the first stage of regression in the service of transcendence and the beginning of the second.

STAGE TWO: ENCOUNTER WITH THE PREPERSONAL UNCONSCIOUS

The difficulties experienced during the first stage of regression in the service of transcendence are primarily problems of dispossession, of loss—loss of the world, of being, of justification, and so forth. In contrast, the difficulties experienced during the second stage are, in a sense, primarily problems of *possession;* they reflect the fact that the mental ego, now destitute and defenseless, is "taken possession of" by forces of the prepersonal unconscious. The mental ego is deeply fearful of these forces; its fundamental stance in being is opposed to them. The mental ego rests on primal repression, on the negation of underlying physico-dynamic life. Accordingly, when the mental ego finally lets go of the false support of primal repression it opens itself to the resurgence of nonegoic life, to the return of the repressed. It is drawn into the stormy underworld of the prepersonal unconscious and brought under the powerful influence of derepressing physicodynamic potentials. The derepression of the Dynamic Ground is at the same time a regression of the ego to the Ground.

Let us now consider some of the principal experiences or phenomena that are part of the ego's regression to the Ground.

BLACK HOLES IN PSYCHIC SPACE

The mental ego maintains internal dialogue so long as the mental-egoic system remains intact (i.e., closed to the Dynamic Ground). In fact, this dialogue tends to increase as disillusionment leads to alienation and alienation to dispossession. For the derealization of the world and the deanimation of identity spur the mental ego to talk to itself as a way of rationalizing its exiled condition, keeping itself company, and, most basically, reassuring itself of its existence. Once primal repression gives way and the Dynamic Ground opens, however, interruptions in internal dialogue may occur. And these interruptions are not periods of restful, much less serene, silence; they are rather moments of trancelike blankness, moments during which internal dialogue is extinguished by currents of gravitational energy. To use a simile, these interruptions are like encounters with black holes in psychic space. The mental ego feels as if it is in the presence of an oppressive gravity that draws the mental ego into an inner, dreadful unknown.

Wilson Van Dusen (1958) describes these black holes, which he has observed in his clinical practice with psychotic patients.[7] He says:

> In the hole one feels one has momentarily lost one's self. What one intended is forgotten. What would have been said is unremembered. One feels caught, drifting, out of control, weak.
>
> These holes and blank spaces are important in every psychopathology. . . . In every case they represent the unknown, the unnamed threat, the source of anxiety, and the fear of disintegration. . . .
>
> It is extremely important to know what people do when faced with encroaching blankness. Many talk to fill up space. Many must act to fill the empty space within themselves. In all cases it must be filled up or sealed off. (pp. 218–219)

Van Dusen believes that these black holes are potentially restorative and creative wellsprings that pose no serious danger to those who experience them. For example, he says: "The findings are always the same. *The feared empty space is a fertile void. Exploring it is a turning point toward therapeutic change*" (p. 219). According to Van Dusen, black holes in psychic space are points of contact between consciousness and the fertile depths of the soul.

Van Dusen points to an important phenomenon: black holes in psychic space are, it seems, access ways to a deeper realm of experience. Van Dusen's conception of these black holes, however, can be questioned. Specifically, his view that yielding to these black holes in all cases brings about positive therapeutic change is, I believe, sanguine. For this view overlooks the real risks involved in submitting to the prepersonal unconscious (i.e., to the nonegoic pole of the psyche in its repressed form). I am not saying that the nonegoic pole of the psyche is never a source of creative and healing upwellings, because in its "trans-expression" it is precisely such a source. However, in its status as the prepersonal unconscious, the nonegoic pole should be regarded as presenting definite dangers to the ego, even to the ego that, mature and strong, is "seaworthy" and ready for regression in the service of transcendence.

Whether or not the ego should yield to black holes, then, depends more on the ego than it does on the black holes. An immature, weak, borderline, or fragmented ego, I suggest, is either unready or unsuited for an encounter with the deep unconscious and may need to find a way to "seal off" the black holes in its subjectivity. A strong and mature ego, on the other hand, may be in a position to yield to black holes. Even a strong and mature ego should proceed with caution, however, because passage through a black hole leads to momentous and uncertain consequences.

Along with black holes, the beginning of the second stage of regression in the service of transcendence may involve dreams of disaster and destruction auguring the end of the world. Dreams of this sort may emerge because the mental ego senses that its existence is seriously undermined: primal repression, the mental ego's terra firma, is giving way and is on the verge of collapse. The mental ego, fearing that its situation is dire, is plagued by the mood of doom and may dream of catastrophic happenings.

Images belonging to this archetypal complex and their likely specific meanings are (1) images of falling or crashing—which mean that the ego no longer stands on firm ground and is in danger of falling through into an underlying realm; (2) images of vortices, gravitational abysses, and sirens of death—which mean that the ego is now exposed to the underlying Ground and to its gravitational and entrancing effects; (3) images of earthquakes, volcanic eruptions, and other violent upheavals—which mean that the psychic underworld, the prepersonal unconscious, is no longer safely contained and is on the verge of breaking through into consciousness; (4) images of floods, violent seas, and raging infernos—which mean that repressed forces are astir and that the ego has begun to sense their destructive potential; (5) images of dark skies and stormy weather—which mean that the mental ego's subjective atmosphere is ominously charged with the power of the Ground; (6) images of a great clash with powers of evil—which mean that the egoic system is in danger of being besieged by the forces of the unconscious; (7) images of wild beasts with wanton appetites, especially oceanic and subterranean monsters—which mean that the id may soon emerge from its nether lair; (8) images of blood, feces, and filth—which mean that the ego is exposed to the rawest and rudest aspects of life; and (9) images of darkness, plague, and death—which mean that the ego is beset with the mood of doom.

These images form a diverse array, but common to them all is the motif of a siege by forces of darkness, a siege that portends the imminent end of the world and death.

FROM ANXIETY TO DREAD

We have seen that anxiety is a feeling state characteristic of the first stage of regression in the service of transcendence. The mental ego experiences anxiety because it is in the process of losing its worldly identity and justification and, consequently, of facing its "nothingness" and "guilt." The mental ego also experiences anxiety because it suffers from a sense of overwhelming possibility and unbearable responsibility. Anxieties such as these continue throughout the first stage of regression in the service of transcendence and frequently carry over into the second stage. Adding to these anxieties, a new anxiety frequently emerges at the beginning of the second stage, an anxiety signaling psychic emergency. The emergency, of course, is the breakdown of primal repression and infiltration into consciousness of the power of the Ground. This crisis situation can set off alarms and trigger into hyperactivity every defensive resource of the mental-egoic system. The mental ego responds with panic as it discovers that it has suffered a deep psychic wound and is defenseless in face of unknown forces.

The second stage of regression in the service of transcendence does not, then, bring the mental ego any relief from anxiety. Anxiety, however, is not the most troublesome affect or mood during the second stage of regression in the service of transcendence. For here anxiety begins to be eclipsed by a new feeling: dread. Anxiety does not disappear entirely as the second stage of regression in the service of transcendence unfolds, but it tends to recede and take a back seat to dread, which becomes the affective state most characteristic of the second stage. Anxiety here gives way to dread because the ego comes increasingly under the influence of a power that, it seems, is utterly dark and alien: the power of the Ground in its repressed, instinctual organization. The anxieties of worldly loss, and even those of psychic damage, are muted as the mental ego is exposed to the *mysterium tremendum* in its manifestation as the "power of the abyss."

Dread and anxiety are very different. Anxiety is a generalized fear reaction: the heart beats faster, adrenaline flows, perspiration breaks out on the brow and palms, and the fight-or-flight reaction is triggered—even though one may not be in any discernible or real danger. With dread, in contrast, rather than alarm and preparation to act, one experiences a sense of being immovably in the grip of something alien, of being overawed and stopped in one's tracks by ominous forces; and rather than palpitation and heated perspiration, one experiences chills, clamminess, bristling sensations, and horripilation. Whereas anxiety is a feeling accompanying the mobilization for defense, dread is a feeling attending the rapt perception of the eerie, ghastly, or strange.

Dread is characteristic of the second stage of regression in the service of transcendence because during this stage the mental ego's overall experience is shot through with a seemingly alien power, the power of the Dynamic Ground. This power infiltrates the mental ego's inner space, causing bizarre sensations and disconcerting states of mind. The power of the Ground is also projected upon the mental ego's world, darkening it and making it forebodingly and grippingly mysterious. Everywhere the mental ego turns, it encounters things bathed in an aura that is at once uncanny and fascinating. The mental ego therefore is entranced in the midst of its experience, which is pervasively strange. Captivated in this way by the uncanny, the mental ego experiences dread. In sum, whereas anxiety is alarm in the face of the dangerous (or what is perceived as dangerous), dread is entrancement is face of the strange.

FROM ALIENATION TO ESTRANGEMENT

Just as flatness is the main feature of the world during the first stage of regression in the service of transcendence, so strangeness is the main feature during the second stage. This strangeness, although pervasive and emphatic, is not easily described, because it is a quality that is both subtle and global and therefore virtually ineffable. Strangeness does not involve an alteration in the specific natures of things in any conspicuous way, and yet it does involve an alteration of the general "look" and "feel" of things. Although in one sense it seems as if nothing in the world has changed, in another sense it seems as if the whole world is entirely, and ominously, different. If in the first stage of regression in the service of transcendence things become *unreal*, losing their old sense and meaning, in the second stage they become *surreal*, acquiring a new, eerie, and as yet uncomprehended sense and meaning.

Strangeness is a matter not only of eerie differentness but also of heightened or exaggerated reality. The power of the Ground, which is now the atmosphere of the world, affects things not only by imbuing them with a haunting newness but also by enhancing and magnetizing them, making them strikingly vivid and compellingly alluring. The power of the Ground supercharges the atmosphere of the world, and consequently everything in the world is amplified in its qualities and rendered hypnotically fascinating in its effect. Everything is endowed with a stunning potency and an entrancing depth. In becoming strange, then, the world changes in a twofold way: it becomes both surreal and superreal. A strange world is at once disarmingly different and prepotently alive. A strange world has the same pervasive character as a dream.

This comparison with dreaming experience is intended to be taken literally. For the surreal-superreal quality shared by the strange world and dreams is due in both cases, I suggest, to the saturation of experience with the power of the Dynamic Ground. When primal repression is in place, the power of the Ground is restricted to the prepersonal unconscious and therefore is discernibly present only in sleep and dreams. The lifting of primal repression, however, liberates this power from its repressed, unconscious organization and allows it to reenter the sphere of consciousness. Consciousness is supercharged with numinous energy, and consequently waking experience is endowed with the eeriness and superabundance characteristic of dreams.

In addition to becoming dreamlike in its general atmosphere, waking experience at this point can also become dreamlike in the character of its imaginal activity: vivid and bizarre images can enter consciousness during the second stage of regression in the service of transcendence. The emergence of such phantasmagoric images indicates that the autosymbolic process, which normally operates during dreams, has become active within the field of consciousness. I shall discuss this expression of the autosymbolic process in more detail later in the chapter.

Thus far two parallels have been established: (1) that dread is to the second stage of regression in the service of transcendence what anxiety is to the first, and (2) that strangeness is to the second stage what flatness is to the first. To these, a third parallel can now be added, namely, (3) that *estrangement* is to the second stage what alienation is to the first. In the first stage, anxiety and flatness are manifestations of the general condition of alienation; in the second stage, dread and strangeness are manifestations of the general condition of estrangement.

Estrangement, like alienation, is a type of relationship between a subject and a setting, and therefore between a person and a world. Alienation, as explained earlier, is a condition that arises when the mental ego, in suffering disillusionment, withdraws energy from the world and thereby reduces the world to a lifeless two-dimensional setting. Estrangement, in contrast, is a condition that arises when the mental ego, in undergoing deep regression, floods an alienated setting with derepressing energy and thereby reanimates that setting, transforming it into a strange new world. Alienation is a consequence of a global decathexis that desiccates the world and saps the ego's interest in the world. Estrangement, in contrast, is a consequence of a resurgence of energy that reenlivens (indeed, haunts) the world and renews the ego's interest (indeed, fascination) in the world. Whereas the person suffering alienation is dissociated from a world that has become unreal, the person suffering estrangement is entranced by a world that has become surreal.

DISTURBING FEELINGS

A major difficulty for the mental ego during the second half of regression in the service of transcendence is that it is liable to be overrun by a host of irrational fears that derive from its wounded and estranged condition. Examples of such fears are the seemingly pathological apprehensions that one is going insane, that one is being possessed by an alien force or entity, that one is transparent to other people, and that one is being conspired against or manipulated by mysterious persons or powers. In light of the mental ego's highly altered condition, it is understandable that the mental ego would be concerned about its sanity and that it would be uncertain about who, or what, is in charge of its inner life. Regression in the service of transcendence is in many respects a psychotomimetic process, and to the person undergoing the process it may seem less like a semblance of psychosis than like psychosis itself.

Also included among the fears that can prey upon the mental ego at this point are a variety of infantile terrors that, long since outgrown, may now spring back to life. Prime examples of such childhood fears are those of darkness, ghosts or other lurking presences, strange people, and haunted places. Without defenses to contain them, and with additional energy to enlarge them, these fears can assume sizable proportions, sometimes becoming debilitating fixations or phobias. People in the second stage of regression in the service of transcendence experience the world as a darkly mysterious realm full of frightening invisible presences.

Fears are not the only feelings to disrupt the personality. Given the amplifying effect of the power of the Ground, together with the mental ego's weakened condition, virtually any feeling can grow large enough to create difficulties. Even feelings that have never before caused problems (e.g., minor embarrassments, irritations, tensions, enthusiasms) can become strong enough to be distressing. And what were powerful affective currents or undercurrents can become overwhelming waves of emotion. The mental ego during the second stage of regression in the service of transcendence is awash in feelings, old and new, and it is powerless to control them, much less contain them.

DISRUPTION OF COGNITIVE PROCESSES

Cognitive processes are disrupted during the second stage of regression in the service of transcendence because the power of the Ground affects the mental ego in ways that interfere with the exercise of active or operational thought. Specifically, the power of the Ground disconcerts the mental ego both by exerting a gravitational influence on it and by supercharging it. The power of the Ground, as a gravitational or magnetic force, decelerates mental activity and draws the mental ego into states of immobile dissociation. And the power of the Ground, as the "fuel" of psychomental processes, accelerates mental activity and throws the mental ego into states of uncontrollable excitation. Mental control is of course not totally lost during this period, but it is seriously disrupted by episodes of inertness and hyperactivity.

Cognition is also disrupted by a dramatic awakening of intuition. The power of the Ground, in drawing the mental ego into states of immobile dissociation, switches the mental ego from the active to the receptive cognitive mode. In arresting discursive thought, the power of the Ground at the same time renders the ego passively open to the unconscious, which is here in the process of derepressing. The ego is thus struck by profound insights, many of them of an unwelcome sort. These insights arrive with great power of impact. They are astounding or gripping disclosures that sometimes cause the mental ego to wince, gasp, or moan. The energy supplied by the Dynamic Ground intensifies cognitive experience generally, which can be overstimulated in its active or operational mode and overpowering in its receptive or intuitive mode.

The awakening of intuition may include a reactivation of the autosymbolic process and, consequently, a reappearance within consciousness of spontaneously produced and highly realistic images. The autosymbolic process is our chief creative faculty, and it is therefore potentially an extremely important contributor to human cognition. However, on those occasions when it reenters consciousness during the second stage of regression in the service of transcendence, this process typically has a negative effect. For at this point the images forged by the autosymbolic process, arising as they do from the prepersonal unconscious, usually take the form of the mental ego's deepest fears and most forbidden desires—"diabolical" tortures or temptations (*makyo*). They present themselves as frightening or alluring apparitions, apparitions that in some instances can be as realistic and full-bodied as hallucinations.

One other way in which mental functioning can be disrupted at this juncture is that the ego can be thrown into seriously deranged states of mind. These states are extreme cases of the dissociations and agitations mentioned previously. They are states of inert vacancy and wild inflation. The former of these two types of states is a condition of mental paralysis and darkness, a condition of denseness, immobility, and blankness of mind that can be compared to being caught in a psychic black hole. And the latter type, in complete contrast, is a condition of riotously overflowing ideation and accompanying affect, of mania and confusion. The state of inert vacancy indicates that the mind has been taken in tow and is held in traction by the gravitational pull of the power of the Ground. The wild inflations, in contrast, indicate that the mind is exposed to the eruptive upsurge of nonegoic life. Deranged states like these are extreme and may be quite rare. Nevertheless, they are possibilities inherent to regression in the service of transcendence, possibilities that should therefore be included in a complete account of the process.

ACTIVATION OF PREPERSONAL SPHERES: THE BODY UNCONSCIOUS

The release of energy from the Ground reawakens the body and reactivates the physicodynamic potentials that had constituted the body unconscious.

The "resurrection" of the body is sometimes signaled by a variety of bizarre physical symptoms. These symptoms, like the deranged states just mentioned, are probably quite rare. They likely appear only in cases of abrupt and powerful awakening. Nevertheless, these symptoms are well known in the tradition of *hatha yoga*, in which they are called *kriyas* (actions of purification).[8] According to the yogic conception, the arousal of the latent power *kundalini*—interpreted here as the opening of the Dynamic Ground—sets off a flow of energy in the body that, in encountering impediments to its circulation, gives rise to unusual bodily sensations and reactions. Among these effects, the following are frequently reported in the yogic literature: (1) sensations of energy currents running through the body; (2) impulsion to assume the bodily postures of *hatha yoga* (*asanas* and *bandhas*); (3) sudden alterations in the breath, especially periods of cessation of breathing (*pranayama*); (4) snapping and popping sensations deep inside the body; (5) spontaneous stretching and tensing of muscles; and (6) a variety of involuntary movements and vocalizations.

These symptoms arise, I suggest, because the energy released from the Dynamic Ground is inhibited in its movement by what remains of the physical infrastructure of primal repression, including the overall postural set of primal repression–primal alienation. The movement of the power of the Ground is impeded by countless petrified tensions and constrictions. In pushing against these obstructions, the power of the Ground may at times feel like a heavy energy current or searing molten liquid. And in breaking through or dissolving specific obstructions, the power of the Ground triggers the discrete and dramatic phenomena that signal purification or release. The long-term results of this process of physical opening are probably entirely beneficial. They include a dismantling of body armor, an opening of the body, a straightening of posture, and a development of atrophied muscles and occluded nerve pathways. Nevertheless, when the process first begins, the mental ego is understandably distressed. For the body seems to be taking on a life of its own, indeed an alien life working in strange and disconcerting ways.[9]

Occurring in conjunction with the "resurrection" of the body is the reawakening of bodily life generally, which once again, as in the earliest years of life, becomes polymorphously sensual. Actually, it is not entirely accurate to describe this initial reawakening of the body as a return to polymorphous sensuality. For such a description implies, contrary to fact, that the ego has once again become completely at home on the level of concrete physical existence. The ego, however, is not yet comfortable with embodied life. Although the body has begun being "resurrected," the ego is not yet "reincarnated," at least not fully or happily. To the ego, which is still basically a *mental* ego, the "resurrection" of the body necessarily seems like a foreign and unwelcome process. The ego, having long fancied itself to be an essentially incorporeal entity, cannot help experiencing the reawakening of the body as an alien affair, an affair in which it, the ego, has no part. As we shall see, the "reincarnation" of the ego—that is, its reidentifying reunion with the body—does not really commence until regression in the service of transcendence is over and regeneration in spirit begins.

Although the ego considers the reawakening of the body to be an alien affair, it nonetheless is drawn to the manifold new sensations that it now experiences. The body, energized and sensitized, tantalizes the ego, and the ego finds it extremely difficult to resist the body's enhanced magnetic appeal. Accordingly, the ego, despite its antiphysical metaphysics and morality, is susceptible to being beguiled and swept off its feet. Indeed, it frequently loses its head (literally!) and plunges into voluptuous sensations. It gives way to engrossments and sensual delights—only later to return to its cerebral heights. At this point, then, the ego's experience is not yet polymorphously sensual in the full meaning of the term. The ego is still a mental ego, but it is an ego that is on the verge of reembodiment.

ACTIVATION OF PREPERSONAL SPHERES:
THE INSTINCTUAL-ARCHETYPAL UNCONSCIOUS

One of the most perplexing aspects of regression in the service of transcendence, especially for those who have approached it from the point of view of a puritan ethic or ascetic spiritual practice, is the arousal of the instincts, especially those of sex and aggression.[10] For someone who has condemned or attempted to conquer the instincts, the stirring of sexual and aggressive impulses can come as an unpleasant surprise. These impulses are nothing new, of course, as sex and violence are in many ways staples of human experience. With the opening of the Dynamic Ground, however, they tend to become completely explicit and distressingly importunate.

Many spiritual aspirants, in experiencing such a reawakening of the instincts, have become convinced that, despite having striven toward the divine, they have succeeded only in delivering their souls into the clutches of demons. Evelyn Underhill describes the experience of St. Catherine of Siena:

> Where visual and auditory automatism is established [when the autosymbolic process is reactivated], these irruptions from the subliminal region often take the form of evil visions, or of voices making coarse or sinful suggestions to the self. Thus St. Catherine of Siena . . . was tormented by visions of fiends, who filled her cell and "with obscene words and gestures invited her to lust." She fled from her cell to the church to escape them, but they pursued her there: and she obtained no relief from this obsession until she ceased to oppose it. (1961, p. 392)

Another striking example, this one from the East, is provided by Swami Muktananda (1978), who in the initial stages of his *kundalini* awakening was repeatedly visited by a vision of a beautiful woman who tempted him to break his vow of chastity. No amount of effort could banish this vision from mind. Only after Muktananda's guru told him that the experience was a necessary part of his spiritual growth did the perplexing episode finally come to an end. Only at this point did Muktananda realize that the vision was in fact an expression of the divine power at work within him.

Many people have observed that spirituality and instinctuality are intertwined in a way that renders spiritually sensitive people prone to contradictory attitudes toward the instincts, to approach-avoidance, hedonistic-ascetic ambivalences and countertendencies. These contradictory attitudes, I propose, are a consequence of primal repression. They derive from primal repression because primal repression not only negates the instincts but also, in restricting the power of the Ground to an instinctual organization, makes the instincts the gateway to spirit. Primal repression forces spirit to keep the company of the instincts and therefore requires the same of anyone who would seek the company of spirit. This coincidence of spirituality and instinctuality is of course not based on any *essential* connection between the power of the Ground and the instincts. It is rather based only on a curious *developmental* conjunction of the two.

This peculiar juxtaposition of spiritual and instinctual possibilities is a source of acute conflict for the mental ego. Every time it opens itself "upwardly" to spirit, it feels the "downward" pull of the instincts. Despite believing that spirit and the instincts are complete opposites, the mental ego now discovers that it cannot aspire to the former without simultaneously opening itself to the latter. The mental ego in this situation faces a perplexing dilemma, a dilemma that has caused many spiritual seekers to experience extreme anguish.

It is noteworthy that regression in the service of transcendence seems in some cases to trigger instinctual systems deriving from prehuman strata of the psyche. The literature on *kundalini yoga*, for example, reports many experiences of *kriyas* that seem to embody the behavior of lower animal life: hissing like a snake, roaring like a lion, neighing like a horse, jumping like a frog, and bristling like a cornered beast of prey. And Stanislav Grof (1975) reports cases of LSD-induced regression that seem to intersect with very early stages of our phylogenesis. Paradoxically, the move toward integration, which aims at the apex of human actualization, may retrace stages from our primitive evolutionary past. This retracing, however, should not be all that surprising. For integration, as the term itself implies, is the unification of the totality of human resources. If anything were omitted, no matter how primitive, integration would not be complete.

Turning from the phylogenetic to the ontogenetic side of the instinctual-archetypal unconscious, the chief consequence of the opening of the Dynamic Ground is that the Great Mother archetype is sometimes reactivated. This return to preoedipal object relations occurs because the ego is here confronted once again with the power of the Ground, which it last experienced, during early childhood, as the inner dimension of the Great Mother. To be sure, the replay of the ego–Great Mother interaction that now occurs differs in significant ways from the original version. Most notably, (1) the ego now clearly knows the difference between the inner and outer dimensions of its experience and therefore between the power of the Ground and any particular human person; and (2) the Great Mother is now perceived through more mature eyes and is therefore more properly a transpersonal Great *Goddess* than a prepersonal Great Mother. Despite these differences, however, it is substantially correct to say that stages of the ego–Great Mother interaction are replayed in new form. Owing to its initial experience of the Ground as an essential dimension of the Great Mother, the ego is predisposed at this point to perceive the Ground through the lens of the Great Mother archetype.

Accordingly, in reencountering the power of the Ground, the ego begins reexperiencing the ego–Great Mother dynamic. Moreover, given its negatively weighted ambivalence toward the Ground, the ego more specifically begins reexperiencing the ego–*Terrible* Mother dynamic. The ego finds itself once again in the presence of a power that is dark, dreadful, and engulfing. The ego fears for its very existence and therefore struggles with every resource at is disposal to free itself from the power it faces. It tries desperately to shore up old defenses and, if at all possible, to reseal the dark Mother-Ground. These efforts, however, the ego learns, are counterproductive; they cause its adversary to grow in size and fury. Digesting this insight, the ego eventually realizes that, in struggling to save itself from the power it faces, it is really only hurting itself. And, in time, the ego realizes why this is so, namely, because it is somehow related to this power as to a deeper and higher part of itself. The ego, that is, arrives at the insight that its adversary, the power of the Ground *qua* Terrible Mother-Goddess, is not something inherently alien and evil, but rather something that is perceived in this manner only because it has been alienated and condemned. For these reasons the ego at last concludes that it cannot, and indeed should not, continue to struggle against the power of the Ground.

Putting this decision into practice, the ego reverses its stand. It ceases attempting to protect itself from the power of the Ground and begins instead to submit itself to this power so that, through this surrender, it might be spiritually reborn. And as the ego yields in this way, it discovers that the Mother-Ground is not at all what it had seemed. It discovers that the Mother-Ground is a creative source rather than a dangerous abyss and that the power of this Ground is a regenerative power rather than a destructive one. The Terrible Goddess is in this way revealed to be more truly a Good Goddess. The power of the Ground is revealed to be the power of spiritual transformation. This emergence of the power of the Ground as spirit signals that the ego has made the turn from regression in the service of transcendence to regeneration in spirit.

Before this turn is made, however, the ego may struggle for a long period with the power of the Ground in its guise as an abyssal-destructive force. Once opened to this power, the ego cannot escape it. The gravity of the Ground draws the ego into the Ground-as-abyss, and the solvent action of the power of the Ground melts the ego's self-boundaries. The ego that has not yet surrendered to the Ground is fearful that it will be drawn into the Ground-as-abyss to a depth from which there is no escape and therefore that it will be completely engulfed and destroyed.

It sometimes happens that the ego *is* destroyed, that regression in the service of transcendence aborts and degenerates into regression pure and simple. The possibility of such regression is the supreme risk of the Way and the primary reason for the many resemblances between psychosis and mysticism. Both the psychotic and the mystic have been cast upon the sea of the prepersonal unconscious. The difference is that the mystic's ego is seaworthy, whereas the psychotic's is not. Accordingly, whereas the psychotic capsizes and loses touch with reality, the mystic is able to survive the voyage to the other side of the sea, finding thereby safe Ground from which integration can be achieved.

CONCLUSION

Regression in the service of transcendence is the first phase of a thoroughgoing psychic reorganization. It is the negative or deconstructive phase that clears the way for the building of a new order. Egoically, it is the phase during which the mental ego is shorn of its false sense of being and value, disabused of its illusions of sovereignty within the psyche, and returned to the underlying Ground. Psychodynamically, it is the phase during which primal repression is lifted and physicodynamic potentials are reawakened. And structurally, it is the phase during which the two poles of the psyche cease being dualistically separated and are brought back into contact with each other. Regression in the service of transcendence is a radical transformation affecting all dimensions of life. It is a process that deconstructs the mental-egoic system so that physicodynamic life can be reawakened and so that, ultimately, the two poles of the psyche can be integrated to form a single, perfected psychic whole.

Given that it is such a radical transformation, regression in the service of transcendence can in many instances be a long and agonizing process. Lest I conclude on too negative a note, however, I should stress again that the overall process is rarely as protracted or severe as the account in this chapter might suggest. Again, I have presented the ideal-typical case of regression in the service of transcendence, and the ideal-typical case is an *exaggerated* case.

8

Regeneration in Spirit

ONCE REGRESSION IN THE service of transcendence has returned the ego
to the Ground, a developmental reversal occurs: the dark night of the
soul comes to an end and a period of psychic renewal begins. The
period of regressive deconstruction is over and the ego enters a period
of healing reconstruction, a period that, adopting traditional terminology, I shall call *regeneration in spirit*. The developmental reversal that
sets the ego on this course has been expressed in a great number of symbolic images. Included among these images are, for example, those that
depict a transformation of violent waters into life-giving springs, infernal fires into the flames of spiritual purification, raging winds into the
breath of life, hell into the purgatorial ascent into heaven, and in general
death into new and higher life.

Among the major historical conceptions of the regeneration process, the one predominant in the West is the Christian account of the
new life breathed in by the Holy Spirit. This new life, prefigured sym-
bolically by the water of baptism, is said to be one that completely transforms a person, washing away sins and dispensing graces that are not
possible for those in the unregenerate or fallen state. An alternative conception of the regeneration process within Christianity is found in the
Roman Catholic and Orthodox conception of purgatory, which is held
to be the place or state of being in which one undergoes the purifications requisite for admission to the heavenly estate. Purgatory is said to
be an eschatological domain in which the soul endures the redemptive
transformations needed to cleanse it of residual contaminations and
thereby prepare it for the blessings of celestial life.

In the West, a second influential conception of the regeneration process is that of alchemy.[1] Alchemy is based on the belief that universal transubstantiation is possible, that is, that any kind of substance can in principle be transformed into any other kind of substance. Assuming universal transubstantiation, alchemy holds that base metals can be transubstantiated into gold—and, in some kind of analogous way, the fallen or "impure" soul can be transubstantiated into a soul that is spiritually perfect. The process by which the soul is transubstantiated is conceived differently in different alchemical systems. Most systems, however, agree that the process has at least the following stages: (1) The soul is subjected to intense inner heat through the practice of rigorous ascetic disciplines. (2) This heat gradually decomposes the soul and reduces it to its substrate condition. (The base metal is reduced to prime matter, which, according to Aristotelian metaphysics, is the universal matter underlying all distinct substantial forms.) (3) After undergoing this reduction process, the soul comes under the influence of the philosopher's stone or elixir (frequently identified with the Holy Spirit) and begins to be regenerated and transubstantiated. And (4) the process of regeneration continues until the soul reaches a state of spiritual perfection, that is, until the soul is no longer merely something that is subject to the transforming power of the philosopher's stone but is itself the full and perfect expression of the philosopher's stone. The alchemical account of regeneration, then, is one that, like our own, describes the regeneration process as a process of psychospiritual reconstruction that follows upon a period of radical psychic deconstruction.

A third important conception of regeneration in spirit, this one from the East, is that of Tantrism.[2] According to Tantrism, the regeneration process begins when the so-called serpent power (*kundalini*) is awakened. This power—conceived here as the power of the Ground in its instinctual and unconscious organization (libido)—is said to lie latent at the base of the spine until it is aroused into activity by means of ascetic and meditative practices. Upon being aroused, *kundalini* manifests itself as the sacred transformative power, *shakti*—conceived here as the power of the Ground in its expression as liberated spirit—which ascends through a central column associated with the spinal cord (*sushumna*), effecting purifications, stimulating subtle psychic centers (*chakras*), and thereby causing extraordinary experiences. The ascent of *shakti* continues until the entire body-mind has been awakened and purified, at which point, it is said, the goddess Shakti unites with her consort Shiva at the crown of the head. At this point the person undergoing transformation is said to experience the highest type of spiritual absorption.

Similar to the Christian and alchemical accounts, the Tantric conception of the regeneration process is one according to which this process is carried out by a supraegoic power as it moves in and through the body. The Tantric conception of *kundalini-shakti* corresponds to the Christian conception of the Holy Spirit, which in turn corresponds to the alchemical conception of the philosopher's stone or elixir. And the Tantric understanding of the body as a *sushumna-chakra* system corresponds to the Christian understanding of the body as the temple of the Holy Spirit, which in turn corresponds to the alchemical understanding of the body as the crucible or alembic of the alchemico-spiritual process.

Christianity, alchemy, and Tantrism are three of the more important historical conceptions of regeneration in spirit. I have made reference to these systems not to provide a survey of historical views but rather to situate the subject of this chapter in the context of historical formulations. The discussion that follows, although indebted in ways to all three of the historical views just mentioned, is not particularly indebted to, or couched in terms of, any one of them. I remain within the framework established in previous chapters and explain regeneration in spirit in terms of the dialectically unfolding interaction between the ego and the Dynamic Ground. Also, in explaining regeneration in spirit, I present what I take to be the ideal-typical case. This case, like the ideal-typical case of regression in the service of transcendence presented in the last chapter, is not intended to be a representative case. It exaggerates the features of regeneration in spirit in order to throw into relief the underlying logic and causality of the process.

I shall first consider some of the general features of the regeneration process; then I shall focus on some of the more specific features.

GENERAL FEATURES OF THE REGENERATION PROCESS

The three most important general features of the regeneration process are the calming of physicodynamic potentials, the purging of mental-egoic resistances, and the mending of the psychic fissure caused by primal repression.

THE CALMING OF PHYSICODYNAMIC POTENTIALS

The conflict between the egoic and nonegoic spheres that occurs during regression in the service of transcendence consists of two simultaneous movements. One of these is an awakening and discharging of physicodynamic potentials. Physicodynmaic potentials, no longer fettered by primal repression, are reactivated and assert themselves in the form of disturbing pulsations arising from the nonegoic sphere. Regression in the service of transcendence can in this respect be compared to a subterranean upheaval that releases volatile gases into the atmosphere. Occurring simultaneously with this upheaval of physicodynamic potentials, however, is an equal but opposite "downfall" of the ego into the prepersonal unconscious, the gravitational pull of which, no longer blocked by primal repression, now acts directly upon the ego. In this respect regression in the service of transcendence is like being sucked into an underlying abyss seething with dark forces. The conflict between the egoic and nonegoic poles occurring during regression in the service of transcendence is therefore both an upheaval of the psyche's repressed underlife and a submersion of the ego in this underlife; and this conflict is both of these movements at once.

This violent double movement continues throughout regression in the service of transcendence. The discharging of nonegoic potentials and the submersion of the ego proceed through ever-deeper and more highly charged levels of the unconscious. The process comes to an end, or at least begins to do so, only after the most deeply underlying and potent levels of the unconscious have been reactivated and after the ego, as it were, has touched bottom. Only at this point does the conflict between the two psychic poles begin to abate and do the prospects of the ego begin to brighten.

This turning point marks the end of regression in the service of transcendence and the beginning of regeneration in spirit. It is signaled in two immediate ways: (1) the ego is released from the abyssal gravity of the Ground, and (2) the violence with which physicodynamic potentials assert themselves diminishes.

The ego is released from the gravity of the Ground not because the power of the Ground ceases being a gravitational force but rather because the ego, in "touching bottom," finally becomes rerooted in the Ground. The ego reestablishes connection with the deepest base of the psyche. It is re-Grounded and consequently is no longer pulled toward the Ground. The ego continues to be affected by disturbing pulsations rising from the physicodynamic sphere, but having completed its descent to the Ground, its *regressus ad originem*, it is no longer subject to the lure of the deep. In the words of Nietzsche's Zarathustra, the ego is here relieved of the "spirit of gravity" and, rooted in Dionysian depths, begins to ascend toward the clear atmosphere of mountain heights.

The release of the ego from the gravity of the Ground is indicated in the disappearance of the trancelike states to which the ego is prone during the second stage of regression in the service of transcendence.

These states, if we remember, are states of inert dissociation that occur when the ego is immobilized by the gravitational pull of the Ground—as if caught in the gravitational field of a psychic black hole. Because these states are consequences of the gravity of the Ground, the ego's proneness to them is not overcome until the ego has completed its return to the Ground and, taking root therein, is released from the Ground's gravitational pull.

When the ego is finally released from the gravity of the Ground, it also begins to be affected less violently by awakening nonegoic potentials. This decrease in violence occurs in part because the most highly charged of nonegoic potentials have by this time fully reasserted themselves and in part because nonegoic potentials, in reasserting themselves, gradually lose, and do not regain, their repressively accumulated energy.[3] The power of the Ground is no longer restricted to a prepersonal organization, and therefore physicodynamic potentials, in asserting themselves, dissipate their repressively accumulated charge without acquiring a new one, that is, without acquiring a new *standing* charge. The derepression of these potentials therefore permanently defuses them; it disburdens them not of energy or life, but of the explosive overload of energy that hitherto they had borne. This defusing, of course, does not happen all at once. Physicodynamic potentials remain "hot" for a considerable period of time. Nevertheless, the direction of change is clear: regeneration in spirit is a movement away from disruptive upheavals and toward more peaceful upwellings of physicodynamic potentials.

The power of the Ground must be distinguished from other physicodynamic potentials—for example, somatic, instinctual, creative-imaginal, and archetypal potentials—because, unlike other such potentials, it is not something that can be defused and rendered tame. The power of the ground is energy, the very energy that, prepersonally organized, accumulates in and then is discharged from (other) physicodynamic potentials. It is that *by* which things are charged and hence cannot itself be depotentiated through discharge. The reassertion of physicodynamic life therefore initiates a pouring of the power of the Ground into consciousness that continues unabated even after other physicodynamic potentials have been defused. The power of the Ground continues to flow into the egoic sphere and, because the ego is not yet fully receptive to the power of the Ground or fully adapted to its supercharging effect, the power of the Ground continues to affect the ego in violent ways: it "pierces," "wounds," ravishes, wildly inflates, and intoxicates the ego. Owing to these violent effects of the power of the Ground, the ego's situation remains unstable well into the regener-

ative period, long after the deepest levels of the prepersonal unconscious have been derepressed and discharged.

This instability, however, is eventually overcome—not because the
power of the Ground recedes or abates in its flow, but rather because
the ego is gradually purged of its remaining resistances to the power of
the Ground and gradually adapts to the "high octane" of this power.
The effects of the power of the Ground upon the ego remain violent to
some degree throughout regeneration in spirit. The violence of these
effects, however, steadily diminishes as the ego becomes more receptive to the power of the Ground.

Moreover, as Ground-induced states diminish in violence, they
begin being experienced by the ego in decreasingly negative and
increasingly positive ways. Although the power of the Ground continues to penetrate, inflate, and inebriate the ego, the ego, as time passes,
feels less and less as though it is being wounded, "blown away," and
deranged by the power of the Ground and more and more as though it
is being ravished, transported, and inspired. Regeneration in spirit,
then, is a period during which Ground-induced states, in becoming
progressively less violent, also become progressively less negative and
more positive in their perceived character.[4]

This reversal in perceived character applies not only to the power
of the Ground but to all other physicodynamic potentials as well. All
such potentials, in being defused, undergo a negative-to-positive reversal. They cease appearing as adversaries of the ego and, at the beginning of regeneration in spirit, begin expressing themselves in decreasingly negative and increasingly positive ways. For example, (1) the
body, which had been a field of newly awakened, disturbing yet en-
grossing sensations, becomes eventually the basis of the ego's own
polymorphously sensual life; (2) the autosymbolic process, which had
been a fabricator of frightening or tempting images, becomes eventually a fashioner of creative visions; and (3) the sexual and aggressive
drives, which had been sources of disruptive impulses, become eventually sources of feelings that enrich and fortify experience. These
changes are merely mentioned here; they will be discussed fully later in
the chapter. It suffices at present simply to note that the basic complex-
ion of these and other physicodynamic potentials changes during
regeneration in spirit. They decrease in violence and, simultaneously,
undergo a progressive change from dark to light. In sum, then, regeneration in spirit can be said to be a decreasingly negative and increasingly positive process.

Regeneration in spirit is a purgative process. It is the process by which all remaining egoic resistances to the power of the Ground are purged and the psyche as a whole is transformed into an unobstructed vehicle of spirit. It is the process of agonizing yet ecstatic opening that renders the egoic sphere completely receptive to spiritual life. Regeneration in spirit is, then, the necessary interim phase that, following the initial reawakening of nonegoic potentials, prepares the way for integrated existence.

As a purgative process, regeneration works to overcome the mental ego's defensive self-encapsulation. Throughout the mental-egoic period the egoic sphere is a self-enclosed domain; the mental ego is the Cartesian ego, an ego that has at once retreated *inwardly* (from the outer-public to the inner-private world) and *upwardly* (from the physicodynamic to the mental plane). The mental ego has retreated from the outer-public domain in that it has withdrawn from others into the protective confines of inner-private space (primal alienation), wherein it hides behind a facade of identity. And the mental ego has retreated from underlying physicodynamic life in that it has buried that life (primal repression) and taken up exclusive residence in the region of the head. The mental ego has withdrawn from interpersonal intimacy and girded itself against intrapsychic spontaneity, and it has thereby reduced itself to an insulated and disconnected state.

Regression in the service of transcendence is the first step in reversing this state of affairs. For the undoing of primal repression—which is at the same time an undoing of primal alienation—divests the mental ego of its protective coverings. It ruptures the seal by which the mental ego had contained the Ground and simultaneously undermines the defenses by which the mental ego had shielded itself from others. The egoic sphere is in this way wrenched open both intrapsychically and intersubjectively. The mental ego is stripped naked; and, not yet accustomed to this state, it feels vulnerable to the core, defenseless against indwelling forces and nakedly exposed to public view.

This process of forcible opening continues as regression in the service of transcendence gives way to regeneration in spirit. As this transition occurs, however, the process—true to the general character of regeneration in spirit—begins to undergo a reversal from negative to positive. The opening of the egoic sphere begins here to change from a predominantly negative process that is dreaded and resisted by the ego into an increasingly positive process that the ego both enjoys and affirms. Specifically, the influx of the power of the Ground into the egoic sphere changes gradually from something that is experienced as an injurious invasion by an alien force into something that begins being experienced as a rejuvenating infusion of spiritual power. And the concomitant opening of the ego to others gradually changes from something that is experienced as a painful exposure into something that begins being experienced as a salutary disclosure. In sum, what the ego had experienced as a harmful infiltration of dark energies, it begins experiencing as a regenerating upwelling of "waters of grace"; and what the ego had experienced as a vulnerability before others, it begins experiencing as an authentic openness to others.

The purgative movement of the power of the Ground as it breaks through inner resistances is a process that is similar to the physical birthing process. Like the birthing process, it is a process by which an emerging life is forcibly delivered into a new sphere of expression. And like the birthing process, this movement of the power of the Ground as spirit is a process that (1) unfolds by way of alternating dilations and contractions and (2) is affectively double-edged, involving both pain and ecstatic joy.

Purgation begins with dilation. The power of the Ground forcibly penetrates the egoic sphere, dilating the aperture between the ego and the nonegoic realm. Assuming that the action of spirit has begun being affirmed, the ego responds to this penetration-dilation in a twofold way. On the one hand, because it affirms spirit, the ego seeks to facilitate the penetration-dilation process. On the other hand, because it is still burdened by deep-seated resistances to openness, the ego, in experiencing the influx of spirit, contracts inwardly and defensively. It opposes the birthing process. In contracting in this way, however, the ego does not cease affirming spirit, and therefore it immediately begins to struggle against its contracted state so that it can again cooperate with the movement of spirit. Spirit again penetrates and dilates the egoic sphere, this time more deeply and widely than before. Again, however, given its remaining resistances, the ego contracts, although this time less violently than before. And so the process unfolds. With each succeeding phase of the purgative process, spirit penetrates the egoic sphere more deeply and dilates it more widely, and the ego, responding to this movement of spirit, contracts less violently. The ego in this way becomes progressively more open and less resistant to the movement of spirit. Residual defenses are gradually dissolved and fears of openness are gradually dispelled. Everything within the egoic system that encumbers the spontaneous movement of spirit is gradually purged until, finally, the ego and spirit begin to function as one.

The dilations and contractions of the purgative process are similar in many ways to those of physical labor. However, they differ from the dilations and contractions of physical labor in two major respects. First, whereas the contractions of physical labor become more frequent and violent as physical labor unfolds, the contractions of spiritual labor become less frequent and violent. The contractions of spiritual labor subside as the process unfolds because the ego becomes progressively more receptive to the movement of spirit. And second, whereas the contractions of physical labor cause the dilations (by exerting pressure on the cervix), the contractions of spiritual labor are caused by the dilations (which trigger the ego's resistance). The causality in the two cases works in precisely opposite directions. This, however, is just as it should be, because physical and spiritual labor are processes that unfold in opposite directions. Physical labor is an expulsive process, spiritual labor an infusive one. Physical labor is the process by which a baby is delivered from the womb; spiritual labor is the process by which the power of the Ground as spirit is delivered into the soul. Physical labor is an out-birthing process assisted by contractions; spiritual labor is an in-birthing process resisted by contractions.

As birthing processes, purgation and physical labor are similar in the feelings they evoke. Both are affectively double-edged, involving both agony and ecstasy. In the case of purgation, the penetration of spirit into the egoic sphere is definitely a painful ordeal, especially in the early going. In being forcibly penetrated and dilated, the ego feels as if it were suffering a mortal wound, and in this sense it experiences agony. This agony, however, is always tinged with ecstasy, for the wound suffered is, in the words of St. Teresa of Avila and St. John of the Cross, a "wound of love."[5] It is a wound that is painful and pleasurable at the same time. Spiritual agony and ecstasy, then, although experiential opposites, are inherently interrelated. Both are feelings of being too deeply touched and moved, too powerfully overswept, too intensely enswooned. Indeed, the primary difference between the two is in the magnitude of the *too*. Agony is as it were too, too much, whereas ecstasy is simply too much. Both are feelings of being inwardly overcome by spirit, but whereas agony is a feeling of being overcome in a painful and injurious way, ecstasy is a feeling of being overcome in a delectable and transporting way.

Although purgation is at first more an agony than an ecstasy, it is never merely an agony but always also an ecstasy. And true to the general direction of regeneration in spirit, it is progressively more an ecstasy and progressively less an agony as the process unfolds.

THE MENDING OF THE PSYCHIC FISSURE

Primal repression cleaves the psyche. It severs the connection between the two psychic poles and restructures the psyche into a dualism of disjoined mental-egoic and nonegoic realms. The undoing of primal repression initiates a process by which this dualistic condition is overcome. It reexposes the two poles to each other and sets them on a course of reunion. At first, this course of reunion is a collision course: physico-dynamic potentials reassert themselves within consciousness, and the ego is drawn into the prepersonal unconscious. This initial phase of interpolar reunion is regression in the service of transcendence.

When regression in the service of transcendence has finished its work, the confrontation between the two psychic poles begins to ease and the long-existing fissure separating these poles begins to mend. This point marks the transition from regression in the service of transcendence to regeneration in spirit. In reaching this point, as we have seen, the ego quits its struggle against the power of the Ground and begins instead to struggle against its own resistances to the power of the Ground; the ego ceases combating the power of the Ground as if it were an alien invading force and begins surrendering to it as spirit, as higher self. The ego here begins to join forces with the power of the Ground and to cooperate with it in its work of psychic healing and integration.

The mending of the psychic fissure, then, is accomplished by the power of the Ground once the ego ceases resisting this power and begins surrendering to it as spirit. The more this power is allowed to express itself within the egoic sphere, the more the two poles of the psyche share in a common life. And the more the ego acts in unison with this power, the more the two poles of the psyche begin to interact in harmonious and functionally coordinated ways. Remaining tensions between the two psychic poles are in this fashion gradually eliminated and a close partnership between the two poles develops. This partnership becomes progressively more intimate until, on the verge of integration, even it is transcended and the psyche at last becomes a true two-in-one, a perfected bipolar system.

In being integrated, the two poles of the psyche retain their distinct natures as opposite poles of a bipolar psyche. In doing so, however, they are no longer alienated from each other, as they were during the mental-egoic period. Nor are they in collision with each other, as they were during regression in the service of transcendence. Nor are they even in cooperative interaction with each other, as they were during regeneration in spirit. Rather, the two poles are here completely wedded to each other as a single life. Accordingly, their oppositeness is no longer one of dualistic (alienated, colliding, cooperative) subsystems; it is rather an oppositeness of fully integrated bipolarity. The two poles of the psyche, in being united in spirit, become a *coincidentia oppositorum*.

This fusion of opposites includes not only the two psychic poles themselves but also all of the specific functions and potentials of these two poles. Hence, not only does the ego unite with the Ground to create an all-embracing coincidence of opposites, but the mind also unites with the body, thought with feeling, operational cognition with creative imagination, and developed personality with instinct to create lesser coincidences of opposites. In each of these unions, a completely harmonious duality is forged—a complementary duality of *yang* and *yin*. And each of these harmonious dualities is itself a facet of the larger harmonious duality that is the fully integrated psyche.

SPECIFIC FEATURES OF THE REGENERATION PROCESS

Regeneration in spirit is an integrative process, and therefore discussion of its various features is in a sense a discussion of integration itself. The features of regeneration that I discuss in this section are features that culminate in integration. Accordingly, in considering these features I shall not just be discussing aspects of regeneration in spirit; I shall also, by way of anticipation, be discussing corresponding aspects of integrated existence.

THE TAMING OF THE INSTINCTS

During regression in the service of transcendence, the instincts are inflated to larger-than-life proportions. We have seen that the reawakening of the instincts is an integral part of regression in the service of transcendence. The undoing of primal repression triggers a return of the repressed. Primal repression disallows the instincts their natural expression and freights them with excess energy as well (by limiting the power of the Ground to a primarily instinctual organization).[6] The removal of primal repression therefore quite understandably can lead to a dramatic assertion of instinctual life. It unfetters the instincts and allows them to express themselves in their repressively accumulated power. As a consequence, the instincts during regression in the service of transcendence can beset the ego with compelling urges and images.

The assertion of the instincts lasts until the instincts have discharged their energy surplus and cease reaccumulating energy according to the prior dynamic organization. Then, no longer burdened by an excess standing charge, the instincts gradually become calm and assume their natural proportions within the psychic economy. Concomitant with this change in magnitude is a change in quality: the instincts cease appearing "depraved." The instincts, like physicodynamic potentials generally, appear to the ego in ways that reflect the ego's attitude toward them. Accordingly, because the mental ego had alienated and condemned the instincts, the instincts, mirroring this attitude, had appeared to the ego as alien and perverse urges, urges rightly kept in repressive containment (a vicious circle!). Once, however, the ego has weathered the derepression of the instincts and has finally accepted them as its own, it begins to experience the instincts in fundamentally positive ways. Specifically, the ego begins to experience sexuality as a healthy erotic vibrancy and "aggressiveness" as a healthy assertiveness of will.

The calming of the instincts signals the beginning of a new dynamic organization: the power of the Ground is now liberated from exclusive association with instinctual life and flows freely through the psychophysical system as a whole. The calming of the instincts therefore is not a merely temporary derepression that, once finished, gives way to a rerepression and reaccumulation of energy in the instinctual systems. Rather, it is a permanent derepression that disburdens the instincts once and for all of an unnatural standing charge. I am not suggesting that the instincts, in discharging themselves, become dead. On the contrary, they continue to be systems that are keenly sensitive to appropriate stimuli. In remaining sensitive, however, the instincts cease being systems that are stimulated in a chronic, smoldering way. They lose the excess of energy that hitherto had made them relentlessly impelling "drives" (*Triebe*) and become systems of experience that, like all others, are at times aroused and engaged and at other times dormant and still.

This new dynamic organization is therefore in no way a noninstinctual organization, much less an anti-instinctual one. The person for whom this new organization is coming into being is every bit as instinctual as before, if not more so. The primary difference is that this person is not ambivalently riveted on sex and aggression. The instincts are in no way weakened, but they now lose their compelling and "unclean" or hostile character. Indeed, in being disburdened of their standing charge and in being accepted by the ego, the instincts become dimensions of truly human experience; they become dimensions of personhood. No longer reduced to unconscious, wanton "drives," they show themselves to be modalities of experience that support and enrich conscious life.

The taming of the instincts has been expressed in mythological and spiritual literature in a variety of ways. The phenomenon is frequently depicted in stories of saints and yogis for whom wild animals have become tame. Wild animals, especially ferocious predators, fittingly symbolize the repressed instincts. The befriending of wild animals by a person of great spiritual power therefore gives effective expression to the kind of instinctual life that emerges through the regeneration process. The taming of the instincts is also expressed in the Tantric conception of the turning upward of the *chakras* that occurs upon the awakening of *kundalini*. Tantrism holds that when *kundalini* (conceived here as the power of the Ground repressively organized as libido) is awakened and begins its psychophysiological ascent in the manifest form of *shakti* (conceived here as the power of the Ground as liberated spirit), the *chakras* (centers of the instincts and of major affective and cognitive systems) are turned from a face-down to a face-up orientation. This inversion indicates that the instincts, freed from the onus of primal repression, are able to express themselves freely and in the service of higher life possibilities.

THE REINHABITING OF THE BODY

The body is reawakened during regression in the service of transcendence. The opening of the Dynamic Ground awakens the power of the Ground, which begins to break through the myriad knots and constrictions that make up the overall posture of primal repression (and primal alienation). In cases of exceptionally intense and abrupt awakening, as we have seen, this breakthrough can give rise to bizarre physical phenomena such as spasms, snapping sensations, and a variety of spontaneous movements and vocalizations. In those instances when the ego is confronted with phenomena such as these, it feels as if an unknown force were working its way through the body, opening the body and returning it to life. To the ego, the body seems to be undergoing a resurrection from the dead, without ever having died in the literal sense of the term. Moreover, as this "resurrection" unfolds, the ego begins to experience many new sensual feelings arising from the body. The body is *aroused*; it plies the ego with new feelings that beckon the ego to abandon its cerebral post and yield to physical delights. The ego is drawn to these new feelings, but it is also threatened by them because they rudely disabuse it, the *mental* ego, of its airs of incorporeality and entice it to return to embodied life.

Just as the "resurrection" of the body is a characteristic feature of regression in the service of transcendence, so the "reincarnation" of the ego is a characteristic feature of regeneration in spirit. During the regenerative period, the ego experiences a reversal in its attitude toward the body and begins a return to concrete bodily life. This reversal is a consequence of the reversal that occurs in the ego's stance toward the power of the Ground. For given that the power of the Ground is a dynamic reality that moves through and enlivens the body, it follows that the ego's reversal in stance toward the power of the Ground—which before the ego had resisted but now affirms—is at the same time a reversal in stance toward the body. If the power of the Ground is the ego's higher spiritual self and if the body is the home of the power of the Ground, it follows—and the ego, notwithstanding its deep-seated Cartesianism, is forced to conclude—that the body is also its, the ego's, home. By surrendering to the power of the Ground, then, the ego at the same time surrenders itself to reembodiment. It drops its airs of incorporeality and commences a reidentifying return to bodily life. The body having been "resurrected," the ego now allows itself to be "reincarnated"; it returns to the body as the temple of its own spiritual life.

Two of the more important ramifications of the ego's "reincarnation" are (1) that the ego becomes more "earthy," less "heady," and (2) that the ego is reestablished in polymorphously sensual life.

During the mental-egoic period, the center of gravity of consciousness is located in the head. The mental ego, dissociated from the body, is stationed in the uppermost regions and conducts life from an elevated, cerebral standpoint, from the "pilot's seat" located behind the eyes and between the ears. To be sure, the body of the mental-egoic period is not a completely insensate appendage; it continues to be a source of physical sensations. These sensations, however—except for genitally based sexual sensations—tend to be of a somewhat muted sort. Moreover, in good Cartesian fashion, they are sensations that the ego experiences from a distance. The mental ego is attracted to or repulsed by bodily sensations, and it capitulates to or defends itself against them. These sensations, however, do not "belong to" the mental ego. In the mental ego's perception at least, they are sensations *of the body* rather than of the mental ego itself.

The head ceases being the center of gravity of consciousness once the body is reawakened and the ego, in yielding to spirit, begins to reinhabit the body. At first, during regression in the service of transcendence, the ego simply falls from its elevated post and descends into the abyss of the prepersonal unconscious (associated with lower instinctual regions). This descent into the abyss, however, finally comes to an end. The ego "touches Ground" (located literally at the seat of the body) and, in achieving contact with the basis of its being, begins being supported and buoyed by the spiritual power that rises from the Ground. The center of gravity of consciousness in this way shifts from above to below. The ego of course continues to conduct mental operations and to interact with the world through the sense organs located in the head. In continuing to perform these functions, however, the ego's existence is no longer limited to the area of the head. The ego's existence now extends throughout the body, and it has its anchor in the dynamic center in the lower body. The ego is now firmly planted in the Ground, and life now has an earthy, visceral, and hearty rather than an exclusively airy and cerebral character.

The reinhabiting of the body also brings about a return to polymorphously sensual life. The ego, in being reembodied, becomes a sensual ego, for the ego's return to the body is at the same time a reowning by the ego of the body's sensations. These sensations, in being adopted by the ego, gradually cease posing a threat to the ego and begin being experienced in fundamentally positive ways. The ego at this point is on closer and therefore better terms with bodily sensations. The ego is no longer seriously disturbed by the awakened body and increasingly experiences the sensations of the awakened body as enriching ingredients of life. The ego now relates to the body as a field of awakened sensual experience in which it is increasingly at home and in which, increasingly, it can operate without being distracted or displaced.

The ego does not become completely grounded in the body until full integration is achieved. Despite its increasing acceptance of bodily life, then, the ego undergoing regeneration in spirit is on occasion still distressed by bodily sensations. This problem, however, is not serious, and in any case it is progressively overcome as the ego becomes more settled on the physicodynamic plane. Once the ego has completed the process of reembodiment, it ceases experiencing any further difficulty with bodily sensations. The ego becomes fully attuned to embodied existence; it becomes intimate with all of the sensations of the awakened body without any longer being troubled by them.

THE HARNESSING OF THE CREATIVE PROCESS

We have seen that regression in the service of transcendence can be attended by a number of disturbances to cognitive functioning: (1) mental immobility and hyperactivity, (2) unwelcome intuitions, (3) menacing or tempting images, and (4) states of inert vacancy and wild inflation. With the exception of the states of immobility and inert vacancy, all of these phenomena continue into regeneration in spirit.[7] In remaining a part of the ego's experience, however, these phenomena change in a way that conforms to the general pattern of the regenerative period: they become decreasingly negative and increasingly positive as regeneration unfolds.

The states of mental hyperactivity result from the sudden injection of the power of the Ground into the egoic sphere. During regression in the service of transcendence, the supercharging effect of the power of the Ground tends to accelerate mental activity to uncontrollable levels. The mind is prone to race frantically from idea to idea. These states of overstimulation, in being characteristic of regression in the service of transcendence, gradually disappear once regression gives way to regeneration. During regeneration, the ego becomes progressively stronger and better adapted to the power of the Ground and therefore begins to be affected less negatively and more positively by this power. Specifically, the "high octane" of the power of the Ground begins to affect the mind less and less by speeding it up and more and more by increasing is vigor and stamina.

The ego is set upon by unwelcome intuitions during regression in the service of transcendence because it has been disarmed, thrown from an active to a passive posture, and forced to observe the airing of the submerged unconscious. The unconscious becomes conscious, and the ego has no choice but to witness the display. This disclosure of previously repressed materials lasts throughout the ego's regression to the Ground; then, as the turn to regeneration in spirit is made, it begins to taper off. The ego undergoing regeneration in spirit of course continues to be struck by insights manifesting from psychic depths, but its captive witnessing of *derepressing* contents is for the most part over. Moreover, because the ego grows in strength during regeneration in spirit, it begins to regain control of its cognitive posture. The ego is no longer helplessly pinned down in the posture of passive openness. It is rather strong enough at this point that it can begin to choose its cognitive mode, whether receptive-intuitive or active-operational.

As we know, the images spawned by the autosymbolic process during regression in the service of transcendence can be vivid and realistic. In some instances they can even take the form of full-bodied apparitions, virtual hallucinations. The prepersonal unconscious is at this point undergoing derepression, and the autosymbolic process sometimes dramatizes derepressing materials by giving them lifelike form. The ego during regression in the service of transcendence is therefore in the curious position of being tormented by its own creative faculty. It is subjected not just to distressing insights into its repressed underlife but also sometimes to a play of realistic images (and voices) embodying this underlife. The ego is subjected to such images until the materials under-

going derepression have been defused or integrated within consciousness, at which time the autosymbolic process ceases for the most part
producing images that disturb the ego and begins producing images
that support and guide the ego. This turning point is, of course, the
transition for regression in the service of transcendence to regeneration
in spirit.

The change in autosymbolic images that occurs at this turning point
can be described by saying that these images, or at least the more realistic among them, are gradually transformed from virtual hallucinations into genuine visions, that is, from manifestations of repressed
materials into manifestations of higher meanings and possibilities.
Autosymbolic images at this point become decreasingly negative and
increasingly positive in their perceived character and effect upon the
ego. They decreasingly depict demons and infernal depths and increasingly depict angels and celestial heights. The images of the regenerative
period are progressively more light than dark, more allies than adversaries. They become progressively more "self" than "other" until,
finally, as regeneration culminates in integration, they drop their appa-
ritional guise and become visions in the strict sense of the term: creative
explorations of the as yet unknown.

The wild inflations that continue into the regenerative period also
observe the general pattern of this period: they too become decreasingly negative and increasingly positive as regeneration unfolds.[8] Specifically, these states are steadily transformed from wild inflations into
calm infusions, from eruptive ecstasies into composed enstasies (Eliade's [1969] term for mature contemplative absorptions). This transformation may move through the following sequence of stages: (1) *cognitive manias*—states of cognitive upheaval that, although not completely
incoherent, are seriously intoxicated and disorganized; (2) *cognitive raptures*—states of inebriated expansiveness that occur unexpectedly and
that are more coherent than cognitive manias; (3) *self-induced transports*—states of creative infusion-absorption that are triggered by the
ego's own mental efforts and that, although still unstable, are more
clear and sustained than cognitive raptures; and (4) *mature contemplations*—states of creative infusion-absorption that arise from disciplined
concentration and that are at once powerfully absorbed and completely
lucid.

Unlike the states of inert vacancy occurring during regression in the
service of transcendence, these ecstatic and enstatic states are cognitive
states in the positive sense of the term: they are alive, indeed overflowing, with cognitive content. They are modes of experience through
which creative cognitions are communicated to the ego. Moreover,

because these states become increasingly coherent, composed, and voluntarily evocable as the regeneration process unfolds toward integration, what happens during the regenerative period is that the ego's capacity for infusion and its ability to pursue imaginal-intuitive inquiry are gradually merged. The ego's infused states become less agitated and more engagedly absorbed, and concomitantly the images and intuitions that appear to the ego lose the character of unexpected manifestations from the blue and become more the fruits of the ego's own contemplative "in-search." The complete union of the capacity for infusion and absorption on the one hand and the ability to access the creative process on the other is achieved in contemplative enstasy. The arrival of contemplative cognition indicates that the ego is at last fully integrated with the nonegoic sources of cognition. The subject of contemplative cognition will be taken up in the next chapter.

In sum, regeneration in spirit is a time during which factors that had seriously disrupted mental functioning become factors that make a positive contribution to mental functioning. It is a period during which causes of mental disorganization become ingredients of a higher mental reorganization. Specifically, it is a period during which dynamic, intuitive, autosymbolic, and ecstatic-enstatic potentials or modes, which had broken through into consciousness in ways mimicking psychopathology, are integrated on a higher level, bringing into being the highest type of human cognition: creative contemplation.

THE PERSONALIZATION OF SPIRITUAL POWER

In surrendering to the transformative influence of the power of the Ground, the ego surrenders to a process that leads both to its own spiritualization and to a personalization of spirit. The ego is spiritualized in that it becomes an expressive vehicle of the power of the Ground. People undergoing regeneration in spirit do not act by egoic means alone; they act, rather, or at least are beginning to act, according to the promptings of spirit. To be sure, the actions of these people are grounded in acquired knowledge and skills and are frequently guided by creative insight. People undergoing regeneration do not act blindly. They do, however, act spontaneously, from sentiments of the heart as well as from considerations of the head. The ego is no longer separated from the Ground, and the power of the Ground now wells up in the ego, animating it and moving it to action. The ego is filled with spirit and therefore is no longer the sole author of its actions. It is now spirit *through the ego* rather than just the ego that acts.

This spiritualization of the ego is at the same time a personalization of spirit. For the ego gives spirit a unique personal form and expression. In personalizing spirit, it should be stressed, the ego does not arrogate spirit; the ego yields to spirit and struggles against its own remaining resistances to the movement of spirit. The ego becomes an instrument of spirit rather than spirit a power of the ego. In personalizing spirit, the ego accedes to spirit rather than laying claim to it.

Although the ego struggles against its remaining resistances to spirit, it does not always succeed in this struggle. Although the ego wants to give itself unconditionally to spirit, it still occasionally contracts against the movement of spirit and sometimes even tries to appropriate the fruits of spirit (and the fruits of other nonegoic potentials as well). Such countermovements and attempted usurpations, however, are quickly corrected. The power of the Ground, having already reasserted itself as the sovereign power of the psyche, brooks no misbehavior from the ego. And the ego in turn, having already acceded to the sovereignty of spirit and having already enjoyed many of the blessings of spirit, accepts such corrections well, realizing that they are the inescapable effects of its own actions and the requisite means of its purgation. Given that the ego is not yet fully aligned with spirit, it is understandable that the ego occasionally reverts to its old egocentric ways. When it does, however, it is immediately set straight, and it suffers this correction in good spirit.

Many specific phenomena are associated with the spiritualization of the ego and the personalization of spirit. Mention has already been made of ecstasies and transports, which are particularly distinctive of regeneration in spirit. To these phenomena can be added behaviors that are the outer manifestations of such spiritual intoxications, for example, exclamations of joy and dances of delight. Perhaps the most intriguing phenomena that are said to accompany spiritual awakening, however, are supernormal powers such as clairvoyance, healing, prophecy, and inspired leadership capabilities. Supernormal powers are by no means a necessary or perhaps even a usual part of the spiritual process. Nevertheless, virtually every religious tradition acknowledges such powers as possibilities inherent to spiritual life.

Different traditions have different attitudes toward these powers. For example, in Hinduism and Buddhism these powers (*siddhis*) are considered dangers that can entrap the spiritual seeker and thus interfere with the proper goal of spiritual life: *moksha* or *nirvana*. In Christianity, in contrast, miraculous abilities or special spiritual gifts are held to possess prima facie value and are considered worthy of cultivation on the condition that they make a positive contribution to the spiritual community. This view at any rate was advanced by St. Paul. Despite having different attitudes like these, however, almost all spiritual traditions agree that supernormal powers should be approached with caution and should always be kept subordinate to spiritual ends. Almost all traditions agree that safeguards should be employed to keep the seeker from becoming sidetracked or inflated by special powers.

AWE, ECSTASY, BLESSEDNESS, AND BLISS

Anxiety and despair are moods or states of mind characteristic of the first stage of regression in the service of transcendence, and dread and trance (immobile dissociation, inert vacancy) are moods or states of mind characteristic of the second stage. Correspondingly, awe and ecstasy are moods or states of mind characteristic of regeneration in spirit.[9] Awe and ecstasy are most pronounced in the early and middle phases of the regenerative period. In later phases, as regeneration culminates in integration, awe is gradually transformed into the sense of blessedness, and ecstasy is gradually transformed into bliss. The whole regressive-regenerative period thus observes the following parallel unfoldings of mood or state of mind: (1) from anxiety through dread and awe to blessedness; (2) from despair through trance and ecstasy to bliss.

The difference between dread and trance on the one hand and awe and ecstasy on the other is just the difference between their respective developmental stages. Dread and trance reflect the ego's experience of being overtaken by a force felt to be alien and dangerous; awe and ecstasy in contrast reflect the ego's experience of being overcome by a force felt to be miraculous and beneficial. Both mood pairs indicate that the ego is not well aligned with the force that it faces and, therefore, that that force deals with the ego in a violent manner. Dread and trance reflect the dark cathectic and gravitational influences of the power of the Ground, which seizes the ego and holds it in a state of uneasy suspension (dread) or heavy inertness (trance). Awe and ecstasy reflect the surging action of the power of the Ground, which stuns or dizzies the ego (awe) or infuses it beyond the bursting point (ecstasy). Both of these pairs of states of mind reflect ungentle treatment of the ego by the power of the Ground in its manifestation as the holy (Otto, 1917), the *mysterium tremendum et fascinans*. Dread and trance are responses to the negative side of the holy: the dark, the eerie, the abyssal; awe and ecstasy, in contrast, are responses to the positive side of the holy: the miraculous, the ethereal, the transporting.

Dread, trance, awe, and ecstasy all seem to have a connection with the autonomic nervous system. All of these states of mind exhibit the paradoxical hot-cold, fever-chill interplay that is characteristic of autonomic activity. Dread and trance are colder states. Dread involves clamminess and bristling chill; trance involves frozen inertness.[10] Even these states, however, show signs of the hot side of autonomic activity, for both are versions of the "cold sweats." Both manifest a psychophysiological precipitation that is ordinarily associated with fever.[11] In contrast to dread and trance, awe and ecstasy show a more even balance— or, more accurately, a more evident mixing or alternating—of hot and cold. Awe is breathless astonishment that mixes both perspiration and chill, palpitation and horripilation, and ecstasy is wild effusion that tends to be alternately hot (feverish frenzies) and then cold (shivers of delight, deluges of tears). Both pairs of states are paradoxical in the way they bring together opposites. No member of either pair, however, truly synthesizes these opposites. Such a synthesis, as we shall see in a moment, is to be found only in the integrated states that succeed awe and ecstasy.

To repeat, awe and ecstasy are violent states. They are stunning impacts or sudden eruptions that indicate that the ego is still not in full alignment with the Ground. These states are most violent in the early phases of the regenerative period; then, as the ego is purged and becomes better attuned to the Ground, they become steadily less violent and more smooth, subtle, and continuous. As the ego becomes more integrated with the Ground, it is better able to tolerate the influx of the power of the Ground without suffering paralysis, inflation, or other types of incapacitation; it is better able to breathe the rarefied air of spirit without being dazzled, dizzied, or intoxicated. As the ego is brought into agreement with the Ground, then, such sudden and dramatic states as awe and ecstasy occur much less frequently and are gradually replaced by states that reflect a more fluid and gentle movement of the power of the Ground. Specifically, awe is replaced by the sense of blessedness and ecstasy is replaced by bliss.

Blessedness resembles awe in being an immediate I-Thou meeting between the ego and spiritual power. Both are intimate beholdings of the power of the Ground in its transcendent aspect as a spiritual reality that presents itself to the ego from a source beyond the ego's own sphere. Related in this way, awe and blessedness differ in two principal regards. First, as we have seen, awe is abrupt and defacilitating, whereas blessedness is not. And second, awe and the sense of blessedness quite evidently differ in tone and meaning. Whereas awe is an ego-eclipsing beholding of the miraculous or sublime (of the power of the Ground as *mysterium tremendum*), blessedness is a serenely joyous and grateful beholding of the beatific or divine. Awe involves a humbling of the ego, a reduction of it to insignificance in the face of a magisterial power; blessedness in contrast involves an exalting of the ego—or of ego-based consiousness—which is allowed to share in the spiritual glory of the world. Awe, although primarily a positive state of mind, is still tinged with fear, which implies that the ego is still ambivalent toward the Ground and, therefore, that the Ground is still bivalent in its appearance to the ego. Blessedness in contrast is a completely positive state of mind in which the ego, completely aligned with the Ground, is no longer ambivalent toward the Ground and in which, therefore, the Ground is no longer bivalent, but is rather wholly positive, in its appearance to the ego. Blessedness as it emerges during the later phases of the regeneration process still has much in common with awe. As regeneration approaches integration, however, blessedness is experienced with increasing fidelity to its nature. It loses all traces of fear and becomes pure reverential joy.

One other way in which blessedness differs from awe is the way in which blessedness synthesizes the hot and cold sensations arising from the autonomic nervous system. Whereas awe evidently mixes, without really combining, hot and cold, fever and chills, blessedness fuses these opposites into a single paradoxical whole. Blessedness thus is in a sense both hot and cold and in a sense neither; it is a synthesis of opposites. Blessedness is "hot" in that it is a radiant happiness. Blessedness, however, is also "cold" in that it involves the delicate shivers and invisible tears that accompany profound gratitude. In its initial emergence, the sense of blessedness usually combines these opposites in an unstable way, taking the form of tearful rejoicing: crying in uncontainable thankfulness for the perfection and beauty of things. In later, more mature stages of its expression, however, the sense of blessedness fuses hot and cold more completely and thereby brings about a more subtle resultant. In the end, as regeneration culminates in integration, the sense of blessedness assumes its final form: glowing gratitude, the sense of being divinely favored.

Closely paralleling the transformation of awe into blessedness is the transformation of ecstasy into bliss. As the state succeeding ecstasy, bliss resembles ecstasy in being an experience of dynamic, upwelling, expansive happiness. Bliss differs from ecstasy, however, in being more continuous and composed; bliss does not come in explosive bursts, and it does not involve wild euphoria. In fact, compared with ecstatic states, which are intoxicated, bliss would have to be considered a state of sobriety. And so it is: it is a state of clarity and composure. If, however, bliss is a state of sobriety in this sense, it is not a state of sobriety in other senses of the term. For in contrast to the seriousness frequently associated with sobriety, bliss is full of good spirit. It is overflowing with joy. In contrast to the mental ego's sobriety, which is gravely earnest, the sobriety of bliss is calmly exuberant. It is a quiet radiance.

Bliss is closely related to blessedness. It is in fact the very same feeling state shorn of its relational, I-Thou, significance. Whereas blessedness is a deeply grateful beholding of the power of the Ground in its ego-transcendent aspect, bliss is the sheer feeling of the power of the Ground as an inner infusive current. Bliss, one might say, is blessedness merely felt, not meant. Bliss lacks the cognitive dimension of blessedness but it shares the same affective composition. In this latter regard, therefore, bliss, like blessedness, is a synthesis of qualitative opposites; it, too, is a serene (cool) delight (warm). More precisely, bliss is a joy that wells up in the soul slowly and smoothly and that has the "feel" of a soothing, sweet liquid. The soul is saturated with the "juice of life," the power of the Dynamic Ground, which bathes the ego coolly and fills it with a sense of glowing well-being. The ego is soothed by an inner ambrosial fluid, a fluid that, in rising from the Ground, gently infuses the ego and then spills out of the soul in ripples of subtle delight. Bliss, like blessedness, combines hot and cold in a way that transcends their contrariety, yielding a paradoxical resultant, a liquid warmth that sets the ego coolly aglow.

Given this union of opposites, it is understandable that the chief symbol for bliss would be honey or nectar. Honey possesses almost all of the right qualities: it is a life-giving substance that flows slowly and smoothly and is both sweet in taste and radiant in color. Honey possesses so many of the right qualities that it is almost a complete symbol for bliss. It is rightly likened to the drink of the gods. The only relevant quality that honey does not possess is cool refreshingness. A substance that does possess this quality, however, along with others essential to the experience of bliss, is milk—which, as *mother's* milk, is in any case already deeply associated with the experience of bliss. Honey by itself, in its warm viscosity, is soothing in a way that suggests sleepy contentment. Milk, in contrast, in its cool moistness, is soothing in a way that suggests rejuvenated alertness. Milk, unlike honey, conveys the higher sobriety of bliss. The perfect symbol for bliss would therefore be a substance that combines the relevant features of both milk and honey. It would be a silvery-gold liquid that flows slowly and smoothly and is vitalizing, refreshing, and sweet. Earthly milk and honey only approximate the divine nectar, the sap of the tree of life.

True bliss belongs only to the integrated stage of life. Nevertheless, states progressively closer to bliss occur during the second half of regeneration in spirit. The direction of change during the second half of the regeneration process is away from episodes of ecstasy and toward the continuous experience of bliss. Just as blessedness gradually becomes a permanent attitude, so bliss gradually becomes a constant underlying feeling state. It becomes the affective ground on which the ego's emotional life is played out.

ENCHANTMENT AND HALLOWED RESPLENDENCE

Whereas flatness and strangeness are the characteristic features of the world during the first and second stages, respectively, of regression in the service of transcendence, enchantment and hallowed resplendence are the characteristic features of the world during the early-to-middle and later phases, respectively, of regeneration in spirit. Accordingly, the transition from regression in the service of transcendence to early phases of regeneration in spirit is marked by a transformation of the world from an environment that is eerie and alien into one that is miraculous and sublime; and the transition from early and middle to later phases of regeneration in spirit (leading into integration) is marked by a transformation of the world from an environment that is miraculous and sublime into one that is sanctified and glorious, of celestial cast and hue.

During the second stage of regression in the service of transcendence, the world is recharged with psychic energy: the power of the Ground, released from the constraints of primal repression, flows out from the soul and becomes the atmosphere of the world. This movement of the power of the Ground invests the world with a numinous aura of a surreal, ominous character. The world as a whole and everything in it is suddenly rendered new, in a strange and frightening way. Just as, during the second stage of regression in the service of transcendence, it seems as though one is being possessed by an alien power, so it also seems as though the world is being haunted by an alien power. The person who, subjectively, experiences dread looks out upon a world that, objectively, is (or seems) uncanny.

Without losing any of its numinosity, the world is in gradual measure relieved of its unnerving alienness once regeneration in spirit begins. For the ego, in being regressed to the Ground, is released from the ominous gravity of the Ground, and correspondingly the world is relieved of its eerie and foreboding darkness. The world is in this way brightened. In being brightened, however, it remains mysterious and pronouncedly "other"—although now in the primarily positive mode of enchantment. The world continues to reverberate with the power of the Ground in ways that are radically unfamiliar and arresting; the world continues to defy comprehension, to be unfathomable, full of hidden depths and meanings. The spiritual power enlivening the world, however, is now sensed to be basically benign; the world is now sensed to be charmed rather than haunted, awesome rather than dreadful, miraculous rather than menacing. It might be said that the ego in this transitional phase has finally found its way out of the deepest and darkest part of the forest and has entered an enchanted wood.

The ego, however, is still in the woods. The enchantment of the world, like the awe and ecstasy of the subject, reflects early and middle phases of regeneration in spirit. Significant purgations of the egoic system are still in order before complete ego-Ground alignment, and therefore integration, is established. The enchanted world for this reason is not the world of the integrated stage, nor even the world of later phases of the regeneration process. The enchanted world is rather an intermediate territory, a transitional domain that leads the ego from the alien land in which it had been wandering to its true and final home, the glorious estate of the integrated stage.

The enchanted world might be said to be the purgatorial space between hell and heaven.[12] Beginning at the exit of the underworld, it is a region still darkly shrouded and frighteningly "other"; entering the central region of its distinctive space, it is a region that is miraculous and sublime; then, ascending to its upper reaches, it is a region that increasingly partakes of celestial splendor. The enchanted world is a world that begins haunted and strange, that becomes magical and marvelous, and that, approaching its far boundary, finally becomes hallowed and resplendent, a heavenly home.

As regeneration nears integration, then, the world begins to lose its enchantment and begins to take on the qualities of an earthly heaven. The world is disenchanted, not in the sense that it is emptied of spiritual power, but rather in the sense that the spiritual power of the world finally loses the last vestiges of darkness, mystery, and foreignness. The world, as intensely alive with spirit as ever, now becomes a gleaming, pellucid, and utterly native domain. The world in this phase ceases being enchanted and becomes *hallowed*; it ceases being marvelous and becomes *resplendent*; it ceases being to any degree alien to the ego and becomes *home*. In approaching integration, the ego returns, on a higher level, to its original Ground, which, no longer the womb of the Great Mother, is now the ego's hallowedly resplendent home.

Hallowed resplendence is the objective correlate of blessedness and bliss. As such, it shares essential features with these states of mind, one of which is the synthesis of qualitative opposites. Blessedness and bliss, as we have seen, fuse hot and cold; similarly, hallowed resplendence fuses fire and ice. Hallowed resplendence combines both brilliant radiance and crystalline cool. A hallowedly resplendent world is one that is bright without being hot and crisp without being cold. Everything in such a world possesses a lustrous, scintillating quality. Everything is accentuated by a luminous sheen, a shimmering aura that imbues things with vibrant power, sharply enhanced qualities, and translucent depth. In a hallowedly resplendent world, everything gleams with dewy newness and glows with a deep, burnished radiance.

Perhaps the chief symbol of resplendence is the sparkling jewel, especially the diamond, which so dramatically synthesizes brightness and coolness, fire and ice. The diamond is utterly translucent and illumined; it has no hidden or dark recesses. Moreover, the diamond is cool to the touch, and its multifaceted brilliance, rather than being blinding, is pleasing to the eye. For these reasons, diamonds—and precious stones and metals generally—are frequently said to be the building materials of the heavenly city, which is envisioned with jewel-bedecked buildings and streets made of gold or rare gems.

Rivaling the jewel, or the jeweled city, as a symbol of hallowed resplendence is the garden paradise, which is a setting characterized by superabundant life, superreal qualities, ethereal atmosphere, and harmony of all life. The garden paradise is an environment pulsating with superabundant life; everything in it is fresh and lush, at once virgin and in full bloom. The garden paradise is an environment embellished with superreal (voluptuous, extravagant) qualities: exploding colors, delicate floral scents, velvety textures. The garden paradise is an environment graced with an ethereal atmosphere; its air is brightened and warmed by an equatorial sun and at the same time kept fresh and cool by gentle showers. And the garden paradise is an environment in which all of the flora and fauna exist in the most benign harmony. Even the serpent is a friend (the instincts are tame), and the central tree is a tree not only of knowledge (the ego) but also of life (the Ground). The garden paradise, so resplendent in every dimension, serves as a fitting symbol for the beatified world that begins to emerge as the ego makes the homeward turn toward integrated existence.

In sum, regeneration in spirit is a period during which the world steadily becomes less foreign and dark, first in the sense of becoming less strange or surreal and more enchanted, then in the sense of becoming less enchanted and more heavenly. The ego gradually finds its way out of the forest it had entered during the second stage of regression in the service of transcendence. At first it finds its way to an enchanted wood, and then, breaking into the open, it finds its way to paradise. The

TABLE 8.1

Ego-Mood and World-Tone Correlations

			Distinctive Mood of Ego	Pervasive Tone of World
			INTEGRATION	
Integration	Permanent		**Bliss:** Serene delight; power of Ground flows smoothly, thickly, sweetly. **Blessedness:** Grateful joy; the sense of being favored to live in a beatified world.	**Hallowed resplendence:** World is beatified. World is coolly radiant, superreal spiritual paradise in which the ego is completely at home.
Regeneration in Spirit	Late		TRANSITION TO INTEGRATION	
			Transition to bliss: Wild inflations subside; higher joyous sobriety emerges. **Transition to blessedness:** Beholding of spiritual power of world becomes less arresting, more exalting. Feelings of humility, reverence, and joy emerge.	**Transition to hallowed resplendence:** World gradually loses its mysterious otherness and becomes a glorious home.
	Early		ENCHANTMENT	
			Ecstasy: Wild inflations; intoxicating transports. **Awe:** Stunning or dizzying encounter with miraculous or sublime.	**Enchantment:** World becomes strange, full of higher, unforeseeable possibilites.
Regression in the Service of Transcendence	Stage Two		ESTRANGEMENT	
			Trance: Immobile dissociations; inert vacant states; ego held in traction by the power of the Ground (also wild inflations). **Dread:** Hair-raising encounter with the eerie and alien.	**Strangeness:** World becomes strange, haunted, surreal. World is full of hidden, sinister meanings and possibilities.
	Stage One		ALIENATION	
			Despair: Loss of hope that world can be reengaged and worldly identity reanimated. **Anxiety:** Fear of losing touch with the world and of losing worldly being and value; vertigo of possibilities.	**Flatness:** World suffers derealization, becomes flat: dead, meaningless.

(Time Line axis on the left side, pointing upward.)

ego, having been lost in darkness, is at last delivered to its glorious destiny.

The completely parallel alterations in (subjective) mood and in the (objective) tone of the world that arise and succeed one another during regression in the service of transcendence and regeneration in spirit are summarized in table 8.1.

CONCLUSION

The regeneration process is of no set duration; nevertheless, it is rarely finished in a short period of time. Doctrines of sudden enlightenment and instant salvation notwithstanding, the regeneration process normally unfolds over a stretch of years. To be sure, spiritual development can be punctuated by dramatic conversions, awakenings, *satori* experiences, and so forth. The potentials that emerge suddenly during episodes such as these, however, take time to be integrated harmoniously with egoic structures and functions. The reawakening of physicodynamic life and its breakthrough into consciousness can be abrupt, but the ensuing transformation of the egoic sphere and reuniting of egoic and nonegoic poles is typically a long-term process.

It is, however, a process with a bright horizon, because it is a developmental change the direction of which is *away* from suffering and *toward* joy. Regeneration in spirit is a process that, although full of difficulties, moves toward a positive end: it is decreasingly negative and increasingly positive as it moves in the direction of integration. The ego undergoing regeneration is therefore confident of its own eventual salvation. The ego senses that the transformation it is undergoing is a positive one, and it can see that progress is being made. The goal toward which the ego is headed is a goal of the progressively actualized sort. Integration is not something that appears suddenly at the end of the regeneration process; it is rather the final realization of that process.

9

Integration

INTEGRATION IS THE CULMINATING stage of human life. It is the stage at which human nature is finally perfected and rendered whole. Integration, then, is the end, *telos*, of human development. It is also, however, a new beginning. For it is only after achieving integration that a person, having completed the developmental process, can begin living a fully human life. Integration is the end of *becoming* human and the beginning of *being* a complete human being.

DUALISM TRANSCENDED: THE *COINCIDENTIA OPPOSITORUM*

Regeneration in spirit is the process by which the two poles of the psyche are reconciled and united. It is therefore only after the regeneration process has completed its work that the two poles begin functioning as a fully developed bipolar system. Prior to this point, the two poles of the psyche are at least to some degree at odds with each other and therefore do not interact in a completely unified and complementary way. It is only with the achievement of integration that the psyche becomes a completely harmonious duality, a *coincidentia oppositorum*.

The integrated psyche possesses a great many facets. Of these, I shall here consider only those that are most basic to it in its character as a bipolar coincidence of opposites.

MIND-BODY INTEGRATION: THE SPIRITUAL BODY

The body is "resurrected" during regression in the service of transcendence, and then the ego is "reincarnated" during regeneration in spirit. By means of these transformations, the mind-body dualism characteristic of the mental-egoic period is overcome and a higher mind-body whole is brought into being. The ego, in being "reincarnated," is rerooted in the body and returns to polymorphously sensual life.

As the "reincarnated" ego approaches integration, it begins to realize that, in a sense, it has *two* bodies: not only the physical body (which is now awakened) but also a subtle energic body (the circulating power of the Dynamic Ground, which does the awakening). The ego, that is, begins to realize that it is not only a material reality but also, and even more essentially, a moving dynamic reality, an inner spiritual body. The existence of such a spiritual body is recognized in many of the world's religions. For example, Christianity speaks of a "resurrection body" (*soma pneumatikon*), Hinduism of a "subtle body" (*sukshma sharira*), and Mahayana Buddhism of a "body of bliss" (*sambhogakaya*).

Issuing from the Ground, located in the dynamic system in the lower body, spiritual power ascends into the body, charging it with a vital current. Much of this power is channeled through a central column associated with the spinal column: the *axis mundi*, the Tree of Life, the *sushumna*, the staff of the symbolic caduceus. Spiritual power, however, also travels through innumerable subsidiary arteries, called *nadis* in Indian yoga. During the mental-egoic stage of life, most of these arteries are closed off by the many constrictions and occlusions that make up the overall posture of primal repression–primal alienation. These blockages, however, are broken open during regression in the service of transcendence and finally dissolved during regeneration in spirit. By the time integration is achieved, the power of the Ground is able to move freely throughout the body. It circulates without inhibition, thereby bringing awareness not only to the body, which it enlivens, but also to itself as a dynamic presence *that* enlivens. The ego in this way becomes aware of itself as having an energy body within the physical body. The body becomes the "temple of spirit," and spirit becomes not only the ego's higher life but also its new transfigured body.

THOUGHT-FEELING INTEGRATION: CONSCIENCE

The disconnection of thought and feeling characteristic of the mental ego is gradually overcome during the transitional periods leading to integration. During regression in the service of transcendence, feelings hitherto repressed begin asserting themselves in consciousness in a way that disrupts thought. This state of affairs improves during regeneration in spirit owing to the pacification and healing that are inherent to the regeneration process. During regeneration, feelings gradually cease disrupting thought, and affective and cognitive life begin being reconciled. By the time integration is achieved, this reconciliation is complete, and feeling and thought begin functioning as one: feeling united with thought is given sight, and thought united with feeling is given life and spirit. Heart and head are united, giving rise to *conscience* as a fully formed faculty of integrated life.

Integrated people, then, are people of conscience. They are people who cannot think about or be witness to something without knowing at once how they feel about the matter. For integrated people, feeling is an integral part of thinking or perceiving. To be sure, some things are more neutral or purely intellectual than others, and integrated people can be dispassionate in their consideration of these. Concerning the many things that bear upon the fortunes or misfortunes of people (and of living beings generally), however, integrated people are by nature concerned and involved. They have clear and immediate responses to such things. They may, for example, be pained at the sight of suffering, anguished or angered by brutality, saddened by hatred, cheered by the happiness of others, and moved by kindness. Integrated people are in full touch with their own humanity, and therefore they feel for humanity as a whole. To be witness to another's experience is, for integrated people, to share in that experience.

Moreover, this immediate response on the level of feeling is accompanied by an immediate response on the level of action: integrated people act unhesitatingly upon the heartfelt insights of conscience. The Socratic equation of knowledge and virtue therefore holds for integrated people, and for integrated people alone. For integrated people, knowledge of the good is a sufficient condition of doing the good. Conscience is a faculty not only of moral knowledge but also of corresponding moral feeling and action.

Given that they are so keenly sensitive to the world, integrated people are in a sense vulnerable in their emotional life. They cannot see or even think about the sufferings and joys of others without experiencing those sufferings and joys themselves. This "vulnerability," however, is not usually a liability, for although integrated people are easily touched and deeply moved, they are rarely overwhelmed by feelings. They have this inner strength because, for them, there no longer exists a repressed unconscious with potentially explosive affects waiting to be ignited. Nor is there any longer any antagonism between feeling and thought; feelings now empower rather than overpower thoughts. Feelings, then, even very strong ones, do not ordinarily affect integrated people in a disruptive manner. Although easily touched, integrated people are rarely shaken, and although deeply moved, they are rarely swept away in emotional outpourings. To the untutored eye, it might even appear as though integrated people are unfeeling or uncaring. Nothing could be further from the truth, however. For if the feelings of integrated people tend not to be loud, that is because they are so deep and so true.

It should be stressed that conscience responds to positive as well as to negative feelings. Conscience is not just a "vulnerability," a susceptibility to co-suffering. As an intimate attunement of thought and feeling, conscience can be as much a source of joy as grief. Of course, in unhappy times integrated people are bound to experience the unhappiness of others. This sensitivity to the unhappiness of others gives rise to feelings of sadness and even mourning; it does not, however, make integrated people "unhappy." Integrated people see, and therefore feel, both sides of life. Moreover, we should not forget that the feelings of blessedness and bliss are inherent to integrated existence. These feelings make up the affective ground of integrated existence, over which pass the pangs and pleasures, sufferings and joys of conscience. Although integrated people are keenly sensitive to the suffering of the world, they feel both an exquisite joy in being alive and an inexpressible gratitude for a world that, despite its serious flaws, is "perfect."

LOGIC-CREATIVITY INTEGRATION: THE TERTIARY PROCESS

Integrated cognition—or to use Silvano Arieti's (1976) term, the *tertiary process*—is a coincidence of opposites in two main respects, namely, (1) in synthesizing operational control and dynamic absorption, and (2) in synthesizing logical rigor and imaginal-intuitive creativity. I shall briefly describe these two syntheses and explain how they draw upon and integrate the resources of the two poles of the psyche.

Operational control and dynamic absorption. The cognitive transports characteristic of regeneration are gradually transformed into more stable and composed states. Explosive bursts of ideation gradually subside and thought becomes increasingly poised and powerfully absorbed. In other words, cognitive ecstasy gives way to cognitive enstasy: contemplation.

Contemplation is a state of dynamic absorption that is compatible with the exercise of ego functions, including operational cognition. It is a state of powerful yet lucid absorption in which the ego, although fully open to physicodynamic potentials and unselfconsciously involved in experience, is nonetheless still able to exercise ego functions. Also, contemplation is a state that the integrated ego can achieve through its own disciplined efforts.

The manner in which the integrated ego achieves contemplative absorption is quite simple: it does so by giving concentrated attention to the matter in which it would become absorbed. Given the integrated ego's harmonious alignment with the Ground, undivided attention has the effect of mobilizing the power of the Ground and channeling it toward the focal datum, which, consequently, is dynamically charged and becomes a cathexis object. As a cathexis object, the focal datum has a gravitational-solvent effect upon the ego, educing it from its subjective reserve and drawing it into an object-based absorption, an enstasy. In this fashion the ego, in being able to mobilize the power of the Ground, is able voluntarily to enter the absorptive state.

The procedure is always the same: (1) the ego gives one-pointed attention to an object (material thing, idea, image); (2) the power of the Ground follows the lead of attention and flows to the object, charging it and investing it with gravitational-magnetic attractivity; and (3) the ego, responding to the "pull" of the object, allows itself to be drawn to the object and to become absorbed in it. The absorption achieved in this way is not an unconscious trance state. It is rather a state in which the ego, although absorbed, remains fully conscious and able to exercise operational and volitional faculties.

This dynamic conception of the contemplative state provides a way of understanding the stages of meditative practice. Patanjali, we recall, distinguishes between *dharana* (effortful focusing of attention), *dhyana* (effortless, continuous one-pointedness), and *samadhi* (absorption, enstasy, contemplation).[1] For the beginning meditator (commencing practice during the mental-egoic period), these three levels of experience mark stages of progress in meditative practice. People just taking up meditation are essentially beginning the practice of *dharana*. Beginning meditators can usually do little more than struggle to fix attention on a meditation object without succumbing to distraction or drowsiness. With continued practice, however, meditators usually succeed in harnessing attention. They learn how to hold the mind still and remain alert at the same time. They are able more and more easily to give sharply focused and uninterrupted attention to the meditation object. That is to say, they achieve *dhyana*.

Dhyana is a transitional stage of practice that indicates not only that the ego has become more disciplined in its attention but also that the power of the Ground has begun to flow to the meditation object, magnetizing it and thereby rendering it attractive to the ego. In *dhyana*, the ego is able to concentrate more effectively in part because the object of meditation is now charged in a way that draws the ego's attention to it. *Dhyana* indicates that the ego's efforts have begun to tap the power of the Ground and have begun to transform the object of meditation into a cathexis object. *Dhyana*, however, is still a transitional stage. In *dhyana*, the ego still stands apart from the object it witnesses; absorption has not yet occurred—nor is it likely to occur so long as the ego remains a *mental* ego, that is, an ego that is repressively self-encapsulated and disconnected from the Ground.

This fact notwithstanding, the attainment of *dhyana* means that absorption is imminent. It indicates that the meditator is on the verge of unsealing the Ground and thereby of coming under the direct, undiminished influence of the power of the Ground. If, therefore, the meditator perseveres in the practice of *dhyana*, it is likely that the Ground will eventually open and that the ego will be drawn into absorption. At this point the meditation object becomes highly charged with the power of the Ground, and the ego, open to the full (cathectic, gravitational-solvent) effect of the power of the Ground, is drawn into the object as a world of experience unto itself. Subject-object fusion occurs. This fusion is *samadhi*.

After initially achieving *samadhi*, the meditator must work at cultivating *samadhi*. Disciplined effort is required to produce absorptive-contemplative states of increasing clarity and power. Upon attaining *samadhi* at a given level, the meditator is able to perform what Patanjali calls *samyama* at that level. *Samyama* is absorption entered by means of a rapid and easy transition through *dharana, dhyana,* and *samadhi*—which are now successive moments of a single meditative experience rather than, as before, long-term stages of meditative practice. To practice *samyama* on something is, then, to enter it absorptively via a direct *dharana-dhyana-samadhi* route. It is to have command of these three levels of the meditative experience so that they can be employed as a single three-step procedure for achieving contemplative enstasy. And again, the causality of this procedure, I suggest, is dynamic. It is because the integrated ego is open to and aligned with the Ground that its focusing of attention has the effect of mobilizing the power of the Ground and consequently of cathecting the object and thereby drawing the ego into an absorption. Conceived in this way, *samyama* is a three-step procedure by which the ego taps the Ground in order to engage in contemplative inquiry.

If contemplative enstasy is usually accomplished with a specific object in mind, it need not always have such a focal anchor. Patanjali indicates that objectless enstasy (*asamprajnata samadhi*) is a real possibility, although he allows that this kind of *samadhi* is a higher and rarer attainment than object-centered *samadhi* or, as he calls it, *samadhi* "with support" (*samprajnata samadhi*).[2] In the case of objectless enstasy, *samadhi* is usually achieved by employing and then dropping a support. By these means the power of the Ground is drawn into the ego's subjective space and the ego in turn is drawn into this power, becoming absorbed in it as a pure power cathexis independent of any cathexis object. An enstasy thus ensues that transcends not only self-reference but reference to objects as well. A dynamic void, or rather plenum, is created. The ego becomes one with the power of the Ground and experiences a state of subjectless-objectless spiritual dynamism.

With progress in meditative practice, contemplation, of both object-centered and objectless sorts, becomes progressively more bright, transparent, and poised. The meditator achieves states that are increasingly powerful and pure, *sattvic* in the language of Indian metaphysical psychology. The goal of the meditative quest, according to Patanjali, is an objectless *samadhi* that is completely pure—no longer clouded or weighed down by unconscious embedded tendencies, by *samskaras* and *vasanas*—and that is able, therefore, fully to reflect the light of consciousness.

Logical rigor and autosymbolic creativity. In making progress in contemplation, the ego also makes progress in learning how to guide the creative process. These two dimensions of cognition emerge simultaneously because the ability to draw upon the power of the Ground is at the same time an ability to draw upon the nonegoic pole of the psyche generally, in all of its resources, including the autosymbolic process. The ego's ability to marshal the power of the Ground is therefore at the same time an ability to engage the instrument of creative cognition. These two abilities coincide and are exercised in the same way, namely, by sustaining focused attention. Because the ego is harmoniously integrated with the nonegoic pole of the psyche, that pole is immediately responsive to the ego's mental efforts. The ego is in a sense the focusing lens of the psyche as a whole; whatever the ego intently focuses on becomes a target for energy cathexis and a subject of imaginal-intuitive exploration. By sustaining focused attention, therefore, the ego not only enters into dynamic fusion with the object of attention but also embarks upon a symbolic-noetic investigation of the object. The ego beholds landscapes of new meaning as the inner nature of the object is imaginally-intuitively probed and disclosed.

The ego in this way learns how to engage the psyche's creative resources. To be sure, these resources remain nonegoic in nature, which means that the ego can never gain the direct control over them that it has over ego functions. Nevertheless, the ego does learn how to set these resources to work on ideas or problems of the ego's own choosing. The autosymbolic process continues to work in a spontaneous way, but the ego learns how to guide its spontaneity.

The primary products of the creative process during the integrated stage are *visionary symbols*. These are symbols that can best be described by contrasting them with earlier products of the creative process and specifically with the protoconceptual symbols that are forged during the period of the body ego and the spontaneous imaginal productions that emerge during the transitional periods leading to integration.

The chief contrast between visionary symbols and the protoconceptual symbols of early childhood lies in their differing relations to concepts: protoconceptual symbols are less than concepts, visionary symbols more. The protoconceptual symbols of early childhood, we recall, are autogenerated images that, in the absence of the distinction between universal and particular, between abstract meaning and concrete instance, are in effect both and neither universals and particulars, meanings and instances. They are particulars attempting to be universals, exemplary instances of meanings serving in the stead of the meanings themselves. Protoconceptual symbols are therefore incomplete concepts. They are strikingly creative but still quite primitive cognitions that, having transcended the level of mere particularity, still lie below the level of abstractly conceived universality.

Visionary symbols, in contrast, are advanced cognitions that presuppose that the level of abstractly conceived universality has already been achieved. As expressions of the tertiary process, visionary symbols presuppose that the ego has already completed the work of constructing a conceptual scheme. Hence, visionary symbols, rather than being incomplete concepts, particulars attempting to be universals, are instead completely instantiated concepts, universals succeeding in being particulars. Visionary symbols are like protoconceptual symbols in being concrete exemplars or models; they are unlike protoconceptual symbols, however, in that their concrete universality is truly symbolic rather than merely protoconceptual. Visionary symbols alone embody a genuine synthesis of the concrete and the abstract, of particularity and universality.

A second important way in which visionary symbols differ from protoconceptual symbols is that only visionary symbols are subject to critical assessment. Unlike protoconceptual symbols, which the body ego accepts at face value, visionary symbols have a hypothetical or exploratory character and are subject to validation or invalidation. Thanks to the mental ego's cognitive accomplishments, the integrated ego is in possession of epistemic tools with which to test its creative envisionings. Most importantly, it possesses conceptual schemes with which to assess new meanings and a body of scientific knowledge with which to assess new facts and possibilities. A creatively envisioned meaning that conflicts with an established conceptual scheme incurs a special burden of proof, as, too, does a creatively envisioned possibility that conflicts with established scientific knowledge. The integrated ego has these egoically forged means at its disposal for evaluating its non-egoically generated symbols. It is able to bring logical rigor to bear upon imaginal-intuitive creativity, to the best advantage of both.

One other way in which visionary symbols differ from protoconceptual symbols is in the range of the meanings they embody. Protoconceptual symbols are extremely limited in this regard, as they draw upon only the meager experience of the body ego. Visionary symbols in contrast draw upon the wealth of meanings contained in the complex theoretical systems established by the mental ego. The abstract universals belonging to these systems seed the autosymbolic process with ideas and questions of exceeding subtlety and power, thus spawning imaginal-intuitive insights of corresponding subtlety and power. The theoretical systems established by the mental ego thus contribute to the autosymbolic process not only in a critical but also in a substantive way. They interact with the autosymbolic process not only at the end of its cycle, by assessing its products, but also at the beginning of its cycle, by impregnating it with germinal ideas.

Visionary symbols can also be contrasted with the images that arise during regression in the service of transcendence and regeneration in spirit. The chief difference here is that visionary symbols are elicited cognitions rather than self-manifesting apparitions. They are creatively spawned images and insights that arise in the ego's exploration of the unknown rather than manifestations that issue transcendently from the unknown. Unlike the products of the autosymbolic process during the regressive and regenerative periods, visionary symbols are responses to the ego's own contemplative explorations. The are *invited creative meanings* rather than *unbidden figments or phantasms*. The integrated ego is able to guide the autosymbolic process and understands full well that the images and insights issuing from this process are products of the psyche's own creative resources.

CIVILIZATION-INSTINCT INTEGRATION: CULTIVATION IN SPIRIT

The mental ego's worldly identity is to a large extent composed of internalized social roles, codes of behavior, and prescribed manners. The mental ego adopts these roles, codes, and manners as its own as part of its identity project. This process of identifying with socially derived patterns of selfhood is, as we know, an important part of the mental ego's development in later adolescence and early adulthood. It is the way in which the mental ego gives form and expression to its "being-in-the-world" and, in doing so, earns a sense of being and value. The mental ego's identity is an important developmental achievement. It is, however, an achievement that rests on primal repression and therefore fails to represent the nonegoic potentials of the psyche, including the power of the Ground. Accordingly, although the mental ego's identity is a vehicle of authentic growth and expression during the first half of adult life, it is not a vehicle for the growth and expression of the whole person. It is an incomplete self posing as the whole self. The mental ego's identity thus contains a seed of inauthenticity. This seed is typically latent until midlife, at which point both primal repression and the worldly identity resting on it lose their developmental warrant and the mental ego begins to suffer self-doubts. At midlife, then—it not earlier—the mental ego begins to have doubts about its worldly identity, which increasingly feels like an inauthentic mask, an outer facade hiding rather than expressing the core self.

The mental ego harbors the fear that, should it fail to maintain its established identity, the consequence would be not only a loss of earned being and value but also a dangerous unleashing of instinctual life. And the mental ego is not entirely mistaken in harboring this fear. For primal repression, on which the mental ego's identity rests, restricts physico-dynamic potentials to a prepersonal organization, reducing them to the level of the Freudian id. The mental ego is for this reason fundamentally Freudian in outlook. It believes, however prereflectively, that civilization (represented by acquired character or ego identity) and physicodynamic life are fundamentally opposed and therefore that the former can be affirmed only through the denial of the latter. The repression of physicodynamic life, the mental ego believes, is the required price, the unavoidable discontent, of civilized existence.

The inauthentic side of ego identity, however, eventually becomes evident. The mental ego's "civilization" is eventually exposed as form without substance. The manner in which the mental ego presents itself to the world is eventually exposed as an empty facade divorced from the spontaneous sources of life. At this point, then, the mental ego's choice ceases being a choice between "civilization" and "savagery" and becomes instead a choice between inauthentic and authentic selfhood. The mental ego comes to realize that in clinging to its identity it is not only protecting itself from frightening nonegoic forces but also, in doing so, closing itself to its own deepest and truest promptings. The mental ego begins to understand that if it is to be authentic and whole it must redeem (or, better, allow itself to be redeemed by) the nonegoic life it has repressed. The mental ego realizes that it must drop its masks, let go its defenses, and bare itself to the forsaken parts of the soul. For the only true self is the whole self: existential integrity requires complete psychophysical-psychospiritual integration. The move toward authenticity, then, requires that the mental ego temporarily let go of its civilized second nature and submit itself to the original nature from which it has been in flight. That is, it requires that the mental ego undergo regression in the service of transcendence.

As we have seen, regression in the service of transcendence involves a derepression of the instincts, which assert themselves upon the ego, frequently in a distressingly insistent manner. The mental ego therefore, in submitting to regression in the service of transcendence, can for a time be confirmed in its fear that beneath the structures of civilized life lies a powder keg of raw libido, the Freudian id. The derepression of the instincts, however, eventually runs its course and the instincts cease disturbing the ego. Once regeneration in spirit begins, the instincts lose their threatening aspect and begin contributing to life in positive ways.

Simultaneously, some aspects of the mental ego's identity, having been deanimated during the mental ego's withdrawal from the world, begin being restored to life in new ways, with roots that now run deep into the psyche. Many structures of the mental ego's identity, of course, are irredeemably antithetical to the expression of nonegoic life and therefore are purged without remainder. Other structures, however, are compatible with nonegoic life, and these structures now begin to be reanimated as vehicles for the spontaneous expression of physicodynamic potentials.

In this way, instinctuality and the acquired structures of personality, which had been opposed, begin intimately to interpenetrate and fuse. The instincts, which in their prepersonal organization had been mindlessly primitive, are invested with personhood; and civilized life, which had been empty and inauthentic, is given power, passion, and drive. The old mutually exclusive disjunction between civilized and instinctual life is therefore refuted. It becomes apparent that true civilization is not a matter of the disciplines of social life overriding instinctuality but rather of social life and instinctuality becoming one.

This integration of civilized and instinctual life, however, is only one dimension of a more complex transformation. For the cultivation characteristic of integrated life is a synthesis not only of socially grounded identity and biologically grounded instinct but also, and even more importantly, of ego and spirit. The integration of the instincts is part of a larger process that also includes the awakening of the power of the Ground as spirit and the regeneration of the ego by spirit. In fact, the assertion of the instincts and the awakening of the power of the Ground as spirit are different phases of the same process: the assertion of the instincts is simply the initial expression of the liberation of the power of the Ground from its repressed, prepersonal organization (i.e., as libido). Accordingly, the ego's instinctualization is also in time its spiritualization. The integrated ego's cultivation is not only a matter of civilization being enlivened by eros but also of personality being purged and sanctified by spirit. True cultivation is above all a cultivation *in spirit*.

The power of the Ground is a force that is inherently "civilized." It needs no disciplining or refining, because it is by its very nature sensitive and other-attuned. The power of the Ground is a force that, in infusing the egoic sphere, transforms the acquired virtues of that sphere into spontaneous graces of character. The power of the Ground as spirit is the deepest heart and eye of the soul; it is the dynamic essence of charity and wisdom. People who are truly cultivated, then, are those whose developed dispositions have been infusively transformed (animated, sensitized, attuned) by spirit. They are people whose acquired structures of personality, no longer in any sense a fabrication, have become the vehicle for authentic instinctual *and* spiritual life.

In dialectical terms, the foregoing analysis can be restated to say that ego identity, as a second nature based on a repressive negation of our original nonegoic nature, must itself be regressively negated before the higher egoic-nonegoic synthesis of integration can be achieved. Accordingly, ego identity, long in the process of formation, is eventually exposed as a false mask and regressively submitted to derepressing nonegoic life. This regressive negation of ego identity, however, is not an annihilation. To be sure, many structures of the mental-egoic personality are purged without remainder, namely, all that are opaque or resistant to the free movement of spirit. The majority of the structures making up ego identity, however, survive its regressive negation and, rooted in nonegoic life, begin to take part in a new and superior synthesis. This synthesis, the integrated personality, is a union of egoic and nonegoic elements, of egoic form, structure, and discipline and nonegoic substance, instinct, creativity, power, and spirit. The acquired structures of the mental ego's personality are regenerated in the native flesh and spirit of physicodynamic life, and in turn the spontaneities of physicodynamic life, no longer confined to a prepersonal organization, are shaped according to the highest forms of social existence and intellectual culture. Our "second nature" is in this way wedded to our original nonegoic nature, and we become genuinely cultivated persons, persons of both form and substance, civilization and instinct, individual identity and transpersonal spirit.

EGO-GROUND INTEGRATION: FULFILLED HUMANNESS

The ego and the Dynamic Ground are the seats of the two poles of the psyche. The ego, of course, is the seat of the egoic pole, the pole that is responsible for monitoring and organizing experience and in general for conducting affairs in the world. And the Dynamic Ground is the seat of the nonegoic or physicodynamic pole, the pole that provides life with flesh, instinct, feeling, creativity, and spirit. Together these two poles include the totality of psychic resources. Everything that is native to the human endowment derives from one or the other of these poles or from the two poles working in unison.

This ego-Ground polarity is the psyche's most basic constitutional structure. From virtually the outset of life, the psyche is a structure with two distinct poles. As we have seen, however, these two poles, although coexistent throughout life, are not always equally developed or harmoniously coordinated. At the outset of life, the ego is almost wholly undeveloped; it exists as little more than a point of departure for further development. And during the ensuing preoedipal period, the ego remains weak, undeveloped, and eclipsed by the Ground. The fledgling ego strives hard for individuation and independence, but it is still so drawn to the Ground and so under the influence of the power of the Ground that it is easily swept away and reembedded in the preindividuated state.

The ego remains unstable throughout the body-egoic period of development. It remains vulnerable to the captivating influence of the Ground until, finally, it takes matters dramatically into its own hands and commits the act of primal repression. In committing this act, the ego, now the mental ego, wins its independence, but only by severing its connection with the Ground. Given this negation of the Ground, the beginning of the mental-egoic period marks a point of reversal in which psychic pole has the ascendant position. The nonegoic pole, which had been ascendant, suffers repression; to a significant extent, it is deactivated and rendered unconscious. And the egoic pole, which had been subordinate, asserts itself as the primary pole, laying claim to sovereignty over the psyche as a whole.

This state of affairs obtains for the duration of the mental-egoic period. Then, beginning with regression in the service of transcendence, another reversal occurs. The mental ego loses the undergirding of primal repression and, reopened to the power of the Ground, is regressed to the Ground. This regression is *in the service of transcendence*, because the ultimate goal of the regression is not to *reembed* the ego in the Ground but rather to *reroot* the ego in the Ground and thereby to open the ego to the transformative action of the power of the Ground. The ego is regressed to the Ground so that it can be regenerated in spirit.

Accordingly, once regression in the service of transcendence has run its course, one last reversal occurs: regression gives way to regeneration. The ego is given a new lease on life and a healing reconciliation between the ego and nonegoic life commences. The final result of this regeneration process, integration, is at last a perfected bipolar system. The psyche, which from inception is bipolar in fundamental constitution, now becomes bipolar in fully actualized fact. At this point both of the psychic poles finally function to the full extent of their powers and in integrated unity, as one.

Integrated egoic-nonegoic polarity is a union of *yang* and *yin*; it is a perfect coincidence of opposites. The two poles of the psyche continue to be opposite in their functions and potentials, their structures and spontaneities, but this oppositeness is no longer plagued by interpolar friction or conflict. For the achievement of integration means that no vestiges of tension remain between the two psychic poles. The ego is no longer resistant to nonegoic potentials, and nonegoic potentials are no longer violent in their effect upon the ego. The achievement of integration, then, means that the two psychic poles have finally become complementary rather than antagonistic opposites.

This integration of opposites, however, is not an integration of equals. The nonegoic pole has primacy over the egoic pole. The ego can enter into union with the Ground only by becoming an instrument of the Ground. The psyche, then, although bipolar, is not truly bicentric. The egoic pole has no true center in itself; it is truly centered only when it is rooted in the Ground. In political terms, the Ground alone is sovereign; the ego is (in all senses) subject. The ego is a self; it is a self-conscious subject with a unique personal identity. As a self, however, it is most truly itself when it is an expressive vehicle of spirit.

THE HORIZONS OF INTEGRATED LIFE

Integration is both rare and excellent. Nothing about it, however, places it beyond the range of native human possibilities. If, however, we look into the far horizon of integrated life, we can see possibilities of experience that are so extraordinary that they must be considered special gifts conferred upon only a few. The three most remarkable such possibilities are prophetic vision, saintly compassion, and mystical illumination.

PROPHETIC VISION

Jung went beyond Freud in understanding that the symbols produced by the unconscious are not just retrospective, harking back to significant events of childhood (or the race), but are prospective as well, forevisioning the course of future development. Jung employed this insight primarily to plot the future and final stages of ontogeny, or individuation. Dream symbols and the symbols that emerge from the process of active imagination, Jung believed, are in many cases suggestive of the imminently forthcoming steps of a person's growth and development. For Jung, our symbolic life is often a few steps ahead of our actual life. Accordingly, to understand the symbols fashioned by the autosymbolic process is in many cases to foreglimpse the future.

Jung's insight into the futural function of the creative process can be extended beyond the ontogenetic or individual level. Humanity, I suggest, has not only memory of its collective roots but also anticipation of its collective future. The autosymbolic process generates images that explore the future not only of the individual but of the community and species as well. In other words, prophecy is an inherent human possibility.

The autosymbolic process, however, is usually unable to attend to possibilities beyond the boundaries of the individual psyche. For primal repression divorces the autosymbolic process from consciousness and forces it to work almost exclusively in the service of private unconscious materials. Primal repression "beheads" the autosymbolic process and reduces it to an enigmatic oracle of the underworld. Primal repression, that is, limits the autosymbolic process to *intra*psychic depths and in doing so keeps it from exploring *trans*psychic possibilities. The autosymbolic process is usually limited in this way until primal repression is lifted and significant progress is made toward integration. Only at this point, typically, can the autosymbolic process become an instrument of prophetic cognition.

In saying that prophecy is an inherent human possibility, I do not mean to suggest that we are capable, potentially, of *infallible* precognition. Prophecy, like everything else that derives from the autosymbolic process, is fallible. The autosymbolic process gives imaginal-intuitive expression to higher meanings and future possibilities, and it does so with immensely creative vision. It does not do so, however, with any guarantee of correctness. The products of the autosymbolic process need to be critically assessed; they need to be reality tested and checked against existing knowledge. Nevertheless, although autosymbolic foresight is not to be accepted as literal and infallible truth, it ought to be taken seriously as a prefiguration of things to come. For under integrated conditions the autosymbolic process is intimately attuned to the rhythms of life (collective as well as individual) and free of all constraints that would render its symbols prima facie suspect.

SAINTLY COMPASSION

Saintly compassion is a *dynamic* phenomenon: it is an expression of the outreachingness and magnetic attractivity of spirit. The power of the Ground is a magnetically attractive force; the ego is drawn to the power of the Ground and to anything in which it is deposited or to anyone from whom it emanates. The magnetic attractivity of the power of the Ground, however, affects not only the ego but also the power of the Ground itself, that is, as one source of this power meets another (e.g., as one magnet attracts another). And the attraction of the power of the Ground to itself is even stronger than is the ego's attraction to it. Spirit flows strongly to spirit and bonds therewith to form a union, a "mystical body," of ego-differentiated spirits. Spirit is irresistibly drawn to itself as it meets itself in others and is thus moved to join in a higher life with others. So powerful is this impulse for some integrated persons—in whom, no doubt, the movement of spirit is exceptionally strong—that they value the spiritual whole more than they do any of its egoic parts, including most immediately themselves. These are persons so utterly devoted to spirit that there is nothing they would not give, including their individual lives, to contribute to humanity's collective life in spirit.

Although prophetic vision is an inherent possibility of integrated life, few integrated people have been prophets. And although conscience is a distinctive feature of integrated life, few integrated people have been saints. Prophets and saints must be considered infrequent exceptions to the rule even among integrated people. Prophecy and saintliness are among the highest, and hence rarest, possibilities of human existence. Nevertheless, prophecy and saintliness *are* real human possibilities. Every age has had its prophets and saints.

MYSTICAL ILLUMINATION

Mystical illumination is the highest form of infused-absorbed experience. There are at least four reasons why this is so. First, mystical illumination is an objectless enstasy: it is an absorption in the power of the Ground itself rather than in any object or activity in which the power of the Ground has been invested. Second, mystical illumination is completely "pure": it is a union with the power of the Ground in its pristine form as spirit rather than in a form admixed with particular feelings or instinctual colorations. Third, mystical illumination is an experience of measureless immensity: it is a beholding so extraordinary in power and grandeur as entirely to eclipse all other experiences. And fourth, mystical illumination is a gift of grace: it is an experience beyond anything the ego can attain or induce on its own.

Mystical illumination needs to be distinguished from other types of objectless states and in particular from (1) the "dead void" states that occur during the mental-egoic period, (2) the empty trances that occur during the second stage of regression in the service of transcendence, (3) the undifferentiated inflations and ecstasies that occur during regeneration in spirit, and (4) the objectless contemplations that are achieved during the later phases of regeneration in spirit and throughout the integrated stage. Of these objectless states, objectless contemplations are the most similar to mystical illumination, but even they fall far short of this supreme "state."

Dead void states differ from mystical illumination in being bereft of the power of the Ground. These experiences are merely episodes of mental vacancy and inactivity, without any degree of dynamic entrainment, infusion, or absorption. Empty trances differ from mystical illumination in being states of cathectic-gravitational entrainment or engulfment rather than states of infusive absorption. Empty trances are dense and dark rather than expansive and bright. Undifferentiated inflations and ecstaties differ from mystical illumination in being wild and "impure." They are explosive infusions that are admixed with derepressing feelings and instincts. And objectless contemplations, although suffering from none of these deficiencies, differ from mystical illumination in being experiences of significantly lesser stature. They fall far short of mystical illumination in the degree to which the ego is infused, illumined, and exalted by spirit.

The difference in degree that distinguishes mystical illumination from objectless contemplations is so great as to constitute a decisive difference in kind. Mystical illumination is not just an experience of illumined absorption, as are objectless contemplations. It is rather an experience of limitless effulgence and bliss. Mystical illumination is an experience of inconceivable magnitude. When mystical illumination occurs, the aperture of the soul opens all the way and spirit, in the fullness of its radiant glory, graces the ego with the ultimate vision. Mystical illumination, then, unlike objectless contemplations, is inherently of the nature of a gift. The ego, by steadfast effort, can voluntarily enter a contemplative absorption, and in doing so it may increase the chance of a mystical experience occurring. Whether or not the ego makes such efforts, however, it is in the last analysis the Ground itself, or perhaps an evolutionary principle regulating the Ground, that determines when an ultimate disclosure will occur. Irrespective of human will, it is spiritual power itself that elects the times and places at which it will bare itself to the ego. Mystical illumination, therefore, like prophetic vision and saintly compassion, is statistically extremely rare, even among integrated persons.

CONCLUSION

Integrated people differ widely from each other. Unlike people at the mental-egoic stage, who live life from the "outside in," internalizing social roles, codes, and categories, integrated people live life from the "inside out," spontaneously following the promptings of their deepest inner nature. Integrated people are the true individuals so lauded in existentialist literature.

Integrated people differ from each other not only in the distinctiveness of their authentically expressed lives but in many other respects as well. As we have seen, only a small minority are prophets, saints, or mystical *illuminati*. Also, few integrated people possess supernormal powers to any significant degree. Integrated people cover a broad spectrum of types, from the seemingly quite ordinary to the truly extraordinary. Except for their outreaching spirit and deep genuineness, most integrated people do not stand out in any way. The only requirement for attaining integrated existence is that one have an ego that is strong enough to reunite with the Ground. Given this single prerequisite, it follows that integration, although rare and of the highest excellence, is a developmental stage from which, a priori, no one can be excluded. Integration is an inherited destiny belonging to the human race as a whole.

Notes

INTRODUCTION

1. Wilber (1979) once held a view similar to this but later abandoned it.

2. The chronological boundaries of the egoic and transegoic stages are indefinite. The beginning of the egoic stage can rather surely be placed at the beginning of latency. The end of the egoic stage, however, is much more difficult to specify, because for many people the transegoic stage never emerges and for some others it appears "early," in early adulthood or even adolescence. The chronological correspondences set forth are therefore only approximations. As a general but by no means universal rule, then, the egoic stage lasts *at least* until midlife. For most people, the transegoic stage begins, if at all, only after the ego-developmental tasks of early adulthood—namely, forging an ego identity and developing an intimate relationship with a significant other or others—have been completed.

1. TRANSPERSONAL THEORY: TWO BASIC PARADIGMS

1. See Wilber 1980a, 1980b, 1981a, 1981b, and especially 1990.

2. The literature on this point is discussed in *Transpersonal Psychology in Psychoanalytic Perspective*, chapter 1.

3. See Brenner (1957) and Madison (1961) for accounts of Freud's concept of primal repression.

4. Stress should be put on the qualification *potentially*. The proviso is necessary to allow for the real possibility that the process will abort and lead only to regression and not to any kind of transcendence or redemptive transformation. In other words, the dynamic-dialectical paradigm implies that ego transcendence involves risks. The dynamic-dialectical and structural-hierarchical paradigms will be contrasted on this issue later in the chapter.

5. It is not clear whether ultimate unity should be considered a *psychic* level, because, as the coincidence of the individual with reality, it seems to be more of a metaphysical than a strictly psychic level.

6. This is the view of Margaret Mahler (Mahler, Pine, and Bergman 1975), which is followed by Otto Kernberg and many others. Psychoanalysis has long focused on the child's struggle for independence as it interacts with parental figures during the preoedipal and oedipal periods. Some recent psychoanalytic

thinkers, however—for example, Daniel Stern (1985)—have sought to shift the focus away from the struggle for independence and toward the achievement of relationship. Both perspectives are essential. I am here following the longer psychoanalytic tradition in focusing on the child's conflict-driven movement toward independence.

2. THE BODY EGO

1. I here gloss over the distinction between ego and self or self-representation as this distinction is struck by psychoanalytic self psychology (according to which the ego is distinguished from a superordinate self or self-regulating principle) and psychoanalytic object relations theory (according to which the ego is distinguished from the ego's own self-representation). My own view that the ego is a small-*s* self has already been presented in a preliminary way and will be developed in this and ensuing chapters. As we shall see, the ego as small-*s* self both develops self-representations (culminating in a mature ego identity) and itself evolves in relation to a superordinate self, the large-*S* Self.

2. Jung and his followers have explained the Great Mother as an archetypal system of the unconscious. Jung (1912, 1938), Neumann (1954, 1963), and others have shown that the Great Mother archetype is basically a *biaxial* system, possessing both positive and negative sides (the Good Mother and the Terrible Mother) and both inner or archetypal and outer or personal dimensions. Proceeding on the basis of this conception, the following account of the Great Mother sets itself apart by identifying the inner dimension of the Great Mother with the Dynamic Ground. Accordingly, the Great Mother is here conceived not only as an archetypal and personal reality but also, and even more fundamentally, as a dynamic reality.

3. Margaret Mahler is the senior author of *The Psychological Birth of the Human Infant*, and the views set forth in the book are based on ideas that Mahler had introduced earlier. Accordingly, I shall follow established practice and cite this work as expressing Mahler's views.

4. Joseph Lichtenberg (1987) reviews the results of neonatal research and stresses that, contrary to views like Klein's, there is no evidence of strong affective polarization in infancy.

5. As I shall explain in the next chapter, this frightening realization occurs because the child begins to understand that objects, including the primary caregiver, can exist anywhere in the vastness of space, whether proximate to or remote from the child's field of experience.

6. For Freud's use of this term, see chapter 1. See also Brenner (1957) and Madison (1961).

7. In hypothesizing that the power of the Ground has its origins in the sexual system, I am not suggesting that it is inherently a sexual power. The power of the Ground, I believe, is essentially a spiritual power; nevertheless, it is a power that, when repressed, is limited to a primarily sexual organization (as libido) and, when awakened, is released and ascends from the underlying

instinctual sphere. I shall discuss the relation of the power of the Ground to the sexual system more fully in chapter 5.

8. In sealing the power of the Ground, primal repression also has the effect of divesting experience of the other benefits of the power of the Ground discussed earlier: intensity and enchantment. Primal repression disempowers and disenchants the world, divesting experience of its all-around abundance and numinosity.

9. In this context it is necessary to drop the gender-neutral term *primary caregiver*. The oedipal triangle can in principle have any gender composition. Historically, however, the oedipal figure has been the father, the primary caregiver the mother.

10. The fact that, historically, the primary preoedipal caregiver has been a women and the primary oedipal authority a man has created gender asymmetries in both the preoedipal and oedipal periods. Feminist psychoanalytic thinkers such as Dorothy Dinnerstein (1976), Nancy Chodorow (1978), and Miriam Johnson (1988) have explored these asymmetries and their long-term consequences. In *Transpersonal Psychology in Psychoanalytic Perspective,* I try to explain how the gender asymmetries discussed by Dinnerstein, Chodorow, and Johnson affect the ways girls and boys make the transition from intimacy to independence.

3. THE BODY EGO: COGNITIVE AND AFFECTIVE DEVELOPMENT

1. This threefold division is a revised formulation of Silvano Arieti's (1967) division of early childhood cognition into stages of exocepts, phantasms, and paleologic.

2. These findings, which have been established in countless studies, are reviewed in most textbooks on early childhood development. On the point of infants learning from experience, see especially T. G. R. Bower (1989).

3. The ensuing discussion of Von Domarus and the notion of predicate identity is indebted to Arieti (1967).

4. THE MENTAL EGO

1. Many of the ideas presented in this chapter were first developed in collaboration with Michael Stark. See Washburn and Stark (1979).

2. The adolescent's sense of guilt also arises from a source deep within the unconscious psyche. For the adolescent's rejection of parents is in certain respects a replay of the primordial sin of divorcing oneself from one's ultimate source or creator, the first instance of which, as we learned in chapter 2, is the original act of primal repression. The adolescent's struggle for independence from parents for this reason has not only personal but also collective, archetypal significance. It incurs a sense of guilt that runs deeper than the adolescent can possibly understand.

5. THE UNCONSCIOUS

1. This statement applies to the mental ego but not the integrated ego, because, as we shall see, the integrated ego is harmoniously rooted in the Ground. Unlike the mental ego, which is susceptible to being *overpowered* by the Ground, the integrated ego is *empowered* by the Ground (except in extraordinary states such as mystical absorption).

2. *Rupture of planes* is Mircea Eliade's (1969) expression to describe a sudden breakthrough of the sacred into the profane plane of existence.

3. For a similar view, see Wilber (1979).

4. The ensuing account of the Great Mother, like the account in chapter 2, is essentially a modification of the Jungian conception. Following Jung (1912, 1938) and Neumann (1954, 1963), the Great Mother is here conceived as a biaxial system, possessing both positive (Good Mother) and negative (Terrible Mother) sides and both inner (archetypal) and outer (personal) dimensions. The present account departs from the Jungian conception, however, in identifying the inner dimension of the Great Mother with the Dynamic Ground and thereby stressing that the Great Mother is not only an archetypal network but also a multifaceted dynamic reality.

5. A good deal of discussion within psychoanalytic circles has been focused on the question of whether aggression should be considered an instinctual drive. In *Transpersonal Psychology in Psychoanalytic Perspective*, chapters 5 and 9, I propose that aggression is better understood as a consequence of primal repression than as an instinctual drive. I refer the reader to that discussion. For convenience of exposition, I shall here continue to speak as if aggression were an instinctual propensity.

6. The prelatency child experiences intense desire and aversion, love and hate, longing and hostility. These feelings, however, I suggest, are better understood as affective responses to bivalent manifestations of the Great Mother than as expressions of active sexual and aggressive drives.

7. For a good general discussion of these and other body therapies, see Marrone (1990).

8. The notion of the embedded unconscious will be discussed more fully in the section on the personal embedded unconscious.

9. These terms are borrowed from Ken Wilber (1980a). Wilber is to be credited for having made the clearest distinction between the submerged and embedded sides of the unconscious.

10. See Goleman (1977), Walsh (1977), and Washburn (1978).

11. Jung's account of the *anima* and *animus* as archetypes of the collective unconscious reflects the patriarchal bias of Jung's own culture and time. Jung's androcentrism has been the target of a good deal of criticism in recent years. In *Transpersonal Psychology in Psychoanalytic Perspective*, chapter 10, I review this criticism and present a revised formulation of the *anima* and *animus* as archetypal structures, a formulation that, I hope, is free of sexist bias.

6. MEDITATION: THE ROYAL ROAD TO THE UNCONSCIOUS

1. Patanjali composed the *Yoga Sutras*. Although most authorities date the *Yoga Sutras* in the second century B.C.E., some have placed Patanjali and his work as late as the fourth century C.E.

2. This contrast needs to be qualified, for although concentrative practices lead more directly to absorbed states, receptive practices can lead to absorbed states as well. On this point, the reader is referred to chapter 11 of *Transpersonal Psychology in Psychoanalytic Perspective*.

3. See *Interior Castle*, Fourth Mansions, chapter 3, and *Way of Perfection*, chapters 28–29.

4. For this view, see "Psychological Commentary on *The Tibetan Book of the Dead*" (Jung 1953, p. 520; CW, 11, pars. 847–848). For a general discussion of Jung's views on Eastern thought and practice, see Coward (1985). Also helpful on this subject is an excellent dissertation by Carol Whitfield (1992), the influence of which I gratefully acknowledge.

5. The hypothesis that meditation reveals the (embedded) unconscious by inhibiting its expression and thereby throwing it into relief was initially set forth in Arthur Deikman's classic paper "Deautomatization and the Mystic Experience" in 1966. This basic idea is applied and extended in various ways in Washburn (1978) and Wilber (1980a).

6. See Buddhaghosa (Buddhist Publication Society, 1975).

7. See *Interior Castle* (Seventh Mansions, chapter 3).

8. As noted previously, other practices that have similar effects are Reichian body work and the body therapies of Alexander Lowen, F. Matthias Alexander, Moshe Feldenkrais, and Ida Rolf.

7. REGRESSION IN THE SERVICE OF TRANSCENDENCE

1. I am indebted to Edith Schnapper (1980) for the example from Islam.

2. Regression in the service of transcendence, conceived as a two-stage process, corresponds closely to St. John of the Cross's two nights of spiritual purgation, the night of the senses and the night of spirit. The account of regression in the service of transcendence presented here draws heavily on Jung's (1912) and Joseph Campbell's (1949) accounts of the night sea journey or heroic odyssey as a process of return to psychic origins. Other important sources are Jean-Paul Sartre's (1956) account of the futility of our basic existential project, R. D. Laing's (1960) phenomenology of the alienated condition, and John Perry's (1974, 1976) and Stanislav Grof's (1985) accounts of the redemptive possibilities implicit in the psychotic process. Since the first edition of this book came out, I have discovered the work of David M. Levin (1985, 1987, 1988, 1989). Levin makes extremely important contributions to transpersonal theory. His "Clinical Stories: A Modern Self in the Fury of Being" (1987) bears significantly on the first stage of regression in the service of transcendence. Also, Edith Schnapper's book *The Inward Odyssey* (1980) should be acknowledged for its

excellent discussion of many of the themes treated in this and the next two chapters.

3. As a diagnostic category, derealization is usually grouped together with depersonalization as one side of a depersonalization-derealization phenomenon. The two-sidedness of depersonalization-derealization is reflective of the two-sidedness of alienation. I shall consider depersonalization more specifically later (when I discuss the deanimation of ego identity). On the depersonalization-derealization phenomenon, see Schilder (1928), Nunberg (1955), Jacobson (1959), Stewart (1964), Arlow (1966), Meyer (1968), Hillman (1985), and Nieli (1987).

4. Transcendental phenomenologists, beginning with Husserl, have stressed that the world is a subjective *construction* in all its basic structures and forms. For transcendental phenomenologists, meaning and value derive entirely from the subject, not at all from the world. For existential phenomenologists, in contrast, meaning and value do not arise out of the subject alone but rather out of the subject's participation in the world. Accordingly, existential phenomenologists such as Martin Heidegger and Maurice Merleau-Ponty see meaning and value as *interpretations* rather than as constructions of the world. Their phenomenology is more hermeneutical than transcendental.

5. What I am referring to here as deanimation is more usually referred to as depersonalization, the inner dimension of the depersonalization-derealization process.

6. Since the first edition of this book was published, I have learned that Michael Eigen (1986) uses this term in a similar way.

7. Many people suffering from psychosis are prey to black holes because they are directly open to the deep unconscious. Also, as Jerome Kroll (1988) reports, people suffering from borderline personality disorder frequently experience heavy trancelike states. Borderlines, I suggest, are subject to the gravitational pull of the Ground because they are inadequately buffered from the deep unconscious.

8. For accounts of spontaneous *kriya* phenomena, see Mookerjee (1983), Muktananda (1978), Sannella (1987), and White (1979).

9. To my knowledge, the most remarkable (and pathologically extreme) case of such bodily awakening is that described by Gopi Krishna in his spiritual autobiography (1971).

10. Again, as in chapter 5, I shall speak of aggression as an instinctual drive. See chapter 5, note 5.

8. Regeneration in Spirit

1. Alchemy is an esoteric teaching that, in its Western form, arose in the Hellenistic period out of Eastern and Greek sources. At the end of the Hellenistic era the practice of alchemy was continued mainly among the Arabs, and it therefore eventually took on the dress of Islam. In the twelfth century, alchemy, along with other ancient and classical teachings, began to make its way into the

West, and a distinctively Christian version of the alchemical quest was gradually developed. Alchemy continued to have devoted practitioners all the way into the eighteenth century, at which time the victory of the new science, which was fundamentally at odds with the Aristotelian assumptions of alchemy, brought an end to alchemy in the West

2. Among the many spiritual systems of the East, I have chosen Tantrism to exemplify regeneration because it is a system that very clearly conceives of the regeneration process as a transformation effected by spiritual power (*kundalini-shakti*). Most Eastern systems, in explaining how ultimate self-realization is attained, emphasize enlightenment and liberation rather than spiritual transformation and purification. Most systems hold that the soul already exists in a state of perfection and needs only to achieve intuitive knowledge of this ultimate fact to be liberated from suffering and rebirth. Tantrism, on the other hand, describes regeneration as a real transformation that is accomplished within the soul by the transformative agency of spiritual power.

3. By repressively accumulated energy, I mean repressively accumulated *potential* energy. If we remember, I proposed in chapter 5 that primal repression works less as a hydraulic container of actual energy than as a countercathexis that reduces energy from an actual to a potential state.

4. As regeneration culminates in integration, Ground-induced states cease altogether being violent and lose their last negative nuances. As the ego grows stronger and becomes more harmoniously aligned with the power of the Ground, the effects of the power of the Ground upon the ego become less wildly effusive and intoxicating. The ego becomes more composed and clear-headed, and the wildness of Ground-induced states progressively calms into a serene dynamism. This change manifests itself in diverse ways. Later in the chapter I shall discuss how, cognitively, the calming of Ground-induced states manifests itself in a transformation of intellectual transport into contemplation and how, affectively, it manifests itself in a transformation of emotional rapture into bliss.

5. St. Teresa and St. John of the Cross speak of infused spiritual life as involving "fiery darts of love" and "wounds of love." Royo and Aumann (1962), expositing Teresa's and John's views, say, "According to St. John of the Cross, the fiery darts of love are certain hidden touches of love which, like a fiery arrow, burn and pierce the soul and leave it completely cauterized with the fire of love. St. Teresa describes this phenomenon as a wounding of the soul, as if an arrow had pierced the soul. It causes the soul great affliction, and at the same time is very delectable. The wound is not a physical one, but it is deep within the soul and seems to spring from the soul's inmost depths.... The wounds of love are similar to the preceding phenomenon, but they are more profound and more lasting" (p. 550). An excellent contemporary example of the intimate interplay of agony and ecstasy in spiritual life can be found in the mystical writings of Simone Weil (1952).

6. Again, the excess energy accumulated by the instincts owing to the instinctual organization of the power of the Ground is a *potential* energy. The

lifting of primal repression allows this standing potential charge to be "ignited" and discharged. See note 3.

7. As observed earlier, states of immobile dissociation and inert vacancy usually disappear at the beginning of regeneration in spirit, because, at this turning point, the ego is released from the gravity of the Ground.

8. Here I am focusing on the cognitive dimension of effusive-ecstatic states. I shall consider the affective dimension of these states in a later section.

9. The affective dimension of ecstasy is considered in this section.

10. The great Rinzai Zen Master Hakuin described the "doubt mass" (a trance induced by *koan* practice) as a condition in which one is frozen in sheets of ice. See Kasulis (1981).

11. In Rinzai Zen, one is said to be on the verge of *satori* when, frozen in a doubt mass, one begins to perspire. The perspiration indicates that the doubt mass is about to thaw or dissolve, triggering a *satori* experience. See Chang (1959).

12. Contrary to the traditional view, according to which hell and purgatory are in no way connected, this view, following Dante's conception in the *Divine Comedy*, places the entrance to purgatory at the very bottom of hell. Purgatory or regeneration in spirit begins after the ego has been regressed to the Ground.

9. INTEGRATION

1. The ensuing account of Patanjali's concentrative meditation (CM) could, *mutatis mutandis*, be applied to receptive meditation (RM) as well. For a more general discussion, including both CM and RM, see *Transpersonal Psychology in Psychoanalytic Perspective*, chapter 11.

2. In the Buddhist system of meditation codified in the fifth century C.E. by Buddhaghosa (Buddhist Publication Society, 1975), objectless enstasy is called *arupa jhana* (formless absorption).

Bibliography

Aranya, Hariharananda. 1983. *Yoga Philosophy of Patanjali.* Albany: State University of New York Press.

Arieti, Silvano. 1967. *The Intrapsychic Self.* New York: Basic Books.

————. 1976. *Creativity: The Magic Synthesis.* New York: Basic Books.

Arlin, Patricia K. 1975. "Cognitive Development in Adulthood: A Fifth Stage?" *Developmental Psychology* 11:602–606.

————. 1977. "Piagetian Operations in Problem Finding." *Developmental Psychology* 13:297–298.

————. 1984. "Adolescent and Adult Thought: A Structural Interpretation." In *Beyond Formal Operations: Late Adolescent and Adult Cognitive Development,* ed. M. L. Commons, F. A. Richards, and C. Armon. New York: Praeger.

————. 1989. "Problem Solving and Problem Finding in Young Artists and Young Scientists." In *Adult Development.* Vol. 1, *Comparisons and Applications of Developmental Models,* ed. M. L. Commons, J. D. Sinnott, F. A. Richards, and C. Armon. New York: Praeger.

Arlow, Jacob A. 1966. "Depersonalization and Derealization." In *Psychoanalysis—A General Psychology: Essays in Honor of Heinz Hartmann,* ed. R. M. Loewenstein, L. M. Newman, M. Schur, and A. J. Solnit. New York: International Universities Press.

Assagioli, Roberto. 1965. *Psychosynthesis: A Manual of Principles and Techniques.* New York: Viking Press, 1971.

Baillargeon, Renée. 1987. "Object Permanence in $3^1/_2$- and $4^1/_2$-Month-Old Infants." *Developmental Psychology* 23:655–664.

Basseches, Michael. 1984a. *Dialectical Thinking and Adult Development.* Norwood, N.J.: Ablex.

————. 1984b. "Dialectical Thinking as a Metasystematic Form of Cognitive Organization." In *Beyond Formal Operations: Late Adolescent and Adult Cognitive Development,* ed. M. L. Commons, F. A. Richards, and C. Armon. New York: Praeger.

Becker, Ernest. 1973. *The Denial of Death.* New York: The Free Press.

Blos, Peter. 1962. *On Adolescence: A Psychoanalytic Interpretation.* New York: The Free Press.

————. 1972. "The Function of the Ego Ideal in Adolescence." *Psychoanalytic Study of the Child* 27:93–97.

————. 1974. "The Genealogy of the Ego Ideal." In *The Adolescent Passage: Developmental Issues.* New York: International Universities Press, 1979.

Borysenko, Joan. 1993. *Fire in the Soul: A New Psychology of Spiritual Optimism.* New York: Warner Books.

Bower, T. G. R. 1982. *Development in Infancy.* 2d ed. San Francisco: W. H. Freeman.

————. 1989. *The Rational Infant: Learning in Infancy.* New York: W. H. Freeman.

Brenner, Charles. 1957. "The Nature and Development of the Concept of Repression in Freud's Writings." *Psychoanalytic Study of the Child* 12:19–46.

Broughton, John M. 1978. "Development of Concepts of Self, Mind, Reality, and Knowledge." In *New Directions for Child Development: Social Cognition,* ed. W. Damon. San Francisco: Jossey-Bass Publishers.

————. 1980. "Genetic Metaphysics: The Developmental Psychology of Mind-Body Concepts." In *Body and Mind: Past, Present, and Future,* ed. R. W. Rieber. New York: Academic Press.

————. 1982. "Genetic Logic and the Developmental Psychology of Philosophical Concepts." In *The Cognitive Developmental Psychology of James Mark Baldwin,* ed. J. M. Broughton and D. J. Freeman-Moir. Norwood, N.J.: Ablex.

————. 1984. "Not Beyond Formal Operations but Beyond Piaget." In *Beyond Formal Operations: Late Adolescent and Adult Cognitive Development,* ed. M. L. Commons, F. A. Richards, and C. Armon. New York: Praeger.

Brown, Daniel. 1986. "The Stages of Meditation in Cross-Cultural Perspective." In *Transformations of Consciousness: Conventional and Contemplative Perspectives in Development,* by Ken Wilber, Jack Engler, and Daniel Brown. Boston: Shambhala, 1986.

Brown, Norman O. 1959. *Life Against Death.* Middletown, Conn.: Wesleyan University Press.

Buddhaghosa. 1975. *Visuddhimagga.* 3d ed. Trans. Bhikku Nanamoli. Kandy, Sri Lanka: Buddhist Publication Society.

Campbell, Joseph. 1949. *The Hero with a Thousand Faces.* New York: Pantheon Books.

Chang, Garma C. C. 1959. *The Practice of Zen.* New York: Harper & Row.

Chodorow, Nancy. 1978. *The Reproduction of Mothering: Psychoanalysis and the Sociology of Gender.* Berkeley: University of California Press.

Coward, Harold. 1985. *Jung and Eastern Thought*. Albany: State University of New York Press.

Deikman, Arthur. 1966. "Deautomatization and the Mystic Experience." *Psychiatry* 29:324–338.

————. 1971. "Bimodal Consciousness." *Archives of General Psychiatry* 25:481–489.

Demos, V. 1982. "Affect in Early Infancy: Physiology or Psychology." *Psychoanalytic Inquiry* 1:533–574.

Dinnerstein, Dorothy. 1976. *The Mermaid and the Minotaur: Sexual Arrangements and Human Malaise*. New York: Harper and Row.

Eigen, Michael. 1986. *The Psychotic Core*. Northvale, N.J.: Jason Aronson.

Eliade, Mircea. 1969. *Yoga: Immortality and Freedom*. Princeton, N.J.: Princeton University Press.

Fairbairn, W. R. D. 1940. "Schizoid Factors in the Personality." In *Psychoanalytic Studies of the Personality*. London: Tavistock Publications, 1952.

Farah, Martha J. 1984. "The Neurological Basis of Mental Imagery: A Componential Analysis." *Cognition* 18:245–272.

Feuerstein, Georg. 1979. *The Yoga-Sutra of Patanjali*. Folkestone, Kent (U.K.): Dawson.

Fraiberg, Selma. 1969. "Libidinal Object Constancy and Mental Representation." *The Psychoanalytic Study of the Child* 24:9–47.

Frankl, Viktor E. 1962. *Man's Search for Meaning*. Rev. ed. Boston: Beacon Press.

————. 1969. *The Will to Meaning: Foundations and Applications of Logotherapy*. New York: New American Library.

Freud, Anna. 1936. *The Ego and the Mechanisms of Defense*. New York: International Universities Press.

Freud, Sigmund. 1900. *The Interpretation of Dreams*. In *The Standard Edition of the Complete Psychological Works of Sigmund Freud*. Vol. 4. London: Hogarth Press, 1953.

————. 1911a. "Formulations on the Two Principles of Mental Functioning." In *Standard Edition*. Vol. 12. London: Hogarth Press, 1958.

————. 1911b. "Psychoanalytic Notes on an Autobiographical Account of a Case of Paranoia (Dementia Paranoides)." In *Standard Edition*. Vol. 12. London: Hogarth Press, 1958.

————. 1923. *The Ego and the Id*. In *Standard Edition*. Vol. 19. London: Hogarth Press, 1961.

————. 1926. "Inhibitions, Symptoms and Anxiety." In *Standard Edition*. Vol. 20. London: Hogarth Press, 1959.

————. 1933. *New Introductory Lectures on Psycho-Analysis*. In *Standard Edition*. Vol. 22. London: Hogarth Press, 1964.

Frobenius, Leo. 1904. *Das Zeitalter des Sonnengotes*. Berlin: G. Reimer.

Gilligan, Carol, and John M. Murphy. 1979. "Development from Adolescence to Adulthood: The Philosopher and the Dilemma of Fact." In *New Directions for Child Development*, No. 5, *Intellectual Development Beyond Childhood*, ed. D. Kuhn. San Francisco: Jossey-Bass Publishers.

Goleman, Daniel. 1977. *The Varieties of the Meditative Experience*. New York: E. P. Dutton.

Greenberg, Mark S., and Martha J. Farah. 1986. "The Laterality of Dreaming." *Brain and Cognition* 5:307–321.

Grof, Christina, and Stanislav Grof. 1990. *The Stormy Search for the Self: A Guide to Personal Growth through Transformational Crisis*. Los Angeles: Jeremy Tarcher.

Grof, Stanislav. 1975. *Realms of the Human Unconscious*. New York: Viking Press.

———. 1985. *Beyond the Brain: Birth, Death, and Transcendence in Psychotherapy*. Albany: State University of New York Press.

———. 1988. *The Adventure of Self-Discovery*. Albany: State University of New York Press.

Grof, Stanislav, and Christina Grof. 1989. *Spiritual Emergency: When Personal Transformation Becomes a Crisis*. Los Angeles: Jeremy Tarcher.

Guntrip, Harry. 1952. "The Schizoid Personality and the External World." In *Schizoid Phenomena, Object Relations, and the Self*. New York: International Universities Press, 1969.

———. 1961. "The Schizoid Problem, Regression, and the Struggle to Preserve an Ego." In *Schizoid Phenomena, Object Relations, and the Self*. New York: International Universities Press, 1969.

———. 1969. "The Regressed Ego, the Lost Heart of the Self, and the Inability to Love." In *Schizoid Phenomena, Object Relations, and the Self*. New York: International Universities Press.

Hartmann, Heinz. 1939. *Ego Psychology and the Problem of Adaptation*. New York: International Universities Press, 1958.

Hegel, G. W. F. 1952. *The Philosophy of Right*. Trans. T. M. Knox. London: Oxford University Press.

Heidegger, Martin. 1962. *Being and Time*. Trans. J. Macquarrie and E. Robinson. London: SCM Press.

Hillman, James. 1985. *Anima: An Anatomy of a Personified Notion*. Dallas: Spring Publications.

Hume, David. 1739. *A Treatise of Human Nature*. Oxford: Clarendon Press, 1888.

Hunt, Harry T. 1989. *The Multiplicity of Dreams: Memory, Imagination, and Consciousness*. New Haven: Yale University Press.

Husserl, Edmund. 1913. *Ideas Pertaining to a Pure Phenomenology and to a Phenomenological Philosophy: First Book.* Trans. F. Kersten. The Hague: Martinus Nijhoff, 1982.

Inhelder, Barbel, and Jean Piaget. 1958. *The Growth of Logical Thinking from Childhood to Adolescence.* Trans. A. Parsons and S. Milgram. New York: Basic Books.

Isaacs, Susan. 1943. "The Nature and Function of Phantasy." In *Developments in Psycho-Analysis,* ed. M. Klein, P. Heimann, S. Isaacs, and J. Riviere. London: Hogarth Press, 1958.

Jacobson, Edith. 1959. "Depersonalization." *Journal of the American Psychoanalytic Association* 7:581–610.

————. 1964. *The Self and the Object World.* New York: International Universities Press.

John of the Cross, St. 1991. *The Dark Night.* In *The Collected Works of Saint John of the Cross.* Rev. ed. Trans. K. Kavanaugh and O. Rodriguez. Washington, D.C.: ICS Publications.

Johnson, Miriam M. 1988. *Strong Mothers, Weak Wives: The Search for Gender Equality.* Berkeley: University of California Press.

Jung, Carl G. 1912. *Symbols of Transformation.* 2d ed. In *The Collected Works of C. G. Jung.* Vol. 5. Princeton, N.J.: Princeton University Press, 1967. This is a translation of *Symbole der Wandlung,* published in 1952, which is an extensive revision of *Wandlungen und Symbole der Libido,* first published in 1912.

————. 1936. "Yoga and the West." In *Collected Works.* Vol. 11. 2d ed. Princeton, N.J.: Princeton University Press, 1969.

————. 1938. "Psychological Aspects of the Mother Archetype." In *Collected Works.* Vol. 9. 2d ed. Princeton, N.J.: Princeton University Press, 1968; originally published in German in 1938; revised 1954.

————. 1953. "Psychological Commentary on *The Tibetan Book of the Dead.*" In *Collected Works.* Vol. 11. 2d ed. Princeton, N.J.: Princeton University Press, 1969.

Kant, Immanuel. 1787. *The Critique of Pure Reason.* Trans. N. K. Smith. Toronto: Macmillan, 1929.

Kapleau, Philip. 1967. *The Three Pillars of Zen.* Boston: Beacon Press.

Kasulis, T. P. 1981. *Zen Action/Zen Person.* Honolulu: The University Press of Hawaii.

Kaufmann, Walter, ed. 1956. *Existentialism from Dostoevsky to Sartre.* Cleveland: World Publishing Co.

Kierkegaard, Søren. 1849. *Sickness unto Death.* In *Fear and Trembling and Sickness unto Death.* Trans. W. Lowrie. Princeton, N.J.: Princeton University Press, 1954.

Kohlberg, Lawrence. 1969. "Stage and Sequence. The Cognitive-Developmental Approach to Socialization." In *Handbook of Socialization Theory Research*, ed. D. A. Goslin. Chicago: Rand McNally.

———. 1976. "Moral Stages and Moralization: The Cognitive-Developmental Approach." In *Moral Development and Behavior*, ed. T. Lickona. New York: Holt, Rinehart and Winston.

———. 1984. *Essays on Moral Development*. Vol. 2, *The Psychology of Moral Development*. San Francisco: Harper and Row.

Kohut, Heinz. 1971. *The Analysis of the Self: A Systematic Approach to the Psychoanalytic Treatment of Narcissistic Personality Disorders*. New York: International Universities Press.

———. 1977. *The Restoration of the Self*. Madison, Conn.: International Universities Press.

Krishna, Gopi. 1971. *Kundalini: The Evolutionary Energy in Man*. Berkeley: Shambhala.

Kroll, Jerome. 1988. *The Challenge of the Borderline Patient: Competency in Diagnosis and Treatment*. New York: W. W. Norton.

Kuhn, D., ed. 1979. *New Directions for Child Development*. No. 5, *Intellectual Development Beyond Childhood*. San Francisco: Jossey-Bass Publishers.

Laing, Ronald. D. 1960. *The Divided Self*. New York: Pantheon Books.

Levin, David M. 1985. *The Body's Recollection of Being: Phenomenological Psychology and the Deconstruction of Nihilism*. London: Routledge and Kegan Paul.

———. 1987. "Clinical Stories: A Modern Self in the Fury of Being." In *Pathologies of the Modern Self: Postmodern Studies on Narcissism, Schizophrenia, and Depression*, ed. D. M. Levin. New York: New York University Press.

———. 1988. *The Opening of Vision: Nihilism and the Postmodern Situation*. London: Routledge.

———. 1989. *The Listening Self: Personal Growth, Social Change and the Closure of Metaphysics*. London: Routledge.

Lichtenberg, Joseph D. 1977. "Factors in the Development of the Sense of the Object." *Journal of the American Psychoanalytic Association* 27:375–386.

———. 1981. "Implications for Psychoanalytic Theory of Research on the Neonate." *International Review of Psycho-Analysis* 8:35–52.

———. 1983. *Psychoanalysis and Infant Research*. Hillsdale, N.J.: Analytic Press.

———. 1987. "Infant Studies and Clinical Work with Adults." *Psychoanalytic Inquiry* 7:311–330.

Loevinger, Jane. 1976. *Ego Development: Conceptions and Theories*. San Francisco: Jossey-Bass Publishers.

Maddi, Salvatore R. 1967. "The Existential Neurosis." *Journal of Abnormal Psychology* 72:311–325.

————. 1970. "The Search for Meaning." In *Nebraska Symposium on Motivation*, ed. W. Arnold and M. Page. Lincoln: University of Nebraska Press.

Madison, Peter. 1961. *Freud's Concept of Repression and Defense, Its Theoretical and Observational Language*. Minneapolis: University of Minnesota Press.

Mahler, Margaret, Fred Pine, and Anni Bergman. 1975. *The Psychological Birth of the Human Infant*. New York: Basic Books.

Mandler, Jean. 1990. "A New Perspective on Cognitive Development in Infancy." *American Scientist* 78:236–243.

Marrone, Robert. 1990. *Body of Knowledge: An Introduction to Body/Mind Psychology*. Albany: State University of New York Press.

Maslow, Abraham. 1968. *Toward a Psychology of Being*. New York: D. Van Nostrand.

————. 1970. *Religions, Values, and Peak-Experiences*. New York: Viking Press.

————. 1971. *The Farther Reaches of Human Nature*. New York: Viking Press.

Meltzoff, Andrew N., and M. Keith Moore. 1977. "Imitation of Facial and Manual Gestures by Human Neonates." *Science* 198:75–78.

Merleau-Ponty, Maurice. 1962. *Phenomenology of Perception*. Trans. C. Smith. London: Routledge and Kegan Paul.

Mookerjee, Ajit. 1983. *Kundalini: The Arousal of the Inner Energy*. 2d ed. New York: Destiny Books.

Muktananda, Swami. 1978. *Play of Consciousness*. South Fallsburg, N.Y.: SYDA Foundation.

Murphy, John M., and Carol Gilligan. 1980. "Moral Development in Late Adolescence and Adulthood: A Critique and Reconstruction of Kohlberg's Theory." *Human Development* 23:77–104.

Neumann, Erich. 1954. *The Origins and History of Consciousness*. Princeton, N.J.: Princeton University Press.

————. 1963. *The Great Mother*. 2d ed. Princeton, N.J.: Princeton University Press.

Nieli, Russell. 1987. *Wittgenstein: From Mysticism to Ordinary Language*. Albany: State University of New York Press.

Nietzsche, Friedrich. 1966. *Thus Spoke Zarathustra*. Trans. W. Kaufmann. New York: Viking Press.

Nunberg, Herman. 1955. *Principles of Psychoanalysis: Their Application for the Neuroses*. New York: International Universities Press.

Ornstein, Robert. 1972. *The Psychology of Consciousness*. San Francisco: W. H. Freeman & Co.

Otto, Rudolf. 1917. *The Idea of the Holy*. Trans. J. W. Harvey. New York: Oxford University Press, 1950.

Perry, John W. 1974. *The Far Side of Madness*. Englewood Cliffs, N.J.: Prentice-Hall.

———. 1976. *Roots of Renewal in Myth and Madness*. San Francisco: Jossey-Bass Publishers.

Piaget, Jean. 1951. *Play, Dreams and Imitation in Childhood*. Trans. C. Gattegno and F. M. Hodgson. New York: W. W. Norton.

———. 1954. *The Construction of Reality in the Child*. Trans. Margaret Cook. New York: Basic Books.

———. 1972. "Intellectual Evolution from Adolescence to Adulthood." *Human Development* 15:1–12.

Piaget, Jean, and Barbel Inhelder. 1971. *Mental Imagery in the Child: A Study of the Development of Imaginal Representation*. Trans. P. A. Chilton. New York: Basic Books.

Reich, Wilhelm. 1942. *The Function of the Orgasm*. Trans. R. P. Wolfe. New York: Farrar, Straus and Giroux.

Richards, Francis A., and Michael L. Commons. 1984. "Systematic, Metasystematic, and Cross-Paradigmatic Reasoning: A Case for Stages of Reasoning Beyond Formal Operations." In *Beyond Formal Operations: Late Adolescent and Adult Cognitive Development*, ed. M. L. Commons, F. A. Richards, and C. Armon. New York: Praeger.

Riegel, Klaus. 1973. "Dialectical Operations: The Final Period of Cognitive Development." *Human Development* 16:346–370.

Royo, Antonio, and Jordan Aumann. 1962. *The Theology of Christian Perfection*. Dubuque, Iowa: Priory Press.

Sannella, Lee. 1987. *The Kundalini Experience: Psychosis or Transcendence?* Rev. ed. Lower Lake, Calif.: Integral Publishing.

Sartre, Jean-Paul. 1956. *Being and Nothingness*. Trans. H. Barnes. New York: Philosophical Library.

———. 1957. *The Transcendence of the Ego*. Trans. F. Williams and R. Kirkpatrick. New York: Noonday Press.

Schilder, Paul. 1928. *Introduction to Psychoanalytic Psychiatry*. New York: Nervous and Mental Disease Publishing Co.

Schnapper, Edith. 1980. *The Inward Odyssey: The Concept of the Way in the Great Religions of the World*. 2d ed. London: George Allen & Unwin.

Segal, Hanna. 1964. *Introduction to the Work of Melanie Klein*. New York: Basic Books.

————. 1991. *Dream, Phantasy and Art*. London: Routledge.

Sinnott, Jan D. 1981. "The Theory of Relativity: A Metatheory for Development?" *Human Development* 24:293–311.

————. 1984. "Postformal Reasoning: The Relativistic Stage." In *Beyond Formal Operations: Late Adolescent and Adult Cognitive Development*, ed. M. L. Commons, F. A. Richards, and C. Armon. New York: Praeger.

————. 1989. "Life-Span Relativistic Postformal Thought: Methodology and Data from Everyday Problem-Solving Studies." In *Adult Development*. Vol. 1, *Comparisons and Applications of Developmental Models*, ed. M. L. Commons, J. D. Sinnott, F. A. Richards, and C. Armon. New York: Praeger.

Stein, Waltraut J. 1967. "The Sense of Becoming Psychotic." *Psychiatry* 30:262–275.

Stern, Daniel. 1985. *The Interpersonal World of the Infant*. New York: Basic Books.

Stewart, Walter A. (reporter). 1964. Panel: "Depersonalization." *Journal of the American Psychoanalytic Association* 12:171–186.

Teresa of Avila, St. 1980. *The Interior Castle*. In *The Collected Works of St. Teresa of Avila*. Vol. 2. Trans. K. Kavanaugh and O. Rodriguez. Washington, D.C.: ICS Publications.

Tolstoy, Leo. 1886. "The Death of Ivan Ilych." Trans. A. Maude. In *The Death of Ivan Ilych and Other Stories*. New York: New American Library, 1960.

Tomkins, Silvan S. 1962. *Affect, Imagery, Consciousness*. Vol. 1, *The Positive Affects*. New York: Springer Publishing Co.

————. 1963. *Affect, Imagery, Consciousness*. Vol. 2, *The Negative Affects*. New York: Springer Publishing Co.

Underhill, Evelyn. 1911. *Mysticism*. New York: E. P. Dutton, 1961.

Van Dusen, Wilson. 1958. "*Wu Wei*, No-Mind, and the Fertile Void in Psychotherapy." In *The Meeting of the Ways: Explorations in East/West Psychology*, ed. J. Welwood. New York: Schocken, 1979.

Von Domarus, E. 1944. "The Specific Laws of Logic in Schizophrenia." In *Language and Thought in Schizophrenia*, ed. J. S. Kasanin. Berkeley: University of California Press.

Walsh, Roger. 1977. "Initial Meditative Experiences: Part I." *Journal of Transpersonal Psychology* 9:151–192.

Washburn, Michael. 1978. "Observations Relevant to a Unified Theory of Meditation." *Journal of Transpersonal Psychology* 10:45–65.

————. 1994a. "Reflections on a Psychoanalytic Theory of Gender Difference." *Journal of the American Academy of Psychoanalysis* 22:1–28.

————. 1994b. *Transpersonal Psychology in Psychoanalytic Perspective.* Albany: State University of New York Press.

Washburn, Michael, and Michael Stark. 1979. "Ego, Egocentricity, and Self-Transcendence: A Western Interpretation of Eastern Teaching." In *The Meeting of the Ways: Explorations in East/West Psychology,* ed. J. Welwood. New York: Schocken, 1979.

Weil, Simone. 1952. *Gravity and Grace.* London: Routledge and Kegan Paul.

White, John, ed. 1979. *Kundalini: Evolution and Enlightenment.* Garden City, N.Y.: Doubleday Anchor.

Whitfield, Carol. 1992. "Jungian Myth and Advaita Vedanta." Ph.D. dissertation, Graduate Theological Union.

Wilber, Ken. 1977. *The Spectrum of Consciousness.* Wheaton, Ill.: Theosophical Publishing House.

————. 1979. "Are the Chakras Real?" In *Kundalini, Evolution and Enlightenment,* ed. J. White. Garden City, N.Y.: Doubleday Anchor, 1979.

————. 1980a. *The Atman Project.* Wheaton, Ill.: Theosophical Publishing House.

————. 1980b. "The Pre/Trans Fallacy." *ReVision* 3:51–71.

————. 1981a. "Ontogenetic Development: Two Fundamental Patterns." *Journal of Transpersonal Psychology* 13:33–58.

————. 1981b. *Up from Eden: A Transpersonal View of Human Development.* New York: Doubleday Anchor.

————. 1982. "Odyssey: A Personal Inquiry into Humanistic and Transpersonal Psychology." *Journal of Humanistic Psychology* 22:57–90.

————. 1983. *A Sociable God.* Boulder, Colo.: Shambhala.

————. 1990. *Eye to Eye: The Quest for a New Paradigm.* Expanded edition. Boston: Shambhala.

Wilber, Ken, Jack Engler, and Daniel Brown. 1986. *Transformations of Consciousness: Conventional and Contemplative Perspectives on Development.* Boston: Shambhala.

Yalom, Irvin D. 1980. *Existential Psychotherapy.* New York: Basic Books.

Index